INDICTMENT

T. C. Campbell & Reg McKay

CANONGATE

First published in Great Britain in 2001 by
Canongate Books Ltd, 14 High Street,
Edinburgh EH1 1TE

10 9 8 7 6 5 4 3 2 1

British Library Cataloguing-in-Publication Data
A catalogue record for this book is available on
request from the British Library

ISBN 1 84195 191 9

Typeset by Palimpsest Book Production Limited,
Polmont, Stirlingshire
Printed and bound by
CPD, Ebbw Vale, Wales

www.canongate.net

I dedicate this book to my cherished children, Tommy, Stephen, Brian, Cheree Anne and Shannon. Raised without their father. That they might come to know me. That I made mistakes, I do not deny, but I have never been a killer. That they may see where I went wrong and perhaps help to pave a better way for their future. All I can say is, 'Please do not follow in my footsteps where I have gone wrong.'

With gratitude to Alistair McIntosh's 'Soil & Soul' for helping me see that I may speak freely and that justice is in the making. To get up and get it done, not merely waiting in vain for it to come.

And to those countless silent heroes unsung.

And to John Carroll and Tommy Sheridan for their tireless efforts on behalf of social justice and equality.

> *For those of us who know the truth as a burden we*
>   *are born to bear.*
> *Of injustice and inequality within a system which*
>   *doesn't care*
> *For those children born in poverty, in ignorance,*
>   *unaware,*
> *Of those victims born of travesty to despair.*
>
> *May you fly high as the eagle, finding freedom*
>   *there,*
> *May your wisdom shine through the darkness of*
>   *despair.*
> *May you always walk in friendship, compassion and*
>   *due care.*
> *May you always give where needed and be fair.*

May all the world embrace you, take you as their own.
May you understand your human errors and atone.
May your children be your future and through your wisdom see,
There is no greater gift than to be free.

Tommy Campbell
14 July 2001

Contents

BOOK ONE

Charmed &
Damned

Da's Hame

Ma had died in 1964 almost twelve months to the day after JFK was assassinated. Da finished his ten stretch in 1968 the year Martin Luther King was assassinated. I was fifteen years old . . .

'So you're big, TC, eh! Think you're a chib man, eh, fuckin chib man do ye? What have I told you about using weapons? It's a coward's get out. Can you not fight a decent square go? Haven't I taught you how to use yourself to best advantage?' Slap, slap, thunk, dunk. He would give me a rapid lesson with his open hand.

'But, Da, it was so a square go. I broke one's nose and the other's jaw.'

'Who were they? Two you say?'

'Aye two brothers fae Haghill in their twenties.'

'What was it about?'

'They were singing The Sash and called me a Fenian bastard because of my Ma.'

'And did ye batter them?'

'Battered them, Da.'

'Where was your brothers?'

'Didnae need them, Da, there was only the two o them.'

'Good boy.'

But before sending me off to bed I was stripped of my new suit, shirt, shoes, the lot into the fire. Can't have bloodstained clothing lying about the house in case the polis came.

Maggie Mac

By 1971 T Rex's Hot Love was top of the charts and I was seventeen . . .

I was seventeen, a confident six-foot tall teenage gang leader who thought he knew it all but didn't even suspect there was any other world beyond those streets, nor any other way of life.

We were walking the block, the equivalent of patrolling the boundaries. I'd teamed up with my big pal, Tamby the Bear, with a few of the troops tagging along behind. Chatting up the birds and keeping an eye open for enemy raiders when I first spotted the gallus big Maggie Mac swaggering towards us. I didn't know it then but was soon to discover she was one of the famous fighting females of the McNeilly clan. She was beautiful – a Robert Palmer's Addicted to Love original but at a time before the video was ever thought of. Long, straight raven black hair parted in the middle, dark mascara on huge oriental green eyes, pale face with baby doll ruby red lips, long black jacket and matching micro mini skirt. Her shoes were black ankle-strapped, high-heeled and pointed. She swaggered – the cutest, coolest, most gallus swagger you could ever hope to see. She radiated an aura of arrogant confidence. This girl knew who she was and knew what she wanted.

She had a bag of chips unravelled open in her left hand and slowed, sort of flicking out with her feet on a hill as we approached. Half turning towards me, her shoulder to Tamby, she offered me a chip from the pack – the street equivalent of taking a date out for a meal I suppose. A definite show of interest. As I plucked a chip Tamby also reached out to help himself but she turned away moving them beyond his reach telling him to, 'Fuck off, poof.'

Tamby looked towards me and I shrugged, indicating that I would remain neutral in this. The ball was at his feet. Turning to her, he tried to give her some lip but she was too quick and too sharp for him. He wasn't coming out of the verbal exchange very well at all. Even when he reverted to fighting talk, thinking that she'd have to back down, still she gave it back and came out best. Finally, in his public humiliation, he resorted to swinging the boot at her to 'Kick her in the crack,' as he'd threatened. Maggie Mac, with supreme cool, simply executed a short fast bow in such a way as to cause her two feet, close together, to shuffle backwards making Tamby miss his target. She straightened up with the heel of his brown terries in the palm of her hand, using the momentum of the kick to continue the motion right into the air. A perfect Ju Jitsu flip, landing Tamby flat on his back on the street. Still holding his foot in one hand with his leg in the air, she parted his legs, stepped neatly between and planted three rapid kicks with her dainty little foot to his exposed balls. Dropping his foot as he curled up in agony, she stepped over him, still holding her chips, and looking down over her shoulder with contempt said simply, 'Poof,' as she casually resumed on her gallus wee swaggering way. Walking the block, eating her chips as if nothing had occurred at all. I about turned, caught up with her and asked, 'So where we goin babe?'

'All the way if you want, big man,' she retorted with a wink.

'Wow!' I thought. 'To the ends of the fucking earth, babe.' Thought I, 'I think I'm in love.'

The Sixty-niners

By 1969 I had been in Borstal, Armstrong was on the moon,
Northern Ireland had erupted and Da died before I was
free . . .

Auld Frankie Vaughan was swinging his grin up by the
Drummy while Clint Easterhouse was slinging his thing
on the silver screen. Acid drops in the rain of the summer
of blood. So cool it was fuckin freezing man.

'As the banner man held the banner high, he was ten
feet tall and he touched the sky and I wished that I
could be a banner man. Oh Glory . . .' The Piranha Pak,
Den Toi, Drummy and Provy Rebels were dumping their
bloody blades, malkies, swords and cleavers for the pitiful
promise of a spankin new big barn to barny in instead
of spillin their blood on the streets. So . . . 'Roll out the
Instigator, Cos there's Some Thin' in the Air. We Gotta
Getta Gether Sooner or Later, Cos the Rev-o-Lution's
here and You Know that It's Right . . .'

All just another big show for the Frankie fullah but
what the fuck did he ever know about the sixtyninas?
Rantin ravin pure dead fuckin mad mental, man. The
only Top Hat we'd ever know would be from the
Clockwork Orange Brigade and the only Cain was Able.
'Gerrintirum,' echoed the war cry in the drab tenement
streets in testimony that the bold Geronimo never died. Jist
remember the fuckin Alamo, man. Remember Culloden?
Yeah! 'Hello, pleased tae meet yeh, hope ye guessed mah
name.' The ragin flame o youth untamed spilled its blood
upon the plain and where did it rain? Napalm Vietnam.
(I thought it was a place like Napal or something.) The

Kennedies are dead, Lennon's in bed and was it King who once said, 'Aye, I had a dream.' This is the real scene. Nae merr fuckin nightmares this trip around.

WOODsTOCK

H*el*T*ee*R-*fuckiN*-*SkelteR.*

'We're havin fun, sittin in the front seat, Huggin anna kissin with . . .' Freddie fuckin Kruger, man. Hit back, hit hard, cut and run. Nae fuckin roses in this gun, chum. Think Pink Floyd. Smash the brain cell walls and free your mind . . .

'All we are sayin is, Give peace a chance.' Men playin golf on the fuckin moon. Miners strike, Aberfan doom. Whit next unner the sun? Apollo 13 unlucky for some. Clint is slingin a bigger gun. Arthur Black the shirt is back. Tartan Tories, flairs annat. Thatcher Snatcher, Ted Heath bequeeth. Nae mare free milk for the weans' relief. Thatcher, Biafra, 'We've got the bomb,' says China. We are the sixtyninas, Carrolinas so what the fuck do we know?

All just another big show for the bold Frankie fullah. Another photo opportunity. The Den Toi, Drummy, Rebels and Pak might march with CND and back but the bloody big US nuclear subs would stay parked up in the auld Holy Loch, so where the fuck do we get off? We are the sixtyninas, chinas. Born to raise hell and die young.

The Tale of Torn Arse

Rid Ronny was spending like he knew tomorrow had been cancelled. He's done about a monkey buying everybody booze. I calculated that he'd only about two ton left from his cut from the last wee turn. They were few and far between for the ginger minge and it looked like he was letting it be known that the tide had turned and that he was the man in the can . . . (people borrow money in the toilet). Then into the bargain, he had a bird on each arm and, even though they had a hand in each pocket, it was still a turn around for the books for the bold yin. Good on him, he deserved a wee break.

Then the manager started fucking him about, taking him down and trying to put him back in his place. Give Rid Ronny his due, I've never seen him so reasonable. He'd even declared his chopper behind the bar as an act of good will. When the bouncers started on him too, they must have assumed he was empty handed but he still had his malky in the top sky pocket. They really took him down. I think it was out of pure embarrassment he finally jumped to his feet ranting with pointed finger in their faces. They jumped him team handed and a barney broke out. I got right in there kicking fuck out of the manager. The bouncers produced coshes from behind the bar.

'Fuck this,' I thought as I whipped out my malky from my own top sky and everybody froze. 'Get the fuck aff ae him,' I growled. They got up off him and Rid Ronny

got up and drew out his own malky. I flicked mine shut
and skied it. Rid Ronny did the same as I walked him
towards the door. From the corner of my eye I saw one
of the bouncers taking a flying dive with a bottle in his
hand. I shouted, 'Sky, edge up,' as I slapped my top
pocket causing the open razor to jump out into my hand
just a fraction quicker than the Rid Ronny fullah's. The
bouncer planted the head on him and bounced the bottle
off his head sending them both careering backwards in a
tangle over the tables onto the benches at the back with
the bouncer on top. The rest had stopped mid stride as
I'd swirled round with the open malky at the ever-ready,
assault and battery style. This cunt was bouncing the
bottle off Ronny's heid and I was shouting, 'Give im it
Ronny! Give im it!' But he was taking a pounding and was
trying to fuckin' reason with the guy, 'Nark it. C'mon,
nark it or I'll do ye'. He wouldn't do the guy and the guy
wouldn't stop doing him. Blood everywhere. I strolled
over, turned my back on the scene of the action to face
the audience and, with the malky behind my back, smiled
sweetly at them while I repeatedly slashed the arse of this
idiot, making him famous with the name Torn Arse.

It was rumoured that he was talking to the polis. So,
Don Don, one of the mad Larinskis, phoned the Co-op.
Death in the family and all that. Torn Arse's address
and with directions. The undertakers arrived with the
coffin and deep condolences for the death of your dear
son, madam. Torn Arse got the message. This is what
would commonly be called a Threatener and no charges
ensued.

Charmed

It was 1972, the death penalty had been abolished in the USA but not for long, Nixon was bugging Watergate, The Godfather was released and Jimmy bloody Osmond sang Long Haired Lover from Liverpool. Me, I was somewhere else . . .

At seventeen I was tall with a Van Dyke beard and everyone assumed I was older so sitting in the pub with Maggie and the troops was not unusual. On this particular occasion, it had been just a few days since someone swinging a sword had lost a few fingers and apparently wasn't too pleased about it.

Drinking bottled beer, large Whitbread or McEwan's Pale Ale, pouring our own the theory being that the bottles were always handy to have around in case of an unexpected attack. So much for the theory for, in reality, when an attack comes unexpectedly, it's the last thing y'think of. I was just having a sip of a pint when I heard these three loud bangs simultaneous with bright flashes and my bobbing head rattling my teeth off the glass, spilling beer down my chin. Putting the glass down and looking up surprised and puzzled, feeling at my mouth for any damaged teeth or tissue. I could see everybody staring in wide-eyed shock, mouths opening and shutting, flabbergasted, whilst others made frantic hand signals, mimicking some TV show, What's My Line, or something.

'What? Three guesses?' said I. 'Eh? Hammer?' Aye, right first time they nodded frantically indicating BIG hammer, pointing at the door behind me. Turning round as I put my hand to my head, seeing the exit door still swinging and feeling the bloody mush of my new hair-do

I soon got the picture. Sure enough, I'd been battered over the head three rapid with a big Thor type hammer as they later described it. The assailant could only be identified by his bloody bandaged hand. I got a matching set of three nine-stitch zips in my concussed skull and a bloody good lesson about sitting with my back to doors. Everyone who had seen it thought they had witnessed my murder and couldn't believe that I hardly felt it, putting it down to bravado. But I had, quite honestly, believed that it had been the room which shook and not I.

It began to seem to me that every time I turned a corner, somebody was having a stab at me with something. Again and again it happened. People leaping out of closes tooled up and team handed in ambush. I think that it was either by pure luck or some kind of survival reflex instinct that I always seemed to come out the better in such encounters. Don't ask me to describe what I did to overcome the odds because I simply don't know. All I do know is that there was no way they were sticking those big blades in me again. I would come out of it with a couple of scratches, maybe holes in my clothing, and two or three people were on their way to the Royal with serious injuries. Possibly in times of extreme danger to life something else takes over, some kind of primitive instinct. I only ever have memories of other people's accounts of the events. For in truth, I really don't know how I managed to come out of such encounters alive. Perhaps, as they say, I had a charmed life. Yet, even if I had nine of them, I'd still be a dozen in debt. There is nothing romantic or glorious about war or the spillage of blood. It's a waste and the ultimate folly.

Charmed & Damned

I was mostly living with Maggie in Dennistoun at this time. Right in the heart of the Orange Powery land and slap bang next door to their headquarters. The famous fighting females being Catholic and myself top of the Powery hit list, it wasn't exactly the ideal spot for a love nest.

Inevitably a team came through the door with axes, choppers and Gurkha knives. Literally through the door, chopping it straight down the middle on entry. There was just the seven of us inside, three guys and four birds. Holly got his throat cut and was lucky to survive. He grabbed a mattress and pulled it over him on the floor while it was hacked to shreds to get at him. Scotty leapt out the window without taking the time to open it, suffering multiple injuries as a result. Both felt lucky to have got away with their lives but that then only left the famous fighting females and me standing our ground.

As the girls tore in with nail and teeth I went ahead with a Malky Frazer. I don't know how I got out of there with only cuts to my head but I did. Fighting my way through a fuckin army out into the street where I was arrested and, having torn the faces off a few, charged with four serious. Eventually I was acquitted on self-defence but whilst bailed pending trial I was to run into these guys again.

They had just hacked Sammy Hutchieson to pieces,

God knows how he lived. His face was torn to shreds, he lost an eye and suffered thirty-six stab wounds as well as slashes and hacks all over his body. Then they captured Kenny Leonard, thinking they had me. He too was hacked to shreds, suffering sixty-three stab wounds and multiple slashes and hacks. By the time they got round to me I was ready, having nipped through the backs to a hidden weapons stash and armed myself with an axe and an open razor. Just stepped out of a close right into them. I felt three dunts to my chest knocking me back with my back to the wall. Putting my hand there and realising that I had been stabbed again, I just went berserk. Charging right in at the ring of armed men surrounding me, focusing on the one who had stabbed me, axe raised and a maniac battle cry echoing in the drab tenement streets. The ring broke formation as they scattered with me in hot stumbling pursuit of my assailant. He ran in the wrong direction, straight into my own rapidly assembling troops alerted by my battle cry. In the darkened streets, he called to them for handers thinking it was his own mob, 'Get him, get him. It's TC he's right behind me.' He slowed on realising his mistake. Time enough for me to catch up and hack at the side of his head with the axe, stumbling as I did so, missing my target but hacking him below the ear slicing through the jaw bone just as he withdrew his knife from his last ever victim. He spun, stumbling backwards as he was going down, terror in his face on the realisation he was about to get what he had just given. He got it and would live but never to stand to fight again.

'Four youths found stabbed and dying on Carntyne Road,' read the Press. The Powery had conspired to murder me in the hospital, only my sisters standing in their way. Time enough for my brothers to arrive with the cry of 'Tongs ya bass' echoing through sterile stone corridors dispersing the enemy for another day.

The next time I was to encounter these guys I was to get sentenced to ten years in the Young Offenders for mobbing and rioting including a series of serious assaults and attempted murders with knives, axes, swords, razors and meat cleavers.

'You, Thomas Campbell, did form part of a riotous mob of evilly disposed persons which, acting of a common purpose, did conduct itself in a violent, riotous and tumultuous manner to the great terror and alarm of Her Majesty's lieges.'

All those assaults with all those weapons? How many hands do they think I have? But it was a crime of art and part complicity, meaning each is guilty of all the acts and crimes of every other.

The day I was sentenced my brother-in-law, wee Shadda, and Joe Steele's brother, Jim, were acquitted for the Stepps Hotel robbery on the 110-day rule. As the law stood then, an accused person must be released after 110 days untried without further proceedings. There had been about seven of us charged and four had been refused bail which meant that the 110-day rule applied to us too. The release on an apparent 'loophole in the law' as the press banner headlines stated was causing a lot of pressure on the prosecution service. Our lawyer at the time came downstairs with a deal for us. If three pled guilty to the one charge of riot the others could go free. We didn't realise that the four untried would be going free anyway leaving the three on bail to answer the charges. The Crown could do without the scandal the next day when our 110 days was up. Everyone turned to me for a decision which in those days would have been accepted without question.

'Right, you, you and you,' I said picking out the three who had done the most damage that night. For whatever reason, the damage I had done personally was not on the charge sheet and everybody knew that.

'No!' the lawyer butted in, looking at me. 'They want you in particular, you and any two others,' he said.

'Fine then,' I said, 'Yous make your own decisions.' Wee Cokey piped up, he was among the two youngest at fifteen and one of the ones refused bail.

'I don't know what to do,' he said. 'Will you ask my Ma?' The lawyer left to let us discuss it among ourselves and to ask wee Cokey's Ma. Joe Mac, the youngest at fifteen, opted to be the second. Nobody would commit themselves to being the third until the lawyer came back with the word from Cokey's mother, no doubt buzzing with sherry in celebration of the prosecution's success in manipulation of the naïvety of youth. He informed Cokey, 'Your Ma said that if it is going to help the others, you have just to plead guilty.' Hence the third was selected – none of the three I had originally picked and who had done the damage on the charges.

Justice was not the issue here. The issue, though we didn't know it, was to save the Crown the embarrassment of another 110-day scandal. Any three would do – me in particular because I was obviously some kind of leader. I got ten and Wee Joe the Jaskit and Cokey got three years each. Justice had been duly served to the wrong people, but I couldn't crib. I felt that, in many ways, it sort of evened the balance of Karma and squared the board.

Back in the YO, however, we were granted an admission visit. Not until then were we informed of the 110-day rule and the scandal that would have seen us walking free the next day. Cokey's Ma came up. She stormed right over to him and belted him a cracker with her open hand right across the face, bringing out the tears. 'What the fuck did you plead guilty for, ya stupid idiot ye? Y'never even done any of it!' she bawled at him for all to hear.

'But, Ma, my lawyer said th'you told me to plead to it.'

'Yer lawyer? Yer lawyer? Who the fuck's yer lawyer? I don't even know who yer lawyer is. I've never even seen him in my life.'

Years later while still serving the ten, I was ranting and raving about the dirty strokes of my lawyer to two good friends of mine from the West End. They were both doing four years for blackmail regarding a scam with prostitutes. They would rush in on non-regulars screaming and shouting about these hapless suckers being in bed with their wife and the guy would have to come up with more dosh to get out of there in one piece. However, they had never even been charged with the greater part of their blackmail scheme which had entailed the secret photographing of select regulars such as judges, lawyers, polis and other prominent pillars of society.

'Have a deco at these, big yin,' I was told with a sly grin.

'Dearie me,' I had never seen such an ugly sight in all my life. This big man with a black hairy chest and legs wearing a pink silk bra flat on his chest, matching pink panties with suspenders and nylons. They told me his name was Susan and that he was a regular who liked to be spanked with a slipper but, dear God almighty, he really was the spitting image of a lawyer I had known. This successful lawyer would go on to hold various high offices. I often wonder whatever became of my friends from the West End and whatever they had done with those pictures. No doubt worth a few quid by now. One thing I do know is that they never ever came back to the jail. One died and was given a big send-off by the Blue Angels weaving their way on motorbikes through the grave stones in their hundreds as tribute to the greatest among their number.

Hari Kari & the Magic Print

This particular incident started as a simple boys' night out to celebrate two things. The first was my recent acquittal at the High Court for what became known as the infamous rope trick where three Cat A prisoners had escaped from Barlinnie – but that's another story. The second excuse for a booze up was Hari Kari's recent liberation on a ten stretch for armed robbery. Hari, as the name may suggest, lacked a certain finesse in as much as he was totally oblivious to any need for caution in any respect. Besides us, there was big Sonny Caveman, Rid Ronny and the Mighty Bug, a small guy with the heart and power of a giant.

The whole thing kicked off from Burns' Howf. Fuck knows how it started – something to do with some bird deciding that she was with us, to the great irritation of her boyfriend and company. I recall the place erupting into a typical bar-room brawl and picking myself up from the floor after taking a dull yin from a bar stool or table to the corner of my right eyebrow. I must have been concussed for I only have hazy memories of being vastly out-numbered and of backing the troops out the door – bang into deeper shit. So on to the Dial Inn, the kiss of chaos planted proudly upon us. I recall trying to pacify Hari Kari, attempting to stop him chibbing a bouncer for some slight or other. Too late and too slow, he planted a dagger in the poor cunt's neck and nearly done him in.

So offski again then at Plompton, I think it was the

Waterloo Bar or something. One of those old fashioned, big long bars. The troops had a table and I was beginning to tipple Hari Kari was too long at the bar getting a round in. I joined him there. As I'd suspected, he was financially embarrassed and needed a tap. What I hadn't expected though was that he'd been standing there contemplating jumping the counter and robbing the place.

'Fuck sake! The fuckin' pitch is mobbed to the gunnels. Y'in a hurry to get back to the nick?' I argued, slipping him a few score notes (from an earlier turn). We stood there, each with a pint, debating the merits like this 'til I got fed up with it and decided to call his huffy bluff. 'Ach, on ye go then but don't expect any back-up from me.' Shit, no sooner said than LEAP he was over the fuckin counter, dagger in hand.

'Move! Move! Get away from the fuckin till, ya fat bastard ye!' and about 200 punters fell silent and turned to watch the show.

'Oh naw!' I groaned, clutching my concussed head. 'Here we go!' The big burly barman burped and backed away shielding the barmaid behind him. Yet instead of going for the dosh Hari Kari, no doubt drawn like a magnet to the fear in their faces, followed them right past the till to the end of the bar. Finally, the poor guy shielding the barmaid unable to squeeze any further back, in sheer panic, grabbed Hari's wrist holding the knife and, with his other beefy big hand, picked him up planting him face-up spread eagled across the bar, landing his massive weight on top of him as he did so. Hari was fucked, immobilised and captured good style. The guy deserved a medal but, shit, I had an obligation.

Rather than jump the counter myself, I walked to the other end of the bar and, just like cheeky-cheeky-chin, lifted the flap and walked in. Considering that I'd just committed myself to a possible charge of art and part in an armed robbery, I wasn't too pleased with the Hari Kari fullah. With all those witnesses staring at me, the walk along the inside of the bar seemed like a mile long. On reaching them, I gripped the barman by his massive biceps and said, 'Right! Let him go. Let him up.'

'The blade, the blade,' he shouted, indicating he wasn't prepared to budge until someone took charge of that very offensive weapon. I held the wrist holding the blade in my left hand, elbowing the barman in the jaw with my right as I did so, repeating my demand and giving him the excuse to let go. Dragging Hari Kari back onto his feet, I turned him around away from the bar staff and pushed him away towards the other end of the bar. Yet instead of just leaving the fuckin place, he decides to finish the job by stopping to rifle the till on the way by. Then as he tried to turn back on the terrified bar staff, I put his arm up his back and took him by the scruff of the neck and exited him, head first, bouncer style, through the swinging doors onto the street and unsuspecting public.

Outside, a fistful of money in the one hand and a dagger in the other, he turns to fight with me. A boot in the balls from the Mighty Bug just as a bus pulled up at the traffic lights behind him, made for a quick change of plan on that score. Opening the emergency exit door, he entered wielding a blade, presenting it at the driver's throat and demanding that he, 'Drive, ya bastard. Go left.' The driver's protestations about one-way systems and the Highway Code meant nothing to him. That system didn't exist when he was last on the streets. I stepped onto the bus just in time to catch him by the crock of the arm mid stabbing swipe at the driver's neck, casually saying, 'You'll have to excuse him, pal, his wee wife's just had a baby. He's on pills for his nerves and the booze has done his head in. It might be better if you just drive, ok?' Hari Kari still ranting and raving gave directions all the wrong ways through the one-way systems. That's how come the old 108 to Arden or somewhere ended up dropping us at Paradise Park in Parkhead. Talk about fly me to Havana? How we didn't get the nick on the spot is beyond me.

Of course, that's not the way it came out in court. Hari Kari got lifted a week later and they caught up with me the week after that. His wife had phoned the coppers on him and he'd put them on to me, reversing the roles which were played, naturally. However, once he was fingered by a string of witnesses at an ID parade even PC Plod couldn't help but know the real score. In any other circumstances, if it had been anyone else, a medal would have been in order for valiantry above and beyond . . . just for sticking with the fuckin' head case to minimise the damage. But, seeing as it was me, the Serious Crime Squad were only too happy to charge me with the lot. Thankfully, the witnesses had other ideas. For though they couldn't help but recognise me, they trooped through the parade, often giving me a wink, but failing to point me out. They had cast me in the role as the hero of the situation.

During police interviews, offers of cups of tea had to be refused because I didn't want my prints on their ceramic cups. An offer of a cigarette which they will light for you is fine. But when they slide over a pack with a lighter for you to help yourself Confucius he say No Ta because those cellophane wrappers are particularly easy to lift fingerprints from for transfer to fuck knows where. Even in the cells the wise man pulls his sleeves down over his hands when handing out dinner plates and the like. As Doctor Dolittle once said, 'The motto of the wise is, always be prepared for surprises.' Still, all such precautions were to no avail due to one simple slip when, gasping for a drink of water, I was told to hand out the plastic mug through the slot on the cell door. Unable to pick it up with my woolly sleeves, I cautiously picked it up by the edge of the handle with the very tips of my index finger and thumb. I was worried, but not too bothered, even when I didn't get the same mug back.

I'd been ID'd once Not Sure by the barmaid which, together with Hari Kari's statement was enough to hold me untried. By the time the trial came up, in the face of the overwhelming evidence against him, Hari pled guilty thus preventing his statement being used against him in court and dragging me down with him. Without ID on the other charges I was acquitted. My problem was with the robbery in the Waterloo. In support of the witness's Not Sure ID the polis had come up with, yes, you guessed it, two fingerprint fragments from a pint glass which matched my right index finger and thumb.

The barmaid told her story and remained unsure in her ID. The twist of this story came out in my QC Donald Findlay's cross-examination of that witness. He took her through it all again, right up to the police arriving and taking statements then beyond that again to her washing up and stacking the glasses before locking up for the night. Beyond again to the following day when the police returned to confirm parts of her statement and, this time, they lifted a pint glass at random from the stack and asked her to sign a label to confirm its origin. Yes, sure enough, that was the glass as confirmed by her signature as produced there in court. Washed, stacked and picked at random the following day, which just happened to have those same fragments of my fingerprints as I'd used in the police cells with that mug.

The jury acquitted me on all charges and I walked out the door a free man. Hari Kari was sentenced to twelve years.

Tamby the Bear

*It was 1979–80 and the winter of discontent. Punk rock was
rolling, national strike, no bread and nothing moving. I was
finishing a ten stretch . . .*

Big Tamby, the Bear, was well known to me long before
we became good pals at about thirteen. We have always
been about the same height and build though he's always
been fitter and faster on his feet than I ever was. People
who say I remind them of Billy Connolly in speech
and mannerism are mistaken because they've never met
Tamby. He is the original Big Yin and Billy Connolly is
the copy.

Tamby was there in all our adventures and always
the fastest on his feet when the polis came. I remember
for instance, the incident which earned him his title
as the Fastest Bear on Two Feet. We'd been mucking
about inside Carntyne dog track, just generally creating
a nuisance, as young teenagers are prone to do. The
bizzies had charged in team-handed and we all bolted
like hound for hare around the track. There must've been
at least twenty of us and Wee Johnny Malloy started
shouting out a running commentary. Though some of
us had the excuse that we couldn't stop laughing, still,
it was a fair heat. 'Aaand TC's off on trap three taking
the field from Von Ryan by a length but Tamby coming
up on the inside it's neck and neck and yes! Tamby takes
the field from track one, TC second, Von Ryan third
going into the final bend. And Tamby streaks ahead
to the finishing line and is the winner of the Carntyne
Cup.' Yeah! His ability as the Fastest Bear on Two Feet

would save his bacon in the years to come, but that's yet another story.

His boyhood troubles really began when the schools turned comprehensive. We were all moved to Whitehill but, for some reason, Tamby was transferred to Smithycroft just outside Barlinnie Prison and within the territorial bounds of the infamous Blackhill Toi. He was isolated with no back-up when the Toi started giving him a hard time so he simply stopped going to school. Eventually Tamby was taken to court and sent to approved school, the equivalent of a juvenile jail, and it was all down hill from there.

At seventeen, while full of hooch, he'd got into a fight with some guys in the Gallowgate. They'd mugged him for the pickled onion from his fish supper then waded in when he gave them a bit of verbal. To this day Tamby still doesn't remember what happened next but witnesses spoke of him standing in the middle of the Gallowgate holding a twenty-one inch steak knife. In the middle of the road staring at the stars surrounded by a big mob. The polis arrived and couldn't persuade him to hand over his blade so they clambered back into one of their Land Rovers and promptly restrained him with their radiator grill, knocking him down with the vehicle. He'd wakened with his broken bones and bandages in the polis cells next day clueless how he'd got there or why. Assuming it was the usual drunk and incapable, which would explain the injuries, he asked the turnkey who told him he was charged with two attempted murders and a serious police assault.

Tamby's victims were his very aggressors who'd mugged him and the boy was looking at two years' borstal. When the charges were reduced to serious assault he reckoned he'd be on the way out again in twelve months. It was quite a shock then when he was sentenced to ten years in a young offenders institution. For one thing, he was never a particularly violent person and, though he couldn't remember anything about the episode, it was believed he'd taken the weapon from his assailants, now the complaining victims. Not a lot can be said about his ten-year sentence in the YOI other than, at last nearing its end, the screws allowed him back to college to finish off his training and qualify as a hairdresser.

My own ten-year sentence finished some time after his and we teamed up again as buddies. Eventually I accepted a couple of insurance jobs. These entailed removing items from warehouse A to warehouse B. The owners would report these goods as stolen, missing and claim their insurance policies. We moved into the removals business for ourselves still doing the same job, sometimes for the same people, with or without their consent. Fridges, cookers, suites, microwaves you name it, we had it and all at half price. No one was ever hurt, except through their rising insurance premiums perhaps. But tough at the top was my attitude to their complaints. They hadn't moaned about the scam when we were doing it for them.

Tamby retired to the pub to become dominoes champ and cut hair for a living while I settled into building a home with the love of my life, Liz. She'd worked all her life from leaving school – the straightest, warmest, kindest person I'd ever known. She'd also saved her dosh all her life and pooling her nest egg and my stash we'd plans to settle down for good and go into business together. It never quite worked out that way, well not at first, as I was to run into a few more wee smidgens of trouble.

Old Anne had invited us to her local social club in Garthamlock as her guests. We were strangers to the place and I certainly hadn't expected to be dug up and verbally abused by the local GY team, not there with my wife. It just wouldn't happen where I come from. It's against the rules and a serious violation of the old street codes but these were cowardly scumbags who knew no code and were just following their predatory instincts. I tried to back down as much as I could for Liz's sake and for the sake of her night out as an invited guest. However, like all scavengers, the more you back down from them the more they smell victory and the more they come on strong. I should have known.

We gathered our coats to leave and Liz headed for the ladies while I waited outside in the foyer for our taxi. They couldn't just leave it at that. They had to come after me. A brawl erupted and, before I knew it I was fighting with the entire fucking club it seemed. When the polis arrived, this being a club and me not a member, the fingers were pointed en masse at TC. I was dragged away bleeding profusely from head and leg wounds and was charged with four serious assaults and a serious police assault. It's not that easy to make the decision to settle down. The decision is not always left to you, as you're left to deal with creeps with no scruples.

Lying as an untried prisoner, it was a pure sickener to be back in the jail. More so when you're in love and just want to get on with your life in peace. Yet they say bad luck lands in threes and the next blow came in news that a pervert with previous had blagged my cash stash that he was blowing with Tamby on a boozing spree. I figured the only way he could have accessed that stash would have been through Tamby. He couldn't have known of its existence other than through him. But surely not? Not my ole pal Tamby? You may expect this sort of thing from a stranger or an enemy but a betrayal by a friend is infinitely more hurtful. Yet it wasn't the worst of it. This pervert McArthur had pulled Liz about by the hair generally abusing her and Tamby had been there and not intervened. They must have expected that I'd be put away for another ten years at least. They must've known I wouldn't stand for it or let it go.

Number three came in the form of a social worker to tell me that he was recalling me on the last two years of the YO licence. I'd done seven of the ten years and been out a year leaving two to do if the licence was revoked – not counting what I'd get if found guilty of any of these five assaults. I disputed with the social worker telling him I was innocent of the charges alleged and expected to be acquitted at trial. He then responded by giving me a detailed account of my actions with the removals firm. I denied all knowledge and told him his info was false. He then said, 'You forget, Mr Campbell, that there are other people out on licence who are more concerned for their liberty than it appears you are.' He told me to forget he'd ever said that but it was pretty obvious I'd been grassed and traded in by somebody close to my business. I returned to my cell pretty pissed off but at least I had postponed the recall until after the trial.

Brain working over time. Who'd done the damage wasn't so hard to fathom. Both the Tamby and the perv McArthur were out on YO licences for a ten and a five respectively. Both had been charged and bailed on no less than three accounts whereas I'd been refused bail first time because of my YO licence. Both had the same social worker. Both knew about the removals firm – the perv would have got the gen from Tamby. Both had blagged my stash. Therefore, both had good reason to want to see me kept in the jail for as long as possible. Either one or both had traded me in for their own freedom and for their own sakes knowing I wouldn't let it go. I figured the principal culprit was the perv but, nevertheless, Tamby must have played a significant part. That was worse than robbing me. That was a betrayal which took advantage of and abused my trust as a friend. The perv would still be the primary target for the fact that he'd laid a hand on Liz. My head was seriously demented by this turn of events at a time when I was trying to settle down and get out of it. Wasn't it Marlon Brando who said, 'Just when you think you're out of it, they pull you back in.' I had very good grounds then, to fall out with Tamby.

The trial came up and they all duly lied for their thirty pieces of silver compensation claims. The last of the Crown's witnesses was a wee guy called Angel and he told the same story as the others. The difference being that under cross-examination when asked if he was lying he simply replied, 'Yes sir,' to the astonishment of everyone. He then went on to give graphic details of the real story and, when asked why he had lied in the first place, told how they'd all got their heads together to get the story straight for the sake of Criminal Injuries Compensation. My defence went on to confirm his final version.

I was acquitted on three charges when the jury accepted that it had been in self-defence. Guilty under extreme provocation on one charge and, guilty 'minus all aggravation' for the police assault. This copper had said that I'd assaulted him and cut his finger as he put his hand up to protect his face. All the other witnesses remembered him coming in after his colleagues had grabbed me. He'd picked up a knife from the floor and nicked his thumb while testing its sharpness. Ah, but see, you don't get compensation for that. The judge explained that an assault to be an assault must have at least one aggravation. This verdict then was not guilty of assault on the police officer. However, they would put it down on record as a technical assault.

I was sentenced to nine months and with that backdated from the day of my arrest I could be home in three months. But within weeks I was notified that I'd been recalled by the Scottish Secretary of State who doled out the remission

of my ten-year Young Offender licence. Having served
seven, been out one, I was then into my ninth year of a
ten and fuming.

> Broken glass pains
> my boiling brains
> tearing my mind apart
> killing me,
> willing me
> driving me insane
> stabbing at my heart.

I appealed against the recall, citing the judge's report
that I was not the aggressor. The judge, God bless him,
backed me saying that he'd been of a mind to admonish
me but had imposed a nine-month sentence backdated
only because of my licence. That it had been within his
power to sentence me to recall, in which case I would've
been required to serve a minimum of twelve months
before being considered for release. That he didn't do
so because he didn't think that the crime warranted it. In
his opinion recall in these circumstances would constitute
double jeopardy.

The appeal process takes some time but after this last
report from the trial judge I was released the next day
after having served a total of twelve months for defending
myself under extreme provocation. By that time, my head
was pure nippin.

The pervert jumped the country and Tamby was giving
me a wide berth, staying well out of my way. I hunted him
night and day. Almost caught him a few times but he was
too fast on his feet. People make the mistake of thinking
that it is through these escapades that he got his name as
the Fastest Bear on Two Feet but that's not exactly true.

Eventually a peace delegation convinced me that I was
in the wrong and that Tamby was an innocent spectator

in all this. I was never entirely convinced and could never fully trust him after that. He could never completely trust me for luring him into a trap and narrowly missing him with a bayonet before he got away by the skin of his teeth. In fact, I'd deliberately missed him because, when it came right down to it, I found that I really couldn't hurt the big guy. Of course, he hadn't known that.

> From the contemplation of a terrible deed
> to the first instance,
> all the interim is,
> like a little insurrection,
> where the conscience of the mortal man,
> and the contemplation of the evil deed,
> wrought havoc in mortal combat.
> (Shakespeare, *Caesar*) TC translation.

In the next few years Liz and I moved away and settled into a happy domestic relationship with our dear wee son Stephen. We'd bought an old clapped out Bedford mobile shop renovating, rebuilding, rewiring and renewing its engine with Liz's savings since my own stash had been pissed up against the wall by the perv. We'd moved into a run in Haghill which was considered not to be viable by others before us. Non-profitable due to the Asian shops on every corner that opened all hours. However, we stocked it as a mobile shop, ordering in anything that was requested. Keeping regular schedules like clockwork, we built up the run and finally began to show increasing profit. Liz had the licence to operate and with me as stock controller it was working out well.

Two incidents occurred which would lead to a change. One was, now that we'd built up the run and made it viable, we were a target for Marchetti pirates who thought they were big enough to run the city. Old Lizzie, the van, was attacked and came limping home to me babysitting

Stephen. She was in a terrible state and Liz wasn't doing too well with her shattered nerves either.

I scoured the streets alone looking for the culprits, tearing £20 notes into two pieces and handing one half over to the local lads with the promise of the other half for information. It wasn't too long in coming and the race was on between myself and the polis to see who would find them first. As it turned out they found me. They sent a messenger, 'Sorry, our mistake.' They'd been hired by Marchetti but hadn't been given the full score. They'd pay for the damage, the bills and all costs. That was the end of it but, while Old Lizzie made a full recovery, her owner, Liz, did not. Her nerves were shattered and she could never quite relax in that area again.

The second incident occurred in Carntyne on my sister's run. Sadie is a small, bespectacled grandmother and a gentle, good-natured soul. She believed that she'd given out credit which just wasn't being repaid. In fact, she'd been paying protection money and hadn't realised it until she refused further credit. Then the hassle started – punctured tyres and broken windows. She didn't tell me what was going on. It had been her driver who'd let it slip.

I had a word with the gangsters. One set his dogs on me. I stabbed one hound through the heart and sent the other howling as I kicked its master up and down the street – the locals cheering me on from their windows. The coppers looking on from their Panda car said nothing but simply gave me a nod as I passed them on the way back home. But now Sadie's nerves were shattered over what I'd done and it led to her and Liz swapping runs. Now that our run was in Carntyne, I was back in my old stamping ground with the bizzies, like vultures, hovering and waiting for the first mistake. But there would never be any.

Myopic Mole – Joe Steele

Auld Andy Steele had passed away leaving the family in abject poverty. Auld Maw Padden, Joe's Granny, was in her nineties and blind. His Ma, Margaret, a dear long-suffering soul, was deaf. Between the two of them they could just about navigate their way through the day. Her two daughters, Lana and Brenda, were married and away from home. Her two older sons, Jim and Johnaboy, were each serving twelve years in Peterhead prison for separate offences, leaving myopic Joe to look after them and the household.

Jim Steele I'd known from old, from his early days' apprenticeship as an armed robber. Johnaboy, not since he was a child living in Carntyne. Joe I hadn't known at all until he introduced himself around mid-1983. There had been no mistaking him though. He had that same odd posture and walk as his brother Jim – often called Brass Neck because his neck appeared so stiff that it affected the posture of his spine causing him to walk with an odd stooped yet rigidly straight back. Groucho Marx would be a slight exaggeration but close.

I didn't know it at the time but was soon to discover that Joe was a petty thief, would-be con man and a drug addict. He was just out of the jail for housebreaking when he came to my door and introduced himself – not as his mother Maggie's son but as Jim's brother. He'd just been up to Peterhead to see his brothers and, apparently, they'd advised him to look me up as a possible resolution to a problem. That their Ma was deep in rent arrears and was due to be evicted was a horrifying prospect to me. I'd have gone to the ends of the earth for this woman. She'd been such close friends with my own mother that they'd been more like sisters and we'd called her Aunty Margaret. She was a rare and sparkling diamond amid the dross. Yes, of course I could help. I would've given this woman my all and my everything, as if she was my own mother, and without hesitation or regret. It was a hefty sum and left me broke but my word was good and I could easily make it up again in the weeks ahead. I handed it over to the Mole.

Any time I ever saw him again was when he was selling rings or bracelets that he'd blagged somewhere or other. He'd sold some pieces to the Craw and he'd borrowed a couple of ton while he was at it. Bragging about how he'd conned him out of the cash but so blind that he hadn't even realised that the Craw was standing right behind him. The Myopic Mole tended to burn his bridges in this way.

Over in Garthamlock to see Agnes one day, I decided to drop by and see how auld Maggie was doing. As usual she was a delightful soul always fussing about making tea and trying to get me to eat something. Memories of those hungry years would never leave her and nothing had changed. Then she started talking about her pending eviction in a matter of fact, fatalistic fashion as if her rent arrears were so huge a bill that a king's ransom couldn't cover it. Massive from her perspective but really it wasn't that bad. She nattered on happily about all the help she was having from all the good people around her who had volunteered to store this and that piece of furniture for her till she could find somewhere to live.

'But that's been sorted, Margaret. There's no eviction,' I told her, thinking maybe she was going senile or something.

'Aye, son? What makes ye say that then?' she answered with a patient smile as if talking to a wistful child.

'Joseph, Margaret. I gave the money to your Joseph. The bill's paid.' She looked up sharply from her fussing.

'Naw! Oh naw! Oh my dear God almighty, ye never gave my Joseph money did ye?' she asked, nervous and alarmed, instantly recognising that if I'd given her Joseph all that money for her rent arrears Joe had ripped it off. She still owed her arrears and Joe hadn't been seen. From her point of view, her alarm was not that she still owed the arrears or that the money had been ripped off but, considering my sense of honour and reputation for violence, her concern was now for what trouble this would entail for Joe. It was just typical of her. She never thought of herself but always of what's best for her children. How could anyone hurt, worry or disappoint someone like that? I paid her bill again and assured her that Joe would be left alone.

I went up to Peterhead to see Jim and Johnny and was not surprised to learn that Joe had never been to visit either of them. Neither was I surprised to discover that Joe had borrowed a neighbour's TV while her man was in the jail and had sold it. Joe thinks these things are funny and clever and that they add to his status, showing how smart he is. King among the rats. Prince of low-lifes. Whereas this is exactly the kind of personality I find repulsive.

'Just stay away from me, son, and don't you or any of your low-life pals come near my door again.' I have taken people like him by the throat just for passing in the street by my window. 'Catch you in this street again, arsehole, I'll break your fuckin neck.' The thought of having such a creature in my house was like finding a rat in my pantry. Dirty little scumbag low-lifes.

Gardi Loo – Hell on Wheels

(The Story of Gary Moore)

Fuck knows how Gardi Loo got his name. So far as I know it means 'Look out below' from the old Glasgow days before flushing toilets, running water and sewers. Trash and sewage would be tipped out of the window with the warning Gardi Loo but whether Gary got the name from such activity or what Gardi would never say. Certainly he was born and brought up in the back streets, in the gutters, amid the less fortunate of society in Glasgow's slum land housing schemes and knows no other.

A powerful and fearless character, he could put a blade between your ribs without hesitation or qualms at the first sign of aggression. Well that's just the way things were in those days. Enlightened education hadn't yet reached into the darker realms of the concrete jungle where poverty reigned. The motto on the Glasgow Cross reads, *Nemo me impune lacessit* which in old Scots reads, *Wha' daur meddle wi me*, which in English means *No one may assail me with impunity*. But which is interpreted as simply *nae messin'* in Glasgow and so far as Gardi was concerned it would be advisable to take that warning seriously.

He'd spent most of his life in the colleges of corrective institutions. A speed freak, his thing was thieving cars, practising handbrake turns at high speed and wrecking vehicles. He would then trade them in at the breakers yard for a few pounds to get about with. In some ways,

I suppose it could be said that he was doing society a favour. Certainly Gardi Loo would agree.

Anyway at this particular time in 1984 he was onto a wee turn, but needed a legit car, which could stand a pull by the police, in which to transport his haul. He'd borrowed one from his girlfriend Marion Reynolds' mother's neighbour. The guy wasn't too happy with the idea, considering Gardi's reputation. Yet on the promise of a few quid coming his way he'd agreed but with one condition – he would hold Marion's mother's TV and video as hostage to ensure that his car was returned in one piece. Of course, the mother wasn't made aware of the terms of this arrangement – the electrical goods could be returned before she came home from her work. It was a done deal then and Gardi Loo set off with his accomplice, Cammy, to earn their daily bread.

It was the Barratt Show Homes Exhibition. One partner would stroll round with the touring group of visitors viewing the new, fully furnished show houses. On inspecting the toilet flushers there, he would open the snib on the window and stroll on through the show. As the group moved on to the next house, the accomplice would follow, one house behind nipping through the windows and out the doors with TVs, hi-fis, videos and what not into the boot of the car. This had always been a successful scank but wheels were an absolute essential. It was no less successful on this fateful day, 29th February, 1984, a leap year. Might have guessed something would go wrong.

On the motorway on the return journey with beaming smiles, Gardi Loo at the wheel became concerned at the erratic driving, screeching tyres, flashing lights and tooting horns in the rear view mirror. Unable to read the frantic hand signals of the other drivers, he dropped his speed to seventy, just in case. To their amazement, a car wheel sped past the passenger side door overtaking them.

Laughing at the chaos it was causing on the motorway, they swerved slightly to the left to avoid it as it veered to the right in front of them. Suddenly they found themselves tilting with the driver's front wheel in the air. Crunching and sparks everywhere.

'FAAAUCK SAKE! It's ours,' Gardi Loo exclaimed, coming back to earth with a thump. They pulled over onto the hard shoulder and legged it off the motorway on the trot to get help.

Back at Marion's mother's there was chaos. The owner of the car wouldn't liberate the TV and video he held hostage, not without his car or a replacement. When Mom came home there would be hell to pay. Thus it came to be that Gardi Loo, Cammy, Marion, her brother Alex and the wife of the owner of the car tagging along borrowed another car to go back to the motorway to remove their haul from the boot to swap back for the hostage TV before Mom came home. Or failing that Plan B – Alex's car as replacement. However, unknown to them, the car they'd borrowed had been driven by one Billy Love who'd just used it in his get-away after firing a shotgun at an ice cream van in Garthamlock. Ignorant of this (they had problems of their own) and on finding that their own get-away car had been towed off the motorway together with their haul, they'd disregarded Love's advice not to go near Garthamlock and put Plan B into effect anyway. Alex's car was at Marion's house in Garthamlock where the shooting had just occurred. Totally oblivious that they'd parked five yards away from the scene of the recent shooting, they all trooped out of the car and headed for Marion's flat as the police pulled up behind Alex, still in the process of switching off the ignition. Seeing the polis, he was spotted ducking and slinking down the seat in an attempt to hide. He was a banned driver.

Meanwhile, as soon as the others trooped into Marion's

front door, they promptly jumped back out the back window. Gardi Loo, Cammy and Marion all had warrants out for their arrests for non-payment of fines. Mrs Wifey also bailed out the back window with the others who promptly bolted through the labyrinths towards unknown destinations, leaving the wee wifey lost and bewildered in no-man's-land. Later, on being questioned at the trial as to why she had jumped out the window, she replied, 'I don't know, everybody else was jumping out the window and I just followed. I was lost, I didn't know where I was and I just followed everybody else.' Thus, she went on to tell how lost and stranded in a strange place without hat, coat, money or bag she had just walked and walked until she came to this big police station. With some relief, she'd entered there and told the sergeant at the desk her woeful story. Harassed and irate he'd said to her, 'My advice to you, hen, is just jump a taxi, give a snide address near your home and once he stops there, nip out and get off your mark. That's what every other fucker seems to be doing.' Astonished and a stranger to the city, that's exactly what she did.

Meantime Alex had been arrested in the car. Nicked as a banned driver and having no idea whose car he'd been driving, he was also under suspicion for two attempted murders for the shooting and had his own warrants to worry about. As a direct result of this, Gardi Loo ended up in the dock charged with the six murders of the Doyle Family and Cammy was charged with the shooting.

'Fuckin' 29th February,' grumbles Gardi Loo. Such is life.

Ode on Morality

I have this wee principle, whether it's right or whether it's wrong, I don't know, nor does it matter. It works for me and has always stood me in good moral balance and stability in the extreme situations I've found myself in in Glasgow's Ganglands. It's nothing new or unique but has helped me through the moral maze and many a quandary on how to deal with any particular situation. It's simply an adaptation of Jesus Christ's most golden rule – do unto others as you would have them do unto you. This rule, when applied universally, answers a million questions better than a million laws. Or as my Ma used to say it, 'Don't do it to others if you wouldn't like it done to you.' My adaptation to that in my environment is, 'Treat people in accordance with the standards of their own rules.' Kind of take people as you find them sort of thing. Thus, those who live by the sword may die by the sword. When dealing with an axe man, have an axe handy. Dealing with an academic or lawyer – sharpen up your pencil. Or when dealing with a backstabbing liar and cheat – no need to feel embarrassed about surprising them and no shame in using their own tactics against them. Hence, it's others who set the extremities of the standards they will be dealt with. 'Judge as thou wilt be judged by,' as yon yin said.

I've never been one for sneaking up on people, the idea of it cringes my soul. All of my escapades, all of my follies have always been face-to-face confrontations. Among those who have known me well, many have commented that I'm too straight. But I can never fully understand that and don't know how to be other than I am. Perhaps I'm in error to assume that it's everyone's aim to try to be as straight and reliable as it's possible to be in the extremes and circumstance of their environment but it's a priority of mine. We're not all the same and we don't all think the same nor come to the same conclusions but how is it possible to be too straight? Perhaps then I'm out of alignment in a bent and twisted environment?

> Must you tear me apart because you're torn apart
> that I'll never again be content
> that I can be free and happy just to be
> while you suffer in the wrath that you rent.

I don't lie and cheat in reality, don't mix it, don't run people down, don't steal from the person. But could you call a man straight who'd find it easier to do an armed wage snatch than to thieve a tenner from a purse? I grew out of thievery very early. Beyond that, blagging from goods trains and the like was more of an adventure than greed or malice.

We all grow up, we all look back and have our regrets for the mistakes we made. We're all embarrassed by our folly and sometimes downright stupidity. I guess that's part of nature's evolutionary plan. Wisdom, so they say, is the province of the aged, the ones who have known past glory but whose day is done. Evil then, is born of ignorance – unfettered ignorance with no regrets. Feelings of regret, embarrassment and shame are known only to the precious soul and the good at heart. That then, surely, is the measure of the man?

The Craw

I first lived in Barlanark when I was about thirteen or fourteen after Ma died. I lived with my sister Sadie and her man Billy. I knew the Craw from that time but never associated with him or the Bar-L. I really got to know him in Housey at fifteen when we were both being trained as plumbers.

He was six-footish, built and dressed like the proverbial scarecrow, always loudly bragging and telling whoppers about these fantastic super deeds of derring-do and criminal enterprise with him at the centre, and which were all just pure fantasy. He's one of those mad, pathological liars who just can't help it. He opens his mouth and out spurts whatever garbology is in his head. A motor mouth speed freak on adrenalin high. The name also comes from the slang term 'shoot the craw' meaning to scarper, crap out, run away. For the Craw, although loudly aggressive in the mouth, always crapped out in face-to-face confrontations. Though this nowadays may be deemed as an indication of early wisdom – then it was taken as the sign of a coward, crap bag, Craw. The fact of the matter is that when cornered with no alternative he could go ahead the same as the rest though seldom coming out on top. In the years to come retired policemen and former associates, no doubt jealous of his massive financial success, would go public and announce to the press that he had been a registered and paid police informer from his very early days. In fact, this had always been the suspicion of most people who knew him. Though nothing could even be proven outright, incident after incident seemed always to point to him as the snake in the grass. Nowadays, nobody doubts it. He has become the role model for the up and coming and the trading in of others is the done thing. No big deal nowadays, it's not simply grassing any more but called pulling a stroke – a new slant on an old adage now meaning to trade people in for your own freedom and immunity from prosecution.

After I finished the ten stretch, I was always being pulled in by the serious faces for some fuckin' thing or other which I hadn't done – usually armed robbery. It turns out that all the Serious Crime Squad codes at the time started with the letters TC for Target Criminal followed by a number and letters of the alphabet. The further along the alphabet you were the more dangerous you were considered to be. Hence the infamous XYY gang. I am the original TC not because I'm a Tough Cunt, nor the Top Cat, nor Tommy-fuckin'-Cooper for that matter. I am TC because it's my name, my initials, but these bastards took it to mean that I was the original and the prime Target Criminal because every time they punched in for data on the usual suspects my fuckin' name popped up. Ping! 'Oh! that bastard again eh!' I was indicted and acquitted five times on fit-ups. On the last embarrassing occasion for the serious faces my lawyer told me, 'Duck! Next time they won't fit you up, they'll just blow your fucking head off.'

So far as I can figure this was because I wasn't playing their game. From the first time they'd pulled me in, when I'd just finished the ten stretch, the questioning was a load of garbage and nothing to do with me. Maybe they just wanted to meet me and to introduce themselves, I don't really know, but it wasn't long before I became more of an amusing curiosity than the station's cat's kittens. They'd grilled me about this and that, none of it any of my business or concern who the fuck killed Cock Robin. I was just tripping off the usual standard No Comment to their genuine amazement and amusement. Then they started shouting in their buddies, the rest of the Crime Squad. 'Hey, c'mere'n see this! Ask him a question. Go on, ask him something.' And they would ask me something:

'Don't know.'
'Not interested.'
'Know nothing about it.'
'Not my problem.'
'None of my business.'
'No Comment.'

Amid the rising hilarity with the assembled squad, the general consensus of opinion was that they had discovered a dinosaur thawed out from the fucking permafrost which, by some freak of nature, was still around. Like Rip Van & the Winkle Pickers band, totally out of fucking orbit. So they took it upon their good selves to educate this poor ignorant Neanderthal man in the ways of the modern Homo sapiens.

'Look you've got to understand that you're a rare bird we thought was extinct. We just don't meet people like you any more. You've been away a long time and it's just not about that anymore. It's about working together, cooperating as a team. It's about getting the information to us first before any other cunt gets it in somewhere else. It's not them and us any more, for we ARE the mob, get it? Now away ye go home and give us a call when you need some cover.'

'Funny,' I thought, 'I get the impression that I was being

recruited but NAAA. I must be para or something.' Aye, I always was a wee bit slow. Like my brothers always said, 'He's no too wide him.'

Sure I'd known that the trade-in scheme had always gone on but for me it had been seen as rare, few and far between amongst scumbags. What I hadn't taken into account was the rate of inflation over the years of my absence. Winters of discontent and all that. The Junk scene had taken a grip and dragged the known standards down with it to the gutter. Thatcher's hard lines sucker policy on law and new order had taken its toll in the deepest, darkest recesses of the social psyche. If that was the evolution of the social structures, sure enough then, I am a dinosaur.

So then, it's not difficult to see how someone with an aptitude and urge to compulsively fib on a wide and monumental scale would thrive under such new order regimes. More especially when such cooperation with the serious fit-up squad turned both ways. I can well imagine those gigantic whoppers being duly and painstakingly noted on file and some paranoid polis duly patting some other paranoid polis on the back, 'Well done, we could never have discovered this dastardly organised crime conspiracy without you. Make sure your grass is well covered and protected.' While all the time the grass is weaving paranoid illusions as a smokescreen for his own activities. Firing in some sucker here and there to keep up his credibility with the mob, all to mutual advantage and personal gain and self-promotion, of course. People always say that the bizzies had the Craw by the short hairs but that's simply not true. The fact of the matter is that they had each other by the balls and were pulling the strokes together. This wasn't rivalry – this was a team. This was the mob that became known as the Caravel Cartel.

They were licensed to operate with impunity and all the way down the line came under the protective umbrella of the Craw. But this was yet to be. Meanwhile back when I was on the street . . .

The Craw & the Blue Doos

Raiding the RSPOs (sub post offices) had always been a good earner. It had been the speciality of the Bar-L team for many a long year before I came on the scene. They were just regrouping an active duty team after a long dry lay-off when the Crime Squad had tipped them that they were under surveillance by Special Branch. Stolen postal orders, stamps and similar items had been turning up all over Northern Ireland in the hands of Orange paramilitary groups, traced back to the raids on RSPOs all over bonny Scotland. The word from the mob was that the heat was off and that the Branch had replanted its roots elsewhere on more fertile soil. Thus the teams were being regrouped.

These were operated like, and to all practical purposes were well organised, well equipped commando style raids on giro banks. The camouflage uniform for urban activity was the obvious dark blue snorkel jacket with chin flap and hood, dark denims, trainers and gloves in which it was legitimate to walk the streets or ride a car, train or bus. This also retained the advantage of camouflage in dark wooded or farmland areas, gardens or domestic hedging. Usually a hit squad of six would make a team, each member with portable multi-channelled short-wave CBs, and had memorised key police codes as well as their own. Bolt cutters, wire snips, jemmies, ignition screws and so on would all be taken out to the turn separately by private hire cab, itself with its code name and tuned into base control for any required early warnings.

The crew themselves would each find their own way to the rendezvous. Nipping out of their own back windows, or taking the dog for a walk to get the evening paper, sending the dog home by itself. Each covertly in their own way vacating their home areas, being picked up at a fixed spot by private hire cab and meeting at a specified location before swapping transport for the target. Each in constant contact with base. If one was picked up by a police tell tail he would be alerted and signed off with the single call sign, Blue Doo. It would then be his task to take his tail as far wide of the target as possible while the others carried on with the job. For this he could still expect his cut at the end of the night as an active member of the team. Fair dos saves blues.

On the turn each was allotted his task. It could be on the edge up, either stationed in the bushes outside the local cop shop ready to radio in the Blue Doo at the first sign of any unusual activity; or on the outback duty watching the roundabouts for incoming patrols which were easily timed so that the dismantled alarm systems and opened steel shutters could be put back into place for the passing patrol, unknowingly watched by six pairs of eyes from the garden hedgerows. Phone systems for the entire area would be put out of action. One time, a new secure system was emplaced so that it couldn't be put out in one stop. A short journey and a heave-ho over an easy wall closed down the phone system for the entire West of Scotland. 'Fuck! yon was a big cable eh!'

Security was good. Anybody showed up in the wrong colour uniform it was a Blue Doo. Either all in green or all in blue but nobody the odd man out. Da once mentioned 'the man in the white bunnit' in reference to a grass. The same idea applied here. Somebody wearing something odd was distinguishable from everyone else. That's an old trick so that when the coppers come on top, he's the one they let escape. It was therefore assumed that if someone turned up in the wrong colour the coppers had been tipped off and the turn would be called off. Yet, even with this level of organisation, the majority of raids were Blue Doos for one reason or another, mostly due to the strict no violence policy which suited me fine. I never did stick at it for very long anyway, jacking it in for more legit employment.

I remember one such turn. I was posted guard on an underpass below a motorway. I'd to step hurriedly back into the bushes because of a courting couple on foot. They presented no risk to the team, heading in the wrong direction for that but temporarily neutralised my post. It seemed he was becoming a wee bit too pushy and demanding and she was getting a wee bit scared. None of my business, just get to fuck past me so I could get back on watch, was my only concern. They wouldn't move past me and she was trying to turn back as if suspicious of the darkened tunnel and secluded wooded area beyond. Either that or she was psychic and had sensed me sitting in the bushes silently mimicking their arguments, 'Yak Yak Yak,' I'd heard it all before. This one, however, turned nasty. She was a definite No and he was a determined Yes.

To cut a long story short, he dragged her through the tunnel to my end, giving her a few heavy dull yins along the way. Next thing they're crashing through my bushes onto the ground near to me. She's suddenly gone awfully quiet. A quick deco saw him with one hand choking the life out of the poor lassie, the other dragging the knickers off her. Then, still holding her by the throat while she turned ten shades of blue, he proceeded to mount her to do the dastardly deed. I stood up – she was looking straight at me, eyes bulging. It must have looked like I came straight up from hell – hood up and big, hooked jemmy held at my shoulder. She must have thought I was the Grim fuckin Reaper himself. Stepping over I said, 'Naw! Fuck you, Jimmy,' as I bounced the jemmy off his noggin. Donk! It hardly budged the fucker but at least he let go of her throat to hold his head and turned to see what the fuck had just happened. Donk! Donk! Donk! I played musical jemmies on his napper, sending him backwards at an angle in dismount as she wheezed to gasp in some precious air. The bastard still got up in a fighting mood. A good boot to the prick and a dull yin to the temple slowed him down but he was still staggering, still on his feet and still looking to put up a fight as I radioed through a civilian Blue Doo alert. I didn't want to hit this guy again, not that I didn't think he deserved it for he deserved a whole lot more. It was just I thought that if I hit him any more I'd probably have killed him.

So far as I was concerned, he shouldn't have been able to take those blows and still be on his feet – staggering and dazed but still conscious and ready to fight. I figured he may already be dead on his feet and just didn't know it yet, like a chicken without a head. The troops came charging round like the household fuckin cavalry. First man decked him with a flying kick without stopping to pause. The guy was still moving on the ground like a toy soldier that didn't know he'd toppled over.

We got her onto her feet, chatting and cracking witty asides to help her recover her composure and hide her embarrassment. She was obviously badly shaken and trembling and never so happy to see such a gang of rogues in her life. She was telling us her name, his name, that she'd only just met him and was he dead? Giving us her address she wouldn't take her eyes off me no matter who spoke to her, burning my face into her memory, giving me the jitters. It suddenly struck me that she thought we were the polis with our radios and all that. It must've occurred to the others too because nobody said anything to make her think different. One of the troops blagged a car and took her home while the rest of us fucked off on our chosen routes home – Blue Doo being the order of the day.

I often wonder what the polis must have thought when they found a safe at the back door of the local post office with no one to claim it then hearing this lassie's story. I'm told the rapist made a full recovery. Pity, it could've been the perfect murder. Still, I'm glad he survived. He is, after all, still some mother's son.

Which again reminds me of old Mrs Dawson as we came to know her. In fact we didn't know her at all. It was just that we'd brought one of the troops along on this job because he was just out of the nick after a long stretch – sort of do him a wee turn, so to speak. Help him get a few quid to furnish the house and get on his feet.

The job itself had gone with the usual clockwork efficiency. The target had been cracked, the box at the back door ready for loading and was reckoned to hold about fifty grand. That's when old Mrs Dawson introduced herself. Mrs Dawson because she looked like Les fuckin Dawson in drag, toothless with the chin touching her nose as she spluttered, 'Ya shower a thieving bastards ye are. Leave that fuckin shop alane.' Shuffling in her wee pink slippers with pom-poms, shaking her fist in the air, more comical than threatening but in total defiance of the odds. Shuffling forward swinging her wee fist. I mean, you're talking potentially dangerous men here in a potentially dangerous situation and she is totally oblivious to any fear. This was her fuckin' turf and nae messin.

The point being that there was one in our team who was indeed a desperate man and needed that cash badly.

He'd just done eight years for less and wouldn't walk away from it that easily. I'd been scouting the outer edges when I got the call sign for a civilian Blue Doo and headed for the locus. Any other Blue Doo call sign and I'd have been going in the other direction, like sharpish.

I'd been called in directly because of Mrs Dawson and the desperado who was being held by the others. For there was just no way he was walking away from the pay at this stage in the game and had decided better to bop her over the napper with a huge pair of bolt cutters. She was still there facing up to him, one hand on her hip and wagging her finger with the other in defiance. I was the only person this guy would pay any heed to and they wanted me to get him back into fuckin line.

'What the fuck'r you up tae?' I stormed in at him as I approached the scene. 'C'mon, let's get the fuck out of here, leave it alane. It's a Blue fuckin' Doo, can you no see it or something?'

'Aye but, aye but,' he stuttered. 'But there's all that money there an that stupid auld bastard.'

'Leave it out, we're out of here. Come on, we're off. Let's move before we're lifted,' I said, taking grip of him and dragging him with me away from the scene. Later it had to be explained to him that it was just not on. It was not the mode of operation so to speak. If civilians, for any reason, got in the way or wandered onto the scene then the turn was aborted. No one need be harmed in these activities – that was the whole point of going to all this trouble. We were taking the same money or more from a breaking and entry as others struggled to get from an armed robbery with guns. This way no one was harmed for no one ever saw the raiders. And the difference between armed robbery and theft was about ten years.

Another screw-up was a social club on the outskirts of

the city. It was more for the fact that it was coming up for the New Year and it was thought to be a good idea to maybe go and pick some up from a not so local supplier and so we should call by at this particular social club and check out their booze stock, fags, and puggies.

It should have been a doddle but forward planning had failed to register one particular aspect of the security system. Namely, that once the outer alarm systems had been dismantled and the pulsar neutralised for entry to the internal system where timing and team coordination were essential, the fucking entire area was automatically flood-lit with a galaxy of heavy-duty spotlights. 'Shit, whit next? If it's no wan damn thing it's another.'

It was decided to carry on regardless, extra men called in from watch duty to add the hands needed to deal with this unforeseen illumination show. Quick thinking, or rather, no thinking – sheer instinct to get out of the glare led to the floodlights being kicked over face down on the grass. Up onto beer barrels, onto the roof so that those too could be faced down onto the asphalt and tarmac. Ah! peace at last as the darkness wrapped itself back around us like a security blanket and we carried on with the job in hand. Filling sacks from the banks of puggies and space invaders, some stocking up the cartons of snout, while others took charge of the booze and still another went to bring round the transport. Christmas time is here and all is well. Dum de dum de dum, 'Ah whistle while you work . . .'

'Hey! shoosht, what's that? Listen!'

Crackle, crackle, snap, pop.

'Well, it's no fuckin' rice crispies.' Nipping outside to have a deco,

'Oh shit!' The heat from the lights had set fire to the fuckin' roof and the whole place was lighting up again like a fuckin' Christmas tree.

It was a punters' club after all, so we were soon on the roof fighting the fire and got it out but what about those fuckin' big lights? The glass was like thick magnifying glass and wouldn't break. 'Got it,' someone said, sliding a concrete slab away and with insulated bolt cutters . . . snip. 'POOOWWW.' He landed on his arse but he'd cut the power. Time for bed, said Zeb. Time to cut and run with what we had but no, the Craw, greedy bastard, wanted it all and fucked about wasting time. The coppers must be on their way by now but he wouldn't just cut and run. Pure greed. Blue lights in the sky. Blue Doo time to go. We went, leaving him still loading up a stolen estate car for himself. There was no way anybody was driving out of that area. We all knew it. He knew it but he just couldn't see it for the greed.

So off he went, just as the Craw flies, straight into the first road block, smashing straight through it and the chase was on. I mean, what is this? It's only a few cases of booze, man! He could've bought the fuckin' place instead of zooming about like a desperado. Overturning on the next roundabout, crawling out of the wreckage and trying to bolt, wrestling with coppers, rolling about the ground. What's got into him? 'He been at that brandy in the cellar?'

He was the only one captured that night. One glance at the modus operandi would have him charged with conspiracy or organised crime. Nothing new. He had been charged with conspiracy and organised crime five times before and they'd never got him as far as court. This time though he was caught on the scene with the goodies. Plus car theft, driving under a ban and fuck knows how many attempted murders of polis through the road-block and chase. They would soon be rounding up the usual suspects.

Once we reached our own home turf we contacted his

wife with the bad news of the casualty on the Field of Rattle but she was way ahead of us. 'It's okay,' says she. 'The mob have been on the blower to say that it's okay, they have it in hand. Not to worry, he'll be home tomorrow. Yous have to just sit tight.' Eh? whit? The fuckin' Crime Squad said whit?

The Serious Crime Squad took charge of the case or cases and he was charged with reset of stolen goods and released the next day – end of story. If someone has that kind of protection well, fair enough, but you've got to ask yourself what was he giving in return? I know a few were getting paid off here and there. Outstanding mortgages? Sorted. Motorbike for their son's Christmas? Sorted. Things like that moved into much bigger and wider areas as time passed with the information super-highway just round the corner.

Round at his place one day sitting on the couch when the phone goes. The Craw's wife answers, 'Right, Jimmy. Okay, Jimmy. Aye, right away, Jimmy. Nae bother, Jimmy. Here he's here, Jimmy,' and hands the phone over to the Craw.

Then HE starts it and all, 'Right ye are, Jimmy. Right away, Jimmy. Soon as ye can then, Jimmy. Cheerio then, Jimmy. See ya.' Putting the phone down, turning to me saying, 'That was Jimmy on the blower there.' Aye? I'd never have guessed it.

More to the point though, Jimmy was one of the rockets in the pocket from the Serious Crime Squad and he'd just tipped him off that the Scottish Crime Squad were presently on their merry way to fit him up. Dearie me! Is that the time already? I need to be on my own merry go lucky fuckin way too. I mean, man, post offices throughout bonny Scotland had been getting rattled right left and centre and it had been causing quite a stir in the Press. This was the province of the national branch of serious faces, the Scottish Crime

Squad, universally famous for their heavy and unique brand of fit-ups with the political nod.

'I'm offski,' I told the Craw.

'Naw!' he says. 'Stay. I'll need witnesses.'

'Whit? Do you need a fuckin' co-accused? No danger stranger, they'll just fit me up alang wi ye.' I made a bolt for the front door. I always was good with my hands.

He did as Jimmy had wisely advised and got all his neighbours in and around him so that by the time the Scottish fit-up squad arrived they were outnumbered three or four to one. They had come, sure enough, three carloads and, following upon the usual orchestrated symphony of slamming doors, they jostled their way team handed into the abode of the Craw only to find that there was now about twenty or so community-spirited neighbours at hand to oversee proceedings. Three or four of them to a man, 'Hey! Whit's that yer taking oot yer pocket, Mister?' 'Is that you trying to put something under that bed?' Christ! If you scratched your arse you'd get done for sexual harassment in there. Well, at least the locals got their panto that year.

I'd headed for the top of the street and stood there on the corner peering round. I was the only one who saw the copper coming out of the house while all this was going on. He walked across the road to the Craw's Granada, pulled out a set of keys and tried the door, giving it a right good jiggle. No luck. No chance with the boot either – everything remained secure and lockfast. If you ever want to screw a car, don't ask a polis, they're pure tits at it. So, hands back in his pockets he walked round the car, looking at the wheels. Stopped, looked around then just toe bashed the hubcap. One tap with his foot and off it dropped to the ground. He picked it up and into it drops a set of keys, a sheaf of paper from his inside pocket and an envelope from his coat pocket. About turned and re-entered the affray, swaggering like a fuckin waiter with the drinks on a tray, whistling, 'I've got you, under my skin. I've got you . . .'

It turned out that the sheaf of paper was cash share-out lists and numbers. The envelope contained survey maps with rings round the post offices that had been targeted and the keys from one or two of those premises. Unable to plant them in the house, he'd thought of the car. Good thinking, Sherlock. Deserve a promotion for that initiative but finding the car inaccessible had improvised further with the hubcap. I mean! A goddamned hubcap for Christ sake! He is supposed to be a crafty villain remember? Rattata-tattling round the streets with a set of fuckin' incriminating keys in his hub cap. Gie's a break!

So, sufficiency of evidence now gathered, the Craw was duly arrested. Okay, so the evidence might be fake but wasn't he guilty anyway? And, don't the Mounties always get their man? Or isn't that for a jury to decide on the facts of the real evidence in a free and democratic society? Is it not the fruit from the poison tree which we must beware of? Is it not that its seed may spread that you or I may fall foul of it too someday? Is it not that these so-called pillars of society, upholders of the law, justice and morality are expected to be above base corruption to set an example to our children and citizenry? Are they not perjurers and perverters of justice on whom you and I rely to be honest and to uphold the law and not to act as judge and jury and executioner? I knew the Craw was guilty. Though even then, mostly by hearsay, but they didn't know. They couldn't know for sure, for that's what a trial and a jury are for. The fact is that they could do it to him without qualms or hesitation as they do to so many others as we sit back in our naïve trust and let them. How would you feel if they did it to you? Do you think a jury would believe you? Do you think truth would win through in the end? Sorry but it doesn't usually work out that way. Try telling the truth in court and I'll see you in the exercise yard and discuss appeal procedures. No way will you get away with such a dastardly character attack upon our boys in blue.

So it was that just as they were bringing the Craw out in cuffs to jeers, sneers and general deriding of the assembled neighbourhood the, by now, very Serious Crime Squad rolled up in two cars. Five of them in all led by the ever faithful Jimmy himself. Slam! Bam! Gonna liberate my man, sang the Doors or was that Abba? No matter, from the stormy mood this was all beginning to look very promising indeed and, by Christ, no one was disappointed. Jimmy and the Mob stormed straight to the point, 'Get those fuckin cuffs off him. You're no fittin him up.' The crowd were in total glee, loving it. Wouldn't you? The atmosphere was electric and ready to blow. 'Things can only get better, since I found you . . .'

'Naw, nae chance,' growls back the Scottish Crime Squad. 'This is our prisoner and it has nothing to do with you, this is our jurisdiction, we ARE the Scottish Crime Squad and we're charging this man with conspiracy and organised crime.'

'Aw no ye'r no. Just get the fuckin cuffs off him, get back into the house and we'll talk about this,' answers the Serious Crime Squad. Makes you wonder if we'll ever see the likes of this again?

They were head to head now out on the pavement by the close, wagging their fingers of so-called authority, cursing and swearing and generally committing a breach of the peace at each other then, BAM. Suddenly it happened. In frustration at not being able to rescue his man, Jimmy stuck the head on the man in charge, a pure dull yin so it was. THUNK, right on the bridge of the nose.

'Yeees!' the crowd let out a single roar as the rammy of

the month ensued. Out came the batons on both sides as the locals tore off the garden railings and they all wellied into each other. Cop against cop. Punter against cop, any fuckin cop. It didn't matter, the excuse was there so get in while ye can. It didn't last long – nae stamina those yins – but by the time they'd all finished rolling about the street and gardens there wasn't an upright hedge left.

The Scottish Crime Squad relented. Took a back seat, in fact. Capitulated, crapped it. They released the Craw into the custody of Jimmy and the serious faces.

'This is not the end of this. Blah! Blah!' moaned the Scottish Crime Squad. But it was. Charges were withdrawn and no further action taken.

The funny thing is, apparently Jimmy had first said that they'd been on their way to fit the Craw up but how did he know? And how did he know that this was what they had done? I mean, how did he know that they hadn't found real evidence? The answer is that he didn't. He'd actually done the right and legal thing but for the wrong reasons. And what does it matter? The insight to me was that here was real protection to a degree that I would never have believed if I hadn't seen it for myself. He wouldn't have acted like that without a nod, at least, from Olympus.

The Weigh-in

The weigh-in originates from a time when cash in the form of copper, brass, silver and gold (pennies, florins, guineas, sovereigns) retained their capital value in weight. Thus, on the scrap yard scales, each knew their due and made damn certain to be there at the weigh-in to ensure their just share of the prize.

Of course, the local cops would always station themselves there at the weigh-in station to take their percentage. They would be weighed-in on the deal, so to speak, for otherwise the haul would be confiscated and all your hard graft would be to no avail or profit. The weigh-in then is one's share out and just due from the scales. At least, originally.

The coppers have their beat. The pubs pay their weigh-in with goods in kind to keep their licences and a blind eye turned where needed. The ice cream van pays in double nougats. The newsagent in newspapers and so on. One way or another they all pay their weigh-in. Whilst, on the other side of the track, the concept was taken just a little further.

It evolved around the scales. The idea of rough justice and just due. As the polis were being weighed-in on one hand, the punters were duly weighed-in on the other. To even the score for a wrong done, the culprit would be duly weighed-in and found to be in deficit and the balance rectified accordingly. Usually with a knife to the gut, a razor to the face or some dull yin over the skull with a hammer or such like. Hence to be weighed-in is simply to be paid one's just due in accordance with the balance of karma. Or, in street terms, the balance of the damage due. Rough justice. Sharp and swift. No appeal.

It's a cultural thing. Those who opt for its codes live by and die by its rules. Coppers who take a weigh-in will do so for the rest of their lives. In other communities it would be called corruption and pay-offs but, in fact, it is no more than insurance premiums paid for protection against loss. A tax on a licence to operate. Never in my life have I known a copper who did not take a weigh-in in return for turning a blind eye or assisting in some criminal enterprise. That's why everyone wants a polis in the family. No to be proud citizenry but simply because it is cheaper in the long run.

To us then, the fact that the Craw was weighing-in the Crime Squad was no big deal and nothing new. They paid their dues in protection and put him on to some good turn from which we all profited. Yet that he was also weighing them in with information on others would not be acceptable or tolerated. That he went on to the actual creation and commissioning of crimes for others to take the fall. Covering for himself and keeping his merry men on the fast track to promotion moves into yet another league. No wonder then he now wears a bullet proof vest. The Glesca kiss is a heeder to the nose but the Glesca kiss-off is a bullet up the arse. They haven't yet been able to make bullet proof underpants y'see . . .

BOOK TWO

Storm Rising

1984

It was 1984. Richard Burton copped his whack, famine raged across Ethiopia and the miners embarked on yet another year-long strike. Frankie Goes to Hollywood kept ranting on about Two Tribes going to war. For most of us it wasn't entertainment . . .

'GLASGOW'S MILES BETTER' blazoned the legend but did anybody ever think to ask, 'Miles better than what? By what comparison?' I suppose, any improvement on the statistics which made us the cancer capital of the word was an improvement worth proclaiming to the tourists. Especially since more people had died of cancers in the city of Glasgow than in the rest of Europe put together. The statistics simply had to improve. When you drop from a population of over a million down to a few hundred thousand things could only get better since there were so few people left still to die. Was it the bad eating habits? The summer sunshine? Or the genocide of fluoridisation of the water supply that was wiping out the rebellious Red Clydesiders? Fuck knows! Glaswegians who used to be those wee bow-leggit, gumsy punters with bunnets and a load of cheek were now strapping six-footers with strong teeth and bones who were all dying of cancer.

Thanks to a whopping great grant from the EU by way of compensation for a dying city, the Necropolis became the thriving Metropolis once again. The City Chambers was sandblasted McClean as a whistle and what became the City of Culture was looking grand. Even if the punters in the streets were no better off at least they now had fine art and architecture to look at as they froze and starved to death in their droves. But, thanks again to Thatcher, we would have the right to buy our own council homes.

'Aye, right hen! Do y'want to gie us the money then?' No work, no pay, no broo money for the young unemployed cast out into the streets b'cos their mammies couldn't afford to feed them, strapping big honey monsters they were at that. Crime figures and youth detention soaring. Hmm! wonder why? Academia pondered philosophically in ivory chambers.

The miners' strike was in full flow. Flying pickets were blocked on the motorway, turned back or arrested. The costs of the emergency measures, latest riot control gear and police overtime could have paid for what the miners were asking but this was not a struggle of economics. This was a struggle of ideologies. Thatcher, the Iron Lady, was out to show the world who was the man of the house by pummelling the miners into submission or oblivion. There were old Tory scores to settle here under a three-line whip whilst Kinnock cringed in whimpers for mercy. Thatcher's hard lines sucker policy on Law and New Order Regime gripped Fortress Britain in the Iron Hand of Fascism.

While the Wapping pickets resisted the baton charges of the mounted police in their struggles for control of the Press and propaganda, the likes of Toxteth and Notting Hill burned in rebellious discontent and Thatcherite armies marched over, under and into every crevice of the land like giant mutant cockroaches. Emergency measures were the new order of the day as miners became prisoners, criminalised under the new order regime. The prisons, overflowing and bursting at the seams, rioted. Socialism outlawed, demonised and trodden underfoot by jack-booted Thatcherites on the march. Armed police at the airports and in the docks of Fortress Britain. The Libyan Embassy siege and the SAS shoot-to-kill policy in the north. The McKenzies, Murdochs, Maxwells, Moloch and Mammon reigned supreme and while the market soared, riots roared and justice was just another commodity we couldn't afford. Que sera . . .

Walking in the streets of downtown Carntyne, I came across these two brothers, about five or six years old, the younger in tears and broken glass at their feet in the gutter between them. As I approached, it became obvious that whatever was up, the younger was getting the blame, reminding me of my own childhood. Tommy Take-the-Blame was my name.

'Am tellin my ma it wiz your fault. She's gonnae batter ye so she wull,' the elder asserted vehemently.

'Naw it wiznae. It wiz your fault,' the younger defended in tears.

'Hey! whit's the score wee man, whit's wrang weh ye?' said I approaching.

'TC, my ma sent us doon tae the darky's weh a gingie fur a single tipped an he drapped it. She's gonnae go aff her heid, she's no got a fag.'

'Can she no get tick aff the van till Monday?' said I digging into a pocketful of loose change.

'Naw! she owes ye a nicker fae a fortnight ago that she got affy Liz an she canny pay it.'

'Fuck sake, is that a? Here!' I says, handing over a couple of quid in change. 'Get her fags aff the van and gee Liz her nicker and pick that fuckin gless up before I get a puncture will ye?'

Telling Rid Ronny about it, he was pissing himself laughing but I couldn't see the joke. 'Gawn ya big sucker ye. Yon's wee Blacky's boys, they're wide as the Clyde. They staun there every night on the same scam. That's their pitch, man. Ah thought ye were wider than that!' Deary me! The world may change, but Glasgow weans remain the same.

My son Stephen was two-and-a-half, a really bright wean with the most beautiful little laugh I've ever heard.

Like tinkling bells. He was the centre of my world and I took him everywhere with me. In the years to come, he'd continue to astound people by pointing to various flowers, trees, birds and things naming them as I'd taught him. His mother was a pure gem and pregnant with our son Brian. We were settled and we were happy. Working as a partnership both at home and in business we shared the load and took the rough with the smooth. Myself in stock control in the mornings to give Liz a long lie in from her evening shift on the van. It was a good run and made a good wage to keep the family off the breadline. We couldn't ask for and didn't expect more. To build a home and a family with a wage and those you love was all I ever hoped to achieve and Liz and Stephen were the greatest thing that had ever happened to me. She was so straight and honest, a wonderful and beautiful person. It wasn't difficult at all for me to stay on the straight and narrow and away from the troubles of old. It was a new life and I have Liz to thank for helping me see that such a life can be achieved.

Of course Thatcher's Britain worried me but she was Middle England, another world away. Yet she was everywhere. Poverty was rife and we'd just got out of it by the skin of our teeth. I'd never met a single soul who would admit to having voted Tory but this was Scotland and we didn't have any say in who controlled our country. So although it seemed to me that George Orwell's 1984 Big Brother annat was naïve, nevertheless it was beyond our control and no point in cryin', 'Ain't gonna work on Maggie's farm no mo' . . .'

Dole queues were long, wages short and labour cheap. The flagship, Spirit of Free Enterprise was resurrected from its watery grave and was steaming its way as a ghost ship out of control towards South Africa.

Eye of the Storm

In 1963 at fifteen years old, Agnes was crippled in one hand by a soldier on leave from the army by the name of Snotter Wray. She'd wrenched a knife from his hand by the blade as he wielded it, disarming him but severing the tendons of her hand across the palm, rendering it dead and paralysed in the process.

At sixteen she was married with a baby daughter. Her man, wee Shadda, was in the nick when Ma died and, as Da was still serving the ten stretch, Agnes became the legal guardian of my sister Patsy (15), Lockey (14), Robert (13), myself (12) and baby daughter Pam. Our Agnes took it all in her stride, we all did. I guess we tend to grow up quicker when needs must.

Through the years to follow, Agnes would never touch alcohol, smoke nor swear. Puritanical in her outlook and strict in discipline, perhaps overcompensating for Da, she wouldn't tolerate bad hygiene, lies, excuses nor any hint of thievery from anyone around her. Not much fun then for us boys used to the rough and tumble of Best Man's Fall down in the Staney, Ring O'Leario down in the Planny or Tom Sawyer adventures with home made rafts along the Monklands canal from Blackhill to the Sugarolly Mountains up by Cranhill and beyond. Not difficult to fathom how Agnes would develop the stereotype matriarchal personality. By her mid-twenties, she'd five children of her own to replace her wayward brothers, by then in the late sixties scattered throughout the land in various corrective institutions.

Around 1983, her eldest daughter having passed her O levels and Highers, Agnes herself returned to college to complete her education with the intention of taking up social work. Always the brightest of the bunch, it had been a great source of sorrow for Da that she'd missed her opportunity to go on to university and better things. Blaming himself for the loss, he'd made her promise to go back to it some day. Now, even though Da was dead, she'd undertaken to fulfil that promise in this, her social work training.

At that time she was also the caretaker of the local drop-in centre for deprived and under-privileged children of whom there were many in the area. Her own experiences were invaluable to the social work department there who couldn't tell the difference between measles and flea infestation and, on being informed of the latter, would yelp and avoid the kids like the plague while Agnes got on with attending to the matter.

It has always puzzled and amazed me that no one ever sees fit to comment that the acrimony in the so-called 'ice cream wars' in Garthamlock centred around Jimmy Mitchell and the Marchetti Bros and not the Doyle family. Old Penny Mitchell and his daughter Irene ran two Marchetti vans in Garthamlock. Penny Mitchell's son, Jimmy jnr, was the manager of Marchetti's who ran a fleet of about sixty vans throughout the city. In Garthamlock, they'd sent in a fleet of six vans to box in and crowd out the competition. Finally, unable to sustain that expense, they'd kept on a third van to do the harassment of the independent non-aligned operator. This third van was driven by Andrew Doyle and the independent non-aligned operator was my sister Agnes.

Her van had been purchased second hand after the

local community residents' association, of which Agnes was a member, had been refused funding to place their own community ice cream van in the housing scheme with the intention of breaking the extortionate monopoly of the Mitchell/Marchetti cartel. Agnes had then decided to go it alone and her van was left wrecked by the roadside for her troubles. Undeterred, a new van was purchased on HP and continued to draw the custom away from the cartel. Mitchell was discovering the cost of robbing his customers over the years. Now they had choice and Mars Bars at 15p rather than 22p make a difference. This throughout the entire stock range made a big dent in their market and the Mitchell/Marchetti cartel couldn't compete on a free trade basis. Their allegation that she was selling stolen goods, though contemptible, was nevertheless serious. Thus when she produced her trump card of manufacturers' price-marked goods, Agnes had won the price war hands down.

On the other hand, Andrew Doyle was, from the Mitchells' point of view, the wrong man for the job or, rather, the wrong boy. For he was only seventeen or eighteen years of age and, though built like the proverbial tank, like so many of his ilk, by nature's balance he was a gentle giant. A non-aggressive, good-natured big lad who always had a smile and a joke for everyone. He'd only accepted this job on the promise from the Mitchell/Marchetti management that it would lead to him having charge of his own van and a run in his own area, Ruchazie, where he and his family lived and were later to so tragically die.

Needless to say, his heart wasn't in this hassle lark. Instead of blocking in and harassing the rival, as was his given task, he just rambled easily around the run following one stop behind while his employers got on with their race towards heart attacks through stress. It was no skin off his nose whoever got to which stop first. He didn't pay the van hire fee or the stock bills. Paid £8 per night as a driver, it wasn't his problem, especially since the Mitchell/Marchetti management had reneged on their promise of allowing him his own van in Ruchazie. At the end of the night, he would draw up alongside Agnes for a friendly chat before saying good night and heading for home. He told her that his employers were always on at him for 'fraternising with the enemy' and asked what fraternising meant. He didn't care what they said. They'd tried to give him a using and had broken their promise, so fuck them.

The Mitchell/Marchetti management however were up to their necks in it. Their monopoly was being smashed wide open by an independent non-aligned private operator. Prices slashed by a third of the cartel's standard going rates. When her old van was wrecked and left demolished by the side of the road, the standard was set. Agnes and her family were the locals, well known, well liked and well respected. Folk would not take kindly to this attack on one of their own and so it proved. From that point, even the kids were throwing stones at every opportunity.

On 12th May, 1984, a month after the Doyle family fire murders, Agnes was arrested along with her husband, wee Shadda, and her teenage son, Thomas. The original petition warrant was that of conspiracy to further business aims. It became known to the press as the 'ice cream wars'. Like history repeating itself, this left Agnes' teenaged daughter to look after her younger school-aged sister and brothers and to manage the household. No easy task since the polis had also arrested the housekeeping cash – the princely sum of £200.

Although Agnes and young Thomas were finally released from prison after ten weeks untried, Agnes remained with one charge outstanding. This was a charge of 'dangerously obstructing traffic' when Irene Mitchell's boyfriend, Dougie Cardil, had mounted the pavement with her van, knocking Agnes down with the vehicle. Of course, the charge was absurd and, on acquitting Agnes at court, the judge ordered an enquiry into why the charge had been brought against her in the first place and not against the driver. By that time, the enquiry was already under way at Glasgow High Court under the newspaper headline of 'Ice Cream Wars'. In view of that, the reason why the victim had been prosecuted rather than the culprit should be obvious. The victim was related to the accused in that trial and the culprit was a witness for the prosecution.

Storm Rising

Sammy Sneak's van had been off the road for some time. The stock was virtually non-existent and there was a rumour that it might be up for sale. I'd been in Fifti's about two year and I couldn't remember ever seeing the guy, didn't know what he looked like. The van was only a couple of years old but it was in a mess from neglect. In the last two weeks it had started to go out to work again, maybe once or twice a week with Sammy's father-in-law at the helm. It looked like they were trying to build up the stock again to get back on the road full time. Good luck to them.

Then one morning up at the garage the Craw says to me, 'See somebody done Sammy McBride's van.'

'Oh aye! Screwed it y'mean?' I said walking between the vans to have a deco. 'Naw, blasted it wi a shotgun,' he told me and sure enough the side serving window was boarded up with plywood. Then came the punchline, 'He's putting it down to you,' said the Craw.

'Ach don't talk shite, I don't even know the guy. Yer kiddin' right?'

'Naw, nae kiddin. I heard he's put it down to you.'

'What the fuck would he say that for? Where is he? I'll talk to the cunt.' But Sammy didn't come up to the garage any more, his father-in-law now ran the show. Someone pointed him out to me and I spoke to him. Ranting and raving on about stupid bastards that don't have a clue what the fuck they were talking about, bringing my name into their fuckin' troubles when I've no fuckin' interest. Blah! Blah! Blah! All the time the Craw standing behind me looking over my shoulder at the guy who didn't look at me but just kept looking over my shoulder while saying to me, 'Don't tell me, son, tell Sammy. You should go down and see Sammy, he wants to see you. Will you go and see him? You need to talk to Sammy.' So we made arrangements for him to take me over to see Sammy later that day. Meantime I'd discovered the copper on the case was formerly of the Serious Crime Squad, now in uniform. I was determined to get this sorted out so off I stormed to Easterhouse polis station to see the man in charge. The Craw had advised against this and I was soon to see why.

'Aye then, TC, y'want to see me about McBride I'm told.'

'Aye, I've just heard I'm getting the blame ae it an ah want tae . . .'

'The blame of what?' he interrupted.

'His windae. I'm told he reported his windae to you an that ah'm . . .'

'Aye his window was panned in.'

'. . . suppose to have done his windae wi a shotgun but ah've got fuck all . . .'

'Before we go any further, TC, and you put yourself any deeper into it tell me this, where did you get your information from?'

'The Craw told me that I . . . What? What ye laughin at?'

'Oh you've just walked right into one,' he says chuckling and shaking his head. 'Don't worry, lucky you came to the right man. Now listen, first things first. Check your fuckin' sources. Have you spoke to Sammy yet?'

'Naw, no yet I'm goin' tae see him later on the day an ah . . .'

'Well make sure you see him because Sammy hasn't made any complaint about any shotgun. He made a complaint about vandalism with an iron bar and he never mentioned your name at all. Off the record, however, he is in no doubt who is behind it. So far as he's concerned it's down to the Craw. Does that surprise you?'

'WHIT!'

'Mind and go see Sammy noo,' he said. What the hell was going on here? Everybody telling me to see Sammy.

'Who the fuck's this Sammy anyway?' I thought as I was shown out the door.

The Craw had told me that Sammy Sneak had got his name as a sneak thief. The vans had been getting screwed late at night and nobody could figure how it had been getting done but the Craw had a good idea. He'd known that the watchman was related to Sammy and that no one else had realised that. So one night he hid himself in his own van with a pick shaft as the garage was locked up for the night and lay in wait for the prowler. Sure enough, in the early hours of the morning the watchman opens up to let Sammy in and they go to work screwing the vans. The Craw leaps out with the pick shaft and pummels them – mystery solved. The watchman was sacked and Sammy hadn't shown face since. Well so sayeth the gospel according to the Craw so you can never be sure which part, if any, is true. The guy is a pathological liar. He can't help himself. To him, the truth is that which is most convenient at the time, and he believes it.

So on to Sammy's then for his side of the story and see what tale he had to tell. And what a tale to open thine eyes it was at that. I knew this guy from somewhere. He was a friend of a friend of mine or something, I just couldn't put my finger on it. He certainly knew me, like he'd read the book or somethin but he was nervous, jumpy, twitchy, badly shaken. He was very delighted to see me, seeming to look upon me as the answer to his prayers – the one man who could stand against the Craw. To him, the Craw was the Moriarty behind every misfortune that had ever befallen him, round every dark corner, under every rock. The paranoia was crawling over his skin, almost visibly.

'What the fuck are you babbling about Sammy?' I said to slow him down.

'He killed my bra, he killed my bra, that wee McGue bastard, McPhee an that mob. They done it for him. Y'mind the cricket bat murder? Aye well that was my bra, they done him in an got out of it. A Not Proven. They killed Fast Eddie tae. Y'mind Fast Eddie? My pal? He was your pal tae. Y'mind Fast Eddie fae the jail? He was a pal of yours in the jail. He's deid. Did ye no know he was deid? They killed him.'

'Fast Eddie's deid? When was this? Who did . . .'

'They killed him. Hit an run. You were back in the jail again an ah knew ye didnae know or you wouldnae even talk to that bastard. That's why I wanted to see you, to tell you. See I've been at war with that bastard for years – me, my bra, fast Eddie, wee Puppet and that. Puppet's deid an aw. Was done in, murdered down in Shettleston. I'm the only one left. They were my back-up and we ran a totale wi him. Ran amok. But noo they're all deid.'

He went on to describe how he had once been the Craw's partner and how they'd waged a bloody war against Marchetti. Paving slabs dropped from bridges onto vans. Vans tipped over bridges, wrecked with baseball bats and pick shafts. Blown up, set alight and so on till Marchetti had backed out and given them what they'd wanted, among other things Ruchazie where Sammy lived. He and the Craw were partners in Ruchazie for a while but the Craw had always wanted it for himself.

He'd become obsessed with it, trying to pull a dirty stroke on Sammy to take his half but, according to Sammy, he'd been too wide for it and had ousted the Craw instead. Ever since, he and the Craw had been at war and he'd been running amok but now everybody was dead. He was the only one left.

I asked him about the thefts at the garage with the vans being screwed and told him the Craw's side of the story. 'That's pure shite,' he said. 'Ye canny believe him. It was a pure set-up. I don't know who was tanning the vans. He probably got somebody to do it so he could set me up and get away with it. I came in oan the van one night, I was last in and the garage wasn't shut yet. I stepped out my van and WHAM what a fuckin doin they gave me. I wasn't expecting it, not in the garage. I had a tool to take down the road with me but it was fuck all to do with the vans getting tanned. It was to do with getting me out of Ruchazie an me fuckin him for his half cos he tried to fuck me for mine. He wants Ruchazie. He's always wanted Ruchazie but now he canny get it except through me and he'll have to kill me tae before I let him get it. He killed my bra, for fuck sake. That's why I wanted to see you. If you get it then he canny get it off you. He'll no take you on.'

'I don't want it Sammy. It's nae good to me. I don't have the time. I don't have the money. I don't have the licences or the workers. It's no good to me, man. I don't want it. Nor do I want the hassle either. There are vans nipping in and out pirating that run because you're not serving it. It's no good to me.'

'Aye, you've got the money all right,' he says. 'You don't even know what I'm asking. Peanuts, man. Ah'm askin' peanuts. Fifteen hunner quid is all I need and all I want. It's all yours – van, stock, run, the lot.'

Now I was interested, not in his precious Ruchazie but

the van itself was worth at least seven grand. What's the catch? It must be owed on HP? It was but he wasn't for telling me that. He had another sorry story to tell.

Since the death of his brother he'd been hitting the booze heavily. His nerves were shattered. He'd knocked a wee lassie down with the van and was charged with it. He'd been drunk, well over the limit. He'd tried to get ice from the fridge and had been sick, vomiting into it and into the sink. The police had sealed up the van. Environmental Health had withdrawn his trader's licence and he'd lost his driver's licence. He owed everybody and couldn't pay to replace the stock and no one would give him credit because he was blacklisted as a bad risk. The Craw hadn't tippled yet but Sammy was beat. All the Craw needed to do was move a van into Ruchazie and there was nothing to stop him.

'He probably thinks I'm ready to go to town an do battle with him but I just don't have it any more. I'm beat.'

What was selling at fifteen hundred quid? A van without a health and safety licence was no good to anybody. Probably owed on HP. The run was already pirated by young Andy Doyle on a part-time basis and Fat Ben was in there too. So the run was worthless. His stock was non-existent. The deal for van, stock and run meant he was selling an illusion. Just a couple of things to check out and I'd get back to him. Fat Ben gave me a lift back over to Fifti's. 'No,' he said, 'if you're buying Sammy out, the run is yours.' He was only covering it part-time while Sammy was off the road and had his own run elsewhere. The boy in the Marchetti van, he assured me, was doing the same but I already knew that. It was young Andy Doyle and I knew of his long-term designs on the run if only Marchetti would give him a van of his own. I said nothing.

Next, on to another contact to check out the HP status on the van and, an unexpected pleasant surprise there. Sure enough, the van was behind payment on the greater part of the purchase. The coachbuilders themselves had covered the finance which was odd but the reason for that became apparent. The registration of the van was LSD 999Y but the purchase owed was to LDS 999Y. On deeper check it was discovered that, according to records, LSD 999Y didn't exist and that the LDS vehicle had been faulted and never left the assembly line. The company was providing their own finance b'cos, it appeared, they were perpetrating a fraud. 'Din din dirain,' said the orchestra in my napper. This may yet be turned to an advantage. It didn't take long for the Craw to catch up with me.

'So what's the score with Sammy?' he says right off, nae messin.

'Ach, he wants to sell out to me but I'm no interested.'

'I'll buy it. I'll buy it.' he says excited, unable to contain himself.

'You're fuckin joking. You're the last person he'll sell out to. He only wants to sell to me to fuck you,' said I, watching his interest mount.

'Get it, get it, get it. Get it for me. Front for me. I'll square you up.' It was agreed that Snadz, his brother-in-law, would run the show up front in partnership with the Craw and that I would front the deal on Snadz's behalf. Snadz being a completely different kettle of fish, a good guy, a straight character and an honest broker – I could seal the deal with Sammy. I got back to Sammy, telling him I might have a deal for him with Snadz. He was happy with that and the deal went through.

We took the van out to Scots of Bellshill for repair and refurbishment for the sake of renewing the hygiene certificate. The first grand was borrowed from my sister Sadie and the Craw came up with his first grand due on the deal. Sadie had been saving for the deposit for a new van to replace her old clapped out Bedford though hadn't quite saved enough yet. But I had other ideas. The refurbishing bill was six ton – I paid that with Sadie's cash. Sammy's outstanding stock bill at the garage was two ton. She paid that too to allow the van to remain garaged there. Sammy was delighted with the remaining twelve ton considering that his deal for fifteen had been for van, stock and run. The van's bills were eight ton, the stock non-existent. With the van owing on HP and the run pirated due to his neglect, Sammy was more than happy with the deal and the more so that the run wasn't going to the Craw – or so he believed.

I then handed over the old Bedford CF to the Craw, with the reminder that my deal with him was for the run. He wasn't happy about it but Snadz was. He just traded it in with the rest of the cash the Craw was due to me and bought a brand new £16,000 A reg Ford, emblazoning it with the legend 'The Ruchazie Boxers' and went to work in Ruchazie. The coachbuilder financier of Sammy's van was happy not to be going to the nick and the finance due was written off. Sadie got a new van. No profit for me but, nevertheless, a job well done. Just one more little matter to clear up yet – who had shot Sammy's fuckin van in the first place?

The answer, though not the entire answer, was Joe Steele. Not the entire answer because the culprits were never all named and the van hadn't been shot at all. It had been blundered . . .

When Sammy's van had been back at work on the run that the Craw wanted so bad – just a couple of nights in the week but building up the stock for a full-time future – having got Sammy this far into a corner the Craw didn't want to see him slipping out of it again. Joe Steele owed him a couple of ton. Therefore, if Joe would rob Sammy, he might only get peanuts, but it would stop Sammy renewing his stock and Joe's debt would be squared.

Joe, the Myopic Mole, had never handled a gun in his life nor carried out a robbery, but on being convinced that it would be only the one stupid old fart, Sammy's father-in-law, decides to step up into the bigger leagues. So he heads for Easterhouse with his pal, a known police informer and child abuser called Ness, and there he borrows a shotgun. Shortly thereafter, he sets out to do the dastardly deed, Ness driving. On reaching the van, Joe dons a rubber mask, but being myopic, can't put his glasses on over the mask and can't see a fuckin thing but bluffs it out anyway. He tries to thrust the gun over the serving hatch in the expectation that there would be someone there – there wasn't. The driver was in the driving seat and the serving hatch window was closed. In his blindness, Joe hadn't noticed. The barrel of the empty gun strikes the serving hatch window, shattering it, as the driver starts the engine and pulls away without even noticing the masked raider. Joe, on the other hand, jumps in shock wondering how the fuck an empty gun could go off and makes a desperate dash back to the car and a getaway driver who can't get the car into gear for laughing. At the next stop, Sammy's father-in-law notices the shattered window and the kids tell him that it was a wee boy with an old man mask and an iron bar. It was then reported to the police as vandalism with an iron bar. Joe, on the other hand, embarrassed by his efforts in the big league, impresses the Craw by telling him that he had blasted the van window with a shotgun and clears his debt.

Joe then heads off down Barrowfield way with Ness. Leaving Ness in the car, he sells the gun to Goofy, watching carefully while Goofy puts it away in his stash and hands over the cash. So far as Goofy is concerned that's his only dealings with Joe and an end to it but little does he know who he's dealing with.

The original owner of the gun is now in hot pursuit of Joe and is not accepting excuses. Under pressure, the Myopic Mole, upon first ascertaining that Goofy was not at home, takes his pal Ness back down to Barrowfield where they raid Goofy's stash, stealing the gun back and helping themselves to the goodies therein. Joe returns the gun to the original owner and it seems that all, at last, is well. Ignorance, as they say, is bliss.

But somewhere on the horizon the thunder roared. A storm was rising.

Wall of the Storm

On Sunday 15th April, 1984, while Andrew Doyle was on his way home, just across the Stepps Road from Garthamlock to Ruchazie where he lived and had been promised the run by the Mitchel/Marchetti management, he'd come head to head with his rival. 'The Ruchazie Boxers' was a brand new £16,000 ice cream van belonging to the Craw and his brother-in-law, Snadz Adams. Snadz was up in C Hall untried for an ice cream war up in Castlemilk. Andrew's van girl gave statements to the police as to what happened next.

She told of The Ruchazie Boxers on their way out of Ruchazie as they were going in. Andy had put his headlights on full beam, blared his horn, put his foot hard down on the accelerator and sped straight at them so that they had to turn away to avoid a collision, while Andy roared with laughter. The Ruchazie Boxers had veered onto the grass verge, two inside wheels sIipping into a drainage ditch causing the van to topple onto its side on a steep grassy hill, and skited along on its side till it came to a stop, scraped and dented but, luckily, in a position where it was easily righted.

Andrew had been driving an old hired Marchetti van. He would've known that the new van would have had to give way in this game of chicken. But more to the point, here in Ruchazie, he had established that these streets were his and that nothing had better stand in his way. From the point of view of The Ruchazie Boxers, something had indeed been established here and it had better be disestablished pretty damn sharpish. This was more than a serious territorial issue, this was a matter of personal fuckin pride and reputations.

Later that night, two junkies had just scored and were hanging about in the close looking into Bankend Street. A silver Mark 5 Cortina cruised on past but the street is a dead end with bollards blocking off the far end from the main road bridging the M8 motorway. It reversed, three point turned back the way it had come and, a few minutes later, cruised past again. Two men inside. It would have to turn around again.

'I know that guy,' says one junkie to the other. 'He's a taxi driver with East End. I'll stop him on the way back and see if he'll give's a lift down the road.' This they did and were in luck for the second guy in the taxi was not a fare. Once inside, they both recognised him. It was the Craw himself. They'd never been introduced but he was well known.

In the course of their journey, Chris the driver had brought up the subject first taken up by the Craw. They wanted a wee job done. A few bob in it for them or anybody handy who could do a wee torch job on a cellar. No big deal, just a wee Threatener, they would make it worth their while.

'Aye! Nae bother,' they'd said with absolutely no intention of torching any fuckin thing. 'We'll ask around, see what we can do, should be no problem pal,' they'd said while thinking, 'Aye that'll be fuckin right.' Once they were dropped off they expected that that would be the last they'd see or hear of any of it. They were very much mistaken.

The girl was going about her normal business in the

early hours of the morning. About half past one it was, she'd told the police, when this wee old Escort type car had come into the all-night service station on Edinburgh Road, where she worked. Two young men had got out and asked for a gallon of petrol in a plastic container. She'd refused to serve them because the boss had told her not to give petrol in plastic containers but he had intervened to say that it was all right and she had served them.

It had been around one forty-five, two o'clockish on the early morning of Monday 16th April, Reg R had told the police at the time. He and his pal and their two girlfriends were driving into Bankend Street where he lived. It is an L-shaped street and just as he came to the corner of the L, an old Ford Escort Popular, he gave its registration, came out the other way at some speed, clipping his off-side wing, and stalled. Three young men and an older man baled out and ran. Reg R had run after them but they'd split up, the older man returning to the Escort and driving it away. He himself had given up the chase and returned to inspect the damage on his own vehicle, but he would know them anywhere he said. One of them signed the broo at the same time as him. It was at this point that he noticed the bright light from the top flat at number 29.

These so-called modern tenements have an open close type stairwell. At each level, the landing extends to the right and left to form an open veranda structure at the front of the building. Each veranda ends in an in-shot for storm doors which were never fitted. The cellars to one side of the in-shot were once used to store coal but are now used for storing any old junk in the new smokeless zones, just as people with gardens would use a bike shed. The front door is at right angles to the cellar door, straight ahead as you step off the veranda into the imaginary storm door area. I know these houses well. I lived in them.

The fire had been set in the cellar with petrol also applied to the main front door. It had burned through the cellar, catching light to chemicals such as turps, too dangerous to be kept in the main house, and igniting car tyres, causing intense flame and dense black smoke. It burned up through the roof causing a lum effect sucking the flame and fumes into and along the attic and down through the ceilings of the household.

The Doyle family awoke to a flaming ceiling and dense black toxic smoke billowing in on all sides of the horror-stricken household. The front door was ablaze and appeared to be the centre of the fire. This was a top flat of a four storey block with no drainage poles down the outside of the building as had most tenements of their type. There was no way out and no escape route. As each member of that tragic family collapsed, two others would move to his rescue, sacrificing their own places at the window to pick him up and place him there before themselves collapsing. This waking nightmare was a situation where, in panic, it would be every man for himself and Fuck you Jack. In this case, the opposite was true as each and every member of that family literally sacrificed their own oxygen for the sake of every other and died as a result of their altruistic endeavour.

Baby Mark was just eighteen months old. His mother, Christine Doyle Halleron, had no time to get to a window. She was in the room closest to the heart of the fire, facing the front door. Her first instinct was for the safety of her child beside her. She was found dead shielding her baby, her back badly burned as she had crouched over her child. Firemen, upon removing her burned body had found the child alive. He lived long enough to reach the first of the arriving ambulances and an oxygen mask. But each ambulance which followed had no oxygen. The ambulance attendants moved the one oxygen mask from patient to patient as they arrived, unconscious and semi-conscious from the horrendous effects of toxic smoke inhalation.

The child's grandmother, Mrs Lillian Peacock Doyle, perched perilously on the narrow window ledge, was rescued on an extended ladder. Her son, Stephen, was stretchered away with multiple injuries having jumped the forty or so feet to the stone paving below.

Day by day they died. Christine Doyle Halleron and Anthony Doyle died as a result of their injuries on 16th April, 1984. Baby Mark Halleron also died on 16th April, at the Royal Hospital for Sick Children. James Doyle jnr died at Glasgow Royal Infirmary on 17th April. Andrew Doyle died at the Glasgow Royal on 20th April. James Bernard Doyle snr died at the Glasgow Royal on 24th April. Each and every one an innocent murdered hero. Each and every one showing their worth and true altruism in self-sacrifice for each other in the face of the ultimate nightmare. A nightmare which most of us could never even imagine and would never want to. They faced that storm in their living reality and, without hesitation or thought for themselves, died horrendously for each other.

Spare a prayer then for the dead and for the surviving mother, Mrs Lillian Peacock Doyle, and her one surviving son, Stephen Doyle. For on hearing the evidence I cry. On remembering the evidence, I cry. I remember a mother in mourning, bravely trying to stem the tide of tears to describe that trauma to the court and beyond, as she left the room and the storms of grief breaking through. I remember clearly her wailing cry of ultimate anguish in her deep, deep soul-wrenching loss echo and resound around those cold, cold corridors of the law.

Spare a thought and a prayer for her for there is no consolation or compensation for a grieving widow who has lost not one but three of her sons, her husband, her dear daughter and darling grandchild in one horrendous firestorm. Forget the Glasgow Two for they live to fight their own battles. Please remember and never let us forget, that terrible tragedy and the heroism of the Glasgow Eight. For those survivors may never for a living moment ever forget 16th April, 1984.

I have my own regrets that my struggle for justice must keep those wounds open, but I beg forgiveness for the fact that my struggles are for more than justice for the Glasgow Two. They are in pursuit of, at least, some measure of justice for the Doyle family too and if I do not pursue it, who shall? Their killers would see me dead too and I am happy with the thought that I am making my mark. For I will not rest till I see them in hell. The difference is that I am ready and I am able for them.

Any time. Anywhere, ya bastards. Look out for me. I'm coming, come hell or high water. They lit that fire in Bankend Street on 16 April, 1984 and it is still burning.

Monday morning, 16th April, while having breakfast with his dad where he'd been dropped off the night before, one of the junkies hears the horn of a car outside in the street. BEEP! BEEP! it insists, demanding attention. His wee dad comes back from the window and says, 'It's that pal o yours with the big fancy car,' and his son nips down the stair to see Chris.

'About last night . . .
you know nothing . . .
you never seen us . . .
you don't know us . . .
you never met us . . .
we never . . .
picked you up . . .'
'Okay!'
'Now how's your pal on this? Is he okay? B'cos if he's

not then we are going to have to deal with him y'know what I mean?'

Y'know what's happened? He didn't in fact have a fucking clue what all this was all about, nor what all the panic was about but just kept saying, 'Aye, cool,' and 'Nae problem,' to keep this Chris character happy. Telling him his pal was 'A hunner per cent cool' till Chris was assured and fucked off. Back upstairs, his puzzlement as to what the fuck Chris was ranting on about was sharply resolved. His dad had just turned the paper around to read the sports pages at the back and there it was blazing right out at him, 'FIRE ENGULFS FAMILY IN TENEMENT FLAT.'

'I told the police at the time', says the garage girl, 'the car had come back that morning. It had a damaged light and when they had got out o the Escort they seen the polis parked there in the garage and just about-turned and got back in the car and drove away. The polis kept coming back to me and saying, "Are you sure it wasn't TC, Tommy Campbell, who bought the petrol?" I kept saying, "No it wasn't Mr Campbell. I know Mr Campbell, he stays near to me and my wee sister sometimes watches his wee boy Stephen." But they kept on and on at me, making me feel bad as if I was a liar or something. I don't know why I wasn't called as a witness.'

'I don't know why we weren't cited as witnesses,' says Reg R. 'I gave the polis full statements to all this and they came back with forensics and took paint scrapings from my car. I expected to see the culprits in the papers when they were convicted, but none of those guys were the guys we seen so I made contact. I'm a car thief and a banned driver. I know cars and I know faces.'

BOOK THREE

Bombed Out & Bewildered

Aftermath

Glasgow went ballistic. A community united in the terrible tragedy of an innocent family and the developing news that this was a fire deliberately set, stirring the soul of the city to outrage. This could so easily have been you or I. This could so easily have happened to any of us and to our families. The perpetrators must be found and dealt with at all cost. The word was on the streets and on every corner of every alleyway, uttered from every lip, 'Find the fire raisers.' Hanging would be too good for them.

But where to begin? Various theories and rumours abounded one after another, doing their turn on the rumour mill until, finally, something the public could grasp hold of, one theory exploded and took off like wild fire itself. So close to the truth yet so twisted by bitterness and blinded by self-interest, warped beyond the reality.

'Ice cream wars' became embedded in the public perception yet how could something so trivial lead to such tragedy? Until this point, ice cream vans had been related to the sound of merry chiming and the happy laughter of children in anticipation of their favourite treat, not with gangsterism, war and murder. Surely then there must be something else behind it? Something more sinister. Drugs perhaps?

The Mitchell/Marchetti management in Garthamlock were telling my sister Agnes day by day to watch for the Daily Record. They'd sold their exclusive story on the back of the Doyle tragedy blasting any other theory out of the reckoning. At that time, I was effectively prevented from seeing the forest for the trees. For they were relating the Doyle family fire to ice cream wars in Garthamlock.

'Gangsters Moving in on the Trade in the Past Two Years.'

'Relatives of the Rivals of Marchetti in Garthamlock.'

Clearly the headlines implied TC to the entire east side of the city. Everybody knew that my sister Agnes was Mitchell/Marchetti's rival in Garthamlock. I'd served a ten-year for gang related riots and been involved with vans in the two years. I knew this to be wrong. Those facts may be right but the implication was wrong. The Doyle family fire was as much of an outrage to me as it was to anybody else, but because the ice cream war theory was now focusing around me and, knowing its source, I tended to disregard the whole idea of any relation to ice cream vans. Thereby missing the forest for the trees. An ice cream war, not related to me or Garthamlock, just didn't enter my head. I put the whole thing down to press sensationalism and the warped self-interest of the Mitchell/Marchettis turning propaganda to their financial advantage. I guess we were all blind-sided and wrong-footed in various ways.

People started moving away from me, avoiding me. My social life had never been so terribly active anyway, too busy at work and home, but what little there was dissolved into nothing. For the first time in my life I began to truly understand the meaning of the word pariah.

Pariah – it means more than merely outcast. It is a process, like some kind of syndrome that somehow feeds on the negative aspects of popular perceptions. Turning and twisting everything beyond recognition till everything you have ever said or done is reinterpreted in the negative. In the back streets of Glasgow we have a game we call the Meegie. It stems from the days of the scarlet fever.

If someone trod upon dog shit, for example, they would be said to have the Meegie. If they touched something or were touched by something dirty they would be accused of having the Meegie and were outcast and avoided as a pariah. The only way to get rid of the Meegie is to touch someone else or hit them with a thrown rag or whatever, thus passing the Meegie on from you to them. This then is pariah syndrome. You have the Meegie and are treated accordingly.

So you see who your friends truly are. Loyalties tested to the limit. I can honestly say I found I'd more than a few. People would come from far and wide just happening to call by for a chat. Finally telling me that I was in the frame for a fit-up, alerting me to the fact that deals were the order of the day. That they had this and that charge to go up for – robbery, drugs, firearms – from as far afield as Greenock and Paisley they came, as well as more locally. They'd been offered deals on their charges – verbal TC, say he said this or that incriminating detail about the Doyle fire and their charges would be dropped, reduced or withdrawn.

'They're fitting you up, big yin. You should split,' was the general message and advice. Yet 'why should I?' was my thought. For the first time in my life I'd settled with a wife and family and was making a living that didn't involve crime. Why should I run? I have never in my life run from anything and wasn't about to start running now, from an illusion. My thinking was, not that they wouldn't fit me up, for they'd tried that on a few occasions before and I knew they were more than capable of it. It was more that I couldn't get it into my head that they'd fit me up for this particular crime. Wide as the Clyde as I thought I was on the subject, I didn't believe they would actually fit me up for murder. Robbery maybe, even plant me with firearms or dope but surely not murder? Surely not the six murders of the Doyle Family? They would want the real culprits for that one and not merely be intent on clearing their books for the sake of public confidence, credibility and personal promotion. However wide as the Clyde as I thought I was, reality has a nasty way of shaking you into a rude awakening. Mine was soon to come.

The foundations for a fit-up were being well and truly laid and the framework of the scaffolding was in construction. All that was required now was a body to drop through the trap and they could all sing and dance at my wake. Only one small problem to overcome first though – for some reason beyond their understanding they couldn't find anyone to say a bad word against me. Right to the very end. The Mitchells and Marchettis could rant and rave and point fingers all they liked but, in actual fact, there was no one who could say a word against me in any evidential sense about anything to do with the alleged ice cream wars. For, in fact, of the three hundred witnesses eventually cited for the prosecution case only one witness would incriminate me in anything – a thrice previously convicted perverter of justice and a virtual stranger to me – William Love.

Local businessmen were pulled in. 'Have you ever seen TC with guns? Bombs? Knives? Has he ever threatened you? Has he ever tried to extort money or take your business from you? Do you know of anyone he may have done that to?' Mostly these people wouldn't have a clue who or what the hell the police were talking about as they didn't know and had never met this TC character. They'd be called liars and told where and when they'd last been observed in my company. 'Oh, that's TC? You're talking about Tommy Campbell? No! I've always found him t'be a nice enough big fullah.'

I was questioned by the police each Sunday for the four weeks leading up to my arrest. That would be two six-hour sessions in police stations under intense interrogation. The police worked in relay teams, checking and cross-checking every word uttered, bringing in everyone mentioned in the course of enquiry. Sammy McBride for example, was given a particularly hard time – pushed and slapped about, and bin lids banged down on him.

'TC. TC. TC,' they'd kept insisting. The Craw, the Craw, he had responded to their deep frustration and annoyance. Most people would tell me that they'd been taken in for six hours and the police had only asked questions about TC. Sammy however had suffered this more than most.

One time, I was one of the many from the ice cream depot being taken in for questioning. I'd pulled up DCS Charlie Craig regarding my name being bandied about all over the place by his mob while interviewing others. He'd simply commented with a sneer, 'Aye! Ye'r a much maligned man.' Anyway, I'd been picked up from the depot and had my own fags and lighter with me, a neat wee gold effort, so I was okay there. No need to worry about planted fingerprints from their fag packets as in the case of Hari Kari, or so I thought.

At one point they took me to another interview room for a few minutes and then brought me back again. 'What the fuck was that all about?' I thought suspiciously to myself. Then, sitting back down lighting a fag, I noticed the wee gold screw from the bottom of my lighter was missing. It wasn't that important, just the wee protective cover for the gas fitting. Then it dawned on me. Shit! I'd left the lighter there on the table with my fags when they'd taken me into the other room. Trying not to scream, 'Ya dirty fit-up bastards,' I pretended to be calm as if I hadn't noticed. They finished their interview and sent me home. Once outside, I headed straight for an old railway embankment and threw the lighter as far away into fuckin orbit as I could muster. Remembering the magic print evidence in the Hari Kari case the motto of the wise is always be prepared for surprises.

Once I got home, they'd take my wife Liz in for the same treatment. They terrorised her, describing the Doyle family as burned black jelly babies like she sells on the van, showing her photos of the dead in the morgue. 'Are you sure he didn't sneak out while you slept?' they would insist. But Liz is such a straight person, if that could've happened, she would have said so.

The last interview was at home. They'd no further excuse to take me to the police station. These coppers were bemoaning what a hard time of it they were having because they were getting nowhere. 'Try barking up the right tree,' I told them. Fifty officers working double time and overtime on the case and they were nowhere. Here is where I'd first heard them say that there had been a point when they'd been sure that I must've been involved somewhere, but their weeks of intense investigation had only removed me further and further away from it. Had I heard any whispers? Any rumours? Had I any ideas at all? Aye, right! The only rumours I'd heard were those started by them about me. As if I was about to start playing that game. 'Have you heard the one about . . . ?'

'No, I haven't heard anything,' I said. So they filled their grubby pockets with doughnuts, gulped down their coffee and left. The next time I saw any of them was the following week, the fourth week of the investigation – 12th May, 1984.

It had been a few years down the line since my last escapades with Tamby the Bear who still lived in Carntyne. I'd got word through Liz on the van that he wanted to see me. The following afternoon, I took a ride down there on the van with oor Stephen, the wean. It was a bright sunny summer's day and, seeing the Bear in the swing park with his son Ian, we parked and joined them there. The Bear looked worried and drawn and I realised that this was not just to say a friendly hi!

'The polis have been up to see me,' he said accusingly.

'So what've you been up to, big yin?' I answered.

'Naw! What've you been up to?' he returned.

'So what's on your mind, big fullah?'

'They're sayin ah done some fuckin shootin on some fuckin van.'

'Garthamlock?'

'Aye! An that you done the Doyle fire. Did ye?'

'Naw, but it looks like they're maybe trying to fit me up for it an . . .'

'So what the fuck's it got to do with me and who done this shootin?'

'None of my business, Tamby, and none of yours either. They're investigating me. Firing my name in all over the place. They probably came up with your name through old association files. Don't worry about it.'

'But what the fuck has any of it got to do with me, man? What the fuck they bringing me into it for? What the fuck do I know about fuckin ice cream vans, man? That's your gemme.'

'Y'want me to tell the bizzies that?'

'Aye!'

'Like you think they'll take my word for it or somethin?'

'Nae offence but if you'd anythin to do with that fire . . . man! Ye deserve all y'get. It's right over the score so it is.'

'Y'think it's my style then, Tamby?'

'Fuck naw! Ah hope no. Nae offence but.'

'It's okay, big yin, ah know what y'mean.'

Tamby once said that he'd grown to dread having to talk to me. That it seemed I was always on the verge of exploding into violence. That it was like, 'playing a fuckin chess game'. He had to be careful of every word in case he put one wrong. This then would be an example. To me, Tamby was indeed walking a fine line, close to calling me a grass on the one hand and a dirty low-life killer on the other. If he'd put a word wrong, only the presence of the weans would have saved him from a Glesca kiss, square to the nose. I guess he knew me too well of old.

The new driver came to the door one bright sunny afternoon when he should've been out on the run selling ice cream. He'd been sent on an errand and had a message for me from a guy I hadn't seen in many a long year. I'll call him Jimmy, a well known UDA activist who sometimes worked in security. Jimmy wanted to see me urgently, he was waiting on me up the road at the van depot at Fifti's. 'Aye, fine, very good then, you just tell him to drop by here and I'll see him then,' I told the driver. 'Then get back on the run right away, you shouldn't have left it.' I wasn't for trotting off to see anyone on mysterious errands since my brother, Robert, had just arrived from down south. I hadn't seen him for quite a while and wasn't about to abandon my guest for this nor any dumb Secret Sam mission.

'Is that yone Jimmy wan?' says Liz, the way women do and started prattling on about all the gossip she'd heard on her rounds in the van – so-and-so's cousin's wee lassie's pal and all that. It happened that Jimmy's girlfriend's mother stayed across the road from Liz's mother and the scandal had emerged from various sources. Jimmy it seemed had bought a car on HP in his poor sick father's name. Sold it off and bought a new one with the proceeds. He'd been running a private taxi with a local firm without a licence, insurance or legitimate tax disc. He'd been stoned on his way to pick up a hire when he'd run over a wee lassie, leaving her in a coma and it was reckoned she'd be left with permanent brain damage. The police were looking for him and no one could get into the house to feed or let his dogs out. They were going bananas with all the neighbours complaining. Jimmy then, was hot on the trot. What the fuck did he want to see me for? The driver had been anxious that I go up there. He said, ' Jimmy said there was big money involved for you.' Fuck that! I know what that means. Who needs it?

Thus by the time Jimmy came to the door, I'd a full guide to his recent history, chapter and verse. Scumbag on the trot for a hit and run on a child. The sun was blazing in the hottest summer in centuries. Boy George was singing something about a chameleon and this nut case was wearing a padded arctic snorkel with fur-lined hood up. Sweat dripping off him in buckets, face flushed and steam rising on his glasses. No he wouldn't sit down, no he wouldn't take the jacket off, no he was just fine but needed to talk to me in private. He kept insisting on privacy but I swept around the room with my hand saying there was nothing he could say to me which could not be said in front of my brother and my wife. Finally, he drew out a clear plastic bag of white powder and lays it on the table telling me that it is an ounce of pure uncut heroin. From the corner of my eye I saw my brother freeze rigid on the couch.

'This,' said Jimmy, 'is yours for £600. It's worth so much more once cut three to one – could be sold off again at around three grand.' If I take this one I can have as much as I want of the same for the same price whenever I want but I have to take this one.

'Naw, Jimmy, I don't have to take fuck all,' I told him. 'I don't know who put you onto me but they've given you a bum steer. I don't do smack an ah . . .'

'OK, £400 then. I'll give it away at four. It's pure, uncut.' He was too nervy scared, too shaky. I picked up the bag from the table weighing it in my hand. My brother staring straight ahead, looking into space, rigid like a dummy. He was conveying a message to me, 'Dummy it. Leave it out, leave it alone.' But I didn't need his warning. I told Jimmy to take his junk and do a bunk, I didn't want his shit and neither did I want him near my door again. He scurried away as my brother let out a huge sigh of relief. I don't think he'd drawn a breath the whole time Jimmy was in the house, nor had he made a sound.

I noticed from the window that Jimmy was heading to the left. He would have to go right for any form of transport. Left was heading across the dual carriageway to the petrol station and beyond into the no-man's-land of the industrial estate at Bartibeith Road. Either he was fuckin lost or this was too curious to miss closer scrutiny.

Nipping into the bedroom I kicked out the tripod on my stargazer telescope and zeroed in on the back of his head. 'Gotcha, right in focus, ya real yin ye. Now let's see what you're up to.' As he approaches the Bartibeith Road, a brown Mark 4 Cortina pulls up in front of him, four Serious Crime Squad inside. They don't look too pleased when he bends down to their window spreading his hands out to the side and shaking his head, 'No dice.' A Mark 5 Cortina pulls up behind them just as they pull away. This time it's three UDA. Jim gets in beside them and they follow the coppers off onto Edinburgh Road heading back towards town.

Back into the living room I started to say what I'd just seen, 'That wee fly bastard's just . . .'

'Ya fuckin bam,' my brother interrupts. 'He was wired for sound. Are you fuckin blind or somethin?' I hadn't actually thought of that though it should've been obvious. 'Your prints are all over that bag, ya stupid cunt ye. Whit's wrang wi ye? Whit the fuck's goin on here?' As usual, my brothers always think I'm a wee bit thick.

'He's no wide,' they would say. I explained what I'd just seen.

'Why up the depot?' he asked.

'I don't know.'

'Do they have security up there?'

'Aye.'

'Cameras?'

'Aye.'

'That's it then. Whether he's handing it to you or you back to him, they'd have you on camera dealing in smack. An with him as the witness you're done. What the fuck's going on, Tommy?' He'd had a call from a friend of his advising him to drop by and see me but not what it was about. I explained the word on the streets about deals being the order of the day and that the polis were trying to fit me for the Doyle fire. 'An yer no goin' tae run are ye? Naw, ah didn't think ye would,' he said. 'Anything I can do?'

'Aye, get your self to fuck as far away from me as you can before the shit hits the fan.'

The proverbial shit hit the fan on 12th May, 1984. Almost four weeks after the Doyle fire I awoke to impatient pounding on the front door. Only the polis would treat another's property like that so it was no surprise when I opened the door and they barged in as if you would be surprised to see them and try to bolt. Watching too much of The Sweeney on TV I suppose.

There never is any of this You're-Under-Arrest nonsense or You-Don't-Have-to-Say-Anything palaver. That's all just a carry on for the courts. It's usually, as in this case, 'Right get a shirt on, ye'r done.' In fact, they seemed intent on keeping the charge a secret, probably as instructed, to fit a presumptuous utterance condemning myself no doubt. I don't know how many times I'd to ask before finally one of them mumbled something about attempted murder. Obviously I wasn't getting any further info until we reached wherever the fuck we were going.

They were tearing the house apart, dragging drawers out, emptying them onto the middle of the floor and just dropping the furniture wherever they stood – not even bothering to sift through the growing heap of contents. Like why bother with the pretence? They already knew they weren't likely to find anything incriminating so had simply brought along their own. I noticed they were picking up all the lighters and checking their bottoms for missing screws. No dice there, Sherlock, sorry! Still, I have no doubt that if I hadn't paid close attention to dear Dr Dolittle's motto about surprises, evidence would later have been produced in court about how they'd found this wee gold screw on the stairwell at 29 Bankend Street and on search of Campbell's home found this lighter which just so happened to fit. Aye right! As if anybody would be that fuckin stupid. Yon lighter had been fired into orbit long since.

My wee Stephen was having a rerr terr. He'd been trying to demolish the house like this since before he could walk. He ran ben the room and dragged out his wee electric polis motorbike to show off to his guests. 'Bottor bike, bottor bike,' he displayed proudly but got in the way and was pushed on his arse, crying more upset than injured.

'Have you any big knives or anything like that around the house?' asked the child abuser.

'If I did, I'd have done you with it before noo,' I snapped, moving to comfort the wean. I fully expected that this would be used as a verbal against me but would be more than pleased to explain the circumstances under which it was uttered. They never did use it though. Obviously they'd better ideas of their own. And so off to Baird Street police station, home of the Serious Fit-up Squad, leaving poor Liz and the wean bawling behind me. I still expected that I would be home after a six-hour interview.

At the polis station I was surprised to see Agnes there with her man and her young son, Thomas. I assumed they were there with Thomas for some juvenile devilment but it turned out that he was seventeen and they were all charged. As were Tamby the Bear and Tam McGraw. The accused were the five Thomases and oor Agnes. We were all taken into separate rooms for processing, as they call it, before being jammed into the can, I supposed.

Charges

Where were you born, first school, mother's name, her mother's name? Blah, blah, blah, blah-bloody-blah. Ancient history. You wonder what anything like this is ever going to be used for in any investigation but in fact it has its practical uses, as you'll find out when a copper tells a jury that he's an old friend of the family and starts rhyming of their history. Like Charlie Craig did to Joe Steele. Makes his evidence come across a little more credible. Thus, perhaps it was fortunate that my interview was interrupted by Inspector Woodini though I confused him at the time with CSI Walker. Woodini came charging into the interview room flustered and spluttering. He'd obviously just spoken with the Craw, pointed at me and shouted at the two polis, 'Cuff that bastard.'

'He is cuffed.'

'Cuff him to the fuckin chair.'

'Okay, boss, there ye go then.'

'See you, ya bastard, eh?

I'm going to fit you up.

I'm goin'a nail you to the fucking wall.

I'm goin'a give you the same justice

you gave to the fuckin Doyles.

D'ye know who ah am eh? Eh?

Ah'm the man th' fitted up yer Da

an ah'm the man that's fittin up you.

Ya cowardly bastard ye.

Ye'r a coward, that's all y'are.

A cowardly bastard . . .'

He spluttered, spraying all over my face as I replied
with controlled anger,

'Take the cuffs off.

Just take the cuffs off then

and we'll see who's the fuckin

coward here.

Take the cuffs off,

gangster that ye are . . .'

He took a dive at my throat, his face so purple with
rage I thought he was going to die of a heart attack. The
other coppers grabbed hold of him, holding him back
with some effort, shouting to get through to him,

'For fuck sake.

He's handcuffed to the fucking chair

for God's sake man!

Get a grip of yourself.'

They took him away but I refused to answer any
questions after that. Not much point in cooperating
when it's out in the open that they're putting you into
the frame regardless.

Aftermath & Charges

They took us all into this big room to be charged, lining us up on one side – the five Thomases – Lafferty, McGraw, Campbell, Gray and Lafferty jnr, with Agnes. The rest of the room was filled with about thirty CID. DCS Norrie Walker read out the charge of conspiring to further business interests and we first heard the name John Campbell as a co-accused but no one as yet had any idea who he was,

'Conspire to intimidate rival ice cream salesmen . . .

Following an ice cream van . . .

Persistently follow an ice cream van . . .

Shout at them . . .

Offer a bottle of wine to damage a van . . .

Persons caused to throw stones at a van . . .

Persons caused to throw stones at . . .

Persons offered inducement to throw stones . . .

Persons caused to throw a bottle . . .

Persons caused to smash a window . . .

Persons pushed out of a queue . . .

Persons threatened in Castlemilk . . .

Persons struck an ice cream van . . .

Persons threw stones at ice cream van . . .

Andrew Doyle assaulted . . .'

He built up to a climax and stopped there leaving it hanging in the air slowly surveying the room full of police, 'Now come on people, we have a lot of work to do and a long way to go. Let's get to it.'

What a load of old nonsense, I thought, is this it? Is this what it was all about? Serious enough but still a load of petty bickering which had nothing to do with me. It struck me that the Castlemilk charge was related to the Craw, the rest might or might not be connected to Shadda's drunken escapades but what had the rest of it to do with anybody else? And who the fuck was John Campbell anyway?

Taking us away, DCS Charlie Craig said to me, 'I hear you're refusing to cooperate, TC. You know that won't do. It won't look good for you on the day.'

'You want me to cooperate in my own fit-up?' I said. 'Norrie Walker said he's fitting me up so fuck that. I've nothin to say.'

'We'll see about that,' he said.

It was all over the papers and the news that six had been arrested for the Doyle family fire murders. Later that day I was taken into a room with Norrie Walker behind the desk and standing behind him were cops we'll call Woodini, Shady to one side, Craig (his real name) to the other, Furlice behind me. These were the five top detectives in the west of Scotland at the time. Walker said right off,

'What's this about me threatening to fit you up TC? Let's get that out of the way first. You know you're making a big mistake here. You're messing with the wrong man and . . .'

'Aye, my apologies. Sorry about that,' I interrupted. 'It wasn't you I meant. I was talking about him,' I pointed. I didn't know his name but Walker looked round from his chair and said, 'Mister Woodini?' Woodini turned bright red, smiled, nodding his head slowly and said, 'Aye that's right, that's exactly what I'm gonna do, all the fuckin way.'

'Now we'll have none of that here, Mr Woodini, ' said Walker turning away, putting his head down into his books embarrassed, as Woodini smirked.

Not for the first time and not for the last I was to be told that there was a time they'd thought that, because of my history, I must be involved in the Doyle fire, but their month of intense investigations had moved me further and further away from any participation or involvement. They'd looked at a possible conspiracy charge and found that this too was not viable. Yet they couldn't get over the thought that I must know who did it and if I didn't say who did it then it must be b'cos I was involved or it was someone so close to me that I wouldn't say. Later I was to be given this same speech, with a few additions, by Furlice but for now it was Walker's turn. I told him that if I had any idea of who'd been involved I would've said so before now. Walker perked up at that. He indicated for the others to leave. I think it was Woodini, Furlice and Shady that left.

Walker referred to statements on his desk, telling me that young Thomas had given three different alibis and each of them had been shown to be false. Reading from the statements he described witnesses having been with young Shadda tanning cars in Queenslie, and of him getting a can of petrol from the garage there on Eddy Road, having last been seen heading towards Ruchazie drunk and saying he was going to torch the Doyles. He read out three different statements to that effect before looking up at me. I was shocked, shattered, flabbergasted, devastated. I would never have suspected this in a million years. One thing, however, nagged at my mind – 'young Shadda'. 'Young Shadda', they'd all called him. Young Shadda. There only ever had been the one Shadda and that was his Da. It means Shadow and it was a name earned, not bestowed or passed on to a son. Nobody called young Thomas Shadda.

'I'd had an idea you were aware of this,' said Walker, 'but I can see by your reaction that you're not.' He went on to tell me what the deal was. I was to be put into the same cell with young Thomas and I was to convince him, by whatever means, to put his hands up to it. If he pled to it, they would charge him with the lesser charge of culpable homicide, he would get three to five years tops and be out in a couple of years. It was, after all, not an intentional killing but a frightener which went too far. Blah-Blah-Blah, he went on and on but my head was spinning, confused and bemused. It was all too much. I was thinking about Agnes, the boy's mother, my sister. This would absolutely shatter her. If it was true, she would be devastated to find her son had in any way been part of that fire and the deaths of the Doyle family.

I said I wouldn't go into a cell with Thomas. I didn't say why. I knew that their intention was that if I couldn't persuade him, I was to beat it out of him. But they hadn't figured that if he'd confessed to me in any circumstances I would have been much more likely just to have broken his fuckin neck. I was returned to my cell.

I spoke to Thomas and his Da through the hatch on the cell door about what had just happened. Thomas said that it was a load of lies. Yes, his alibi had been that he'd been screwing cars in Queenslie earlier that night but there were eleven people to say that he'd returned to the scheme. There only ever was one alibi and it had checked out because it was true. It turned out that he was telling the truth. I believed him then but the proof of it was yet to come.

At one point they had us all in one room except for Agnes. Thomas spoke of the deal he'd been offered. If he pled to it they'd charge him with culpable homicide and he'd get three to five years max. His Ma, his Da and his Uncle Tommy would be set free, everyone would walk right out the door and all he had to do was sign the confession. He'd said he wanted to ask his Ma but they wouldn't let him speak to her. His Da interrupted him to say, 'What has you Ma already told you?'

'Not to sign anythin to get her oot,' said Thomas.

'Aye, ya dotty-heeded daftie, listen to her wull ye.'

Tamby butted in to ask, 'Did y'dae it?'

'Naw ah fuckin' didn't, right!' Thomas shouted back at him.

'Well what the fuck are ye talking about then. Plead to fuck all,' said the Bear.

Thomas just explained that it might have been worthwhile to get everybody out the nick and had wanted their opinion and advice on what to do. The only person who agreed that he should take the deal was the Craw but nobody there had ever paid any attention to him anyway.

I had one more encounter that day, this time with Furlice. He too gave me all that stuff about their belief that I must've had something to do with the Doyle fire, but their investigation surely and firmly eliminated me from their suspicions. However, 'We can't get over the fact that you must know who did it and if you don't tell us who did it then you yourself are the perfect target.' He went on to talk about my previous cases. 'Previous attempted fit-ups y'mean,' I said. He ignored me and went on about a reputation which I didn't know I had. About all the cases I'd been acquitted of since the ten-year sentence and a long list of many others before that sentence many of which didn't even get as far as the courts. This, according to Furlice, told him that I was a very clever man and knew what I was doing in court. That I'd make a very good policeman. That I'd a reputation for having nine lives and as the man they couldn't put down, on the one hand . . . and on the other, as a violent, razor-slashing monster. That sure, it was a reputation created for my own defence, he appreciated that, he said. But nevertheless, it was this part of that reputation they could use against me. That monster, he said, could be turned against me so that it would take my fuckin head right off.

'So make no mistakes about it – we can and will use it against you. If you don't tell us who did it, if you don't help us now, then you yourself are the perfect target. All we have to do is to charge you. Prejudice will do the rest.'

There was just no point in telling these people there was no way I could help them because I was totally in the dark myself. If I could've helped I would have. I told him anyway and I told him that it wasn't me who created the reputation. I hadn't asked to be fitted up five times in row and that it wasn't me who bungled each time. It was him and his mob, not me or mine.

Into the cells for the rest of the weekend. A stinking stone box, rubber mat for a bed and a rancid smelly army blanket. Light on all night and wakened up every hour just to remind you where you are. If this is designed to degrade and demoralise, it works and there's only one way to counter it. The box is an echo chamber – use it and sing. This must be where Phil Spector got his ideas from. It sounds great. So sing your fucking heart out. If they don't like it, what are they gonna do? Jail ye for breach? The only problem is that I'm a great singer and I pick good songs. It has a much better impact when the singer is crap, sings crap songs and the coppers have to listen to it. So for now, it's Bob Dylan and Chimes of Freedom, 'For each and every gentle soul caged inside a jail . . .'

After the police cells Barlinnie – a bath and a bed, even on death row – is a luxury. First day, going out to the exercise yard, this guy approaches, storming up to me saying, 'You TC?' Thinking I was about to get into a fight, I corrected my balance for a quick dig as I nodded, 'Aye, that's right.' But it wasn't a fight he was looking for but an introduction.

'I'm your co-accused,' he says with a smile presenting his hand. 'John Campbell. Do y'have a copy of the charge on ye? Ah've no seen it yet.'

I gave him my copy of the petition warrant as we started to walk the yard, Gary Moore joining on. Cammy, as John Campbell was commonly known, laughing all the more as he read through the charges. 'Christ! I knew it was crap,' he says, 'but this's gonna be a pure farce, man. I was in the jail for every wan of these.' He went on to explain that he was Billy Love's co-accused and had only been charged with us for that reason, as if that would explain things to me. It didn't. He and Gary then had to explain to me, and Tamby and Shadda who'd joined us, that Billy Love had made a deal with the polis to fit us up and that he'd been released as we were arrested. People were passing us in the yard, telling us, 'Billy Love's fitting y'up. Billy Love's fitting y'up.' They would shout it down from the gallery, 'Billy Love's fitting y'up.'

'Aye right!' I'd call back. Turning round to Shadda and Cammy, 'Like am I supposed to know who the fuck this Billy Love is anyway?' Cammy just throws his head back and laughs. It was all very well for him, an outsider on the inside seeing the absurdity of it all, but for the rest of us, myself and Tamby in particular, it was all so fuckin confusing. I say in particular because we didn't know any of the characters involved. None of the names. They all knew each other. No doubt young Thomas and Agnes would have known them all too. They were all from

Garthamlock which was like a village but it wasn't our village. So who the fuck was this Billy Love then?

'Aye, you'll know him,' Shadda would say. 'You'll know him when y'see him. He's the guy tha wiz wi Ronny Carlton when he sorted Agnes's van mind?' No, I didn't remember and couldn't figure how someone who didn't know me could be fitting me up. Cammy, Gary and others from Garthamlock would tell us not to worry. Love had no intention of appearing in court. That he was pulling a stroke and intended to get off his mark as soon as he got out the door. The polis had offered so many of them the same deal – verbal TC for their freedom – and they'd all refused. Love had discussed it with them as a possible escape plan but had been advised against it. No one had believed he would actually try it but he had. So, here we all were.

Shadda tells me that the first time that I would ever have seen Billy Love would've been the time Ronny Carlton was fitting a new gearbox to Agnes's old Bedford CF up at the depot. I remember the occasion and that there'd been another guy with him who'd sat in the transit and had run us down to the weigh station in Brigton. Shadda tells me that this other person was Billy Love. He and Ronny were scrap merchants and besides the £30 payment for the job they'd also had a couple of old gear boxes thrown in.

Joe Steele tells me that Billy Love had accompanied him to my house on one occasion when he'd gone there to borrow or sell me something. I recall that Joe always had someone with him who'd driven him over from Garthamlock but, once again, this was someone in the background that I paid no particular attention to. I also recall Ronny Carlton and another approaching me in the Netherfield pub one weekday afternoon when I was down that way to pick up my son Stephen from his Gran's who lived in that area. They'd just acquired an aluminium box

Transit and asked if I could put them on to any local traders who would either trade it for a flatbed pick-up truck or else convert their vehicle, removing the box and adding a motorised winch. The price for the job would be that they could keep the aluminium box. I'd directed them to either Robbie's yard, a local truck dealer, for a possible trade or else to Smiddy's the local blacksmith, for the conversion job.

This guy with Ronny had returned soon after and his face had been familiar as one of that Garthamlock crew. He'd driven me and my son Stephen home, dropping us at the bus stop on Edinburgh Road directly opposite my house on his way home.

I hadn't known his name then and would've sworn I'd never met anybody called Billy Love but would, as Shadda had said, recognise him when I saw him again. This would be when he walked into court as the chief prosecution witness against me for a series of serious offences including the mass murder of the Doyle family. Isn't life strange?

Our next court appearance was Wednesday 16th May for judicial examination. This was when I first heard the police verbal and wasn't too pleased at all. Here's how it went.

INDICTMENT

CASE No. C4745/84

UNDER THE CRIMINAL PROCEDURE (SCOTLAND) ACT 1975

as amended by the

CRIMINAL JUSTICE (SCOTLAND) ACT 1980

and relative Act of Adjournal

TRANSCRIPT OF PROCEEDINGS AT JUDICIAL EXAMINATION

WITHIN THE SHERIFF COURT OF GLASGOW AND STRATHKELVIN AT

GLASGOW

RELATING TO

THE QUESTIONS ASKED AND ANSWERS GIVEN, INCLUDING

DECLINING TO ANSWER, UNDER SECTION 20A

in the Petition of

Procurator Fiscal Glasgow

and Strathkelvin against	THOMAS LAFFERTY
	AGNES CAMPBELL or LAFFERTY
	THOMAS McGRAW
	THOMAS CAMPBELL
	THOMAS CLARK GRAY
	THOMAS LAFFERTY
	JOHN CAMPBELL
DATE	16 May 1984
SHERIFF	Gordon
NAME OF ACCUSED	
APPEARING	THOMAS CAMPBELL
FOR THE PETITIONER	Mr D Spiers, Procurator Fiscal Depute.
FOR THE ACCUSED	Mr R T McCormack,
	54 Gordon Street, Glasgow
SHERIFF CLERK	Mrs Gillian Sweeney Sheriff Clerk Dpt
Sheriff	Mr Campbell, have you received a copy of the charges against you?
Accused	Yes.
Sheriff	Do you understand these?
Accused	Yes.
Sheriff	The Procurator Fiscal is going to ask you some questions about them. You are not obliged to

	answer any of his questions but anything that you do say will be taken down in shorthand and on the tape and may be used in evidence. On the other hand if you decline to answer any questions this morning and at a subsequent trial you, or any witness called by you, gives evidence telling the Court things that you could have told us about by answering the questions this morning, then the fact that you declined to say anything this morning can be commented on at the trial. Do you understand that?
Accused	Yes.
Sheriff	You are entitled to consult your solicitor before You decide whether or not to answer any questions. If you are going to say anything would you please speak slowly, clearly and loudly so that we can get an accurate recording . . . Mr Fiscal.
Procurator Fiscal	Yes my Lord.
Procurator Fiscal	Your name is Thomas Campbell is that correct?
Accused	Yes.
Procurator Fiscal	And your date of birth is 4 November 1952?
Accused	Yes.
Procurator Fiscal	You have already agreed that you have received a copy of a petition containing a charge of conspiracy and other acts committed in furtherance of the conspiracy and that you understand that?
Accused	I understand the charge yes.
Procurator Fiscal	Have you also received a written record of an extrajudicial confession allegedly made by you?
Accused	I received this today yes.
Procurator Fiscal	If I can refer you to the Petition Mr Campbell, you will see that it is alleged that you and others including Thomas Lafferty, Agnes Lafferty, Thomas McGraw, Thomas Clark Gray, Thomas Lafferty junior and John Campbell conspired with each

	other and with others meantime unknown to further your business interests in ice cream sales vehicles. Have you anything to say with regard to the allegation firstly that you have business interests in ice cream sales vehicles?
Accused	Do I have an interest in ice cream vans? Well my wife has an ice cream van yes.
Procurator Fiscal	Have you anything to say with regard to the allegation that you conspired with other named persons and perhaps others?
Accused	No I did not conspire with anybody. I don't even know John Campbell.
Procurator Fiscal	That is the last person who is named on the Petition?
Accused	Yes.
Procurator Fiscal	So you deny having formed a conspiracy to intimidate rival ice cream van salesmen and women?
Accused	Deny that completely yes.
Procurator Fiscal	Have you anything to say with regard to the allegation that in furtherance of a conspiracy a Donna Logan and Stephen Timoney were followed persistently in their ice cream van?
Accused	I don't know anything about that at all.
Procurator Fiscal	Have you anything to say with regard to the allegation that on 30 September 1983 in various streets in Garthamlock a Jaimes (sic) Lockhart and an Andrew Doyle, now deceased, who were in an ice cream van, were persistently followed?
Accused	I don't know anything about that either.
Procurator Fiscal	And that they were shouted at?
Accused	I have never shouted at anybody in any ice cream vans in Garthamlock or anywhere.
Procurator Fiscal	Have you anything to say with regard to the allegation that between 1 and 31 December

in furtherance of a conspiracy William Hamilton, Andrew Early and Paul Devlin were all offered and given a bottle of wine on condition that they damage a Marchetti brothers ice cream van?

Accused
I don't know any of these people at all. I may know Paul Devlin to see. It's either him or his brother I know. Did'nt (sic) offer anybody anything to do anything.

Procurator Fiscal
It is alleged you see that may have been done in furtherance of a conspiracy perhaps by someone else but in furtherance of a conspiracy you were involved in. Have you anything to say with regard to that?

Accused
I know nothing about it, I can't see how I could possibly be involved.

Procurator Fiscal
It is alleged further that on 4 December 1983 in Tattershall Road, persons were caused to throw stones at a Marchetti ice cream van being used by Douglas Cardle and Catherine Rankine. Have you anything to say about that?

Accused
No. I don't know these people at all or anything about the incident.

Procurator Fiscal
Have you anything to say with regard to the allegation that on the same date and place persons were caused to throw stones at another Marchetti ice cream van being used by James Mitchell?

Accused
I don't know anything about this either.

Procurator Fiscal
Charge 6 narrates that between 2 and 31 January 1984 in the Barge public house in furtherance of a conspiracy Robert Byrne and John McNamara were both offered payment as inducement for them to damage Marchetti ice cream vans?

Accused
I don't believe I was ever in the Barge public house in January of that year. I don't know Robert Byrne or McNamara.

Procurator Fiscal	You know neither Byrne nor McNamara?
Accused	No.
Procurator Fiscal	It is alleged further that on 21 January 1984 in Porchester Street William Hamilton was caused to throw a bottle through a window of a Marchetti ice cream van. Have you anything to say about that?
Accused	I know nothing about it no.
Procurator Fiscal	Then on 18 March it is alleged that the same William Hamilton and Allan Todd were caused to smash a window of a Marchetti ice cream van?
Accused	I don't believe I know these people. I know nothing about the incident.
Procurator Fiscal	It is alleged that between 1 and 31 March in Dudhope Street in Glasgow an Angela Kane was assaulted by being pushed out of a queue at a Marchetti ice cream van and told to go to another ice cream van. Do you know anything about that?
Accused	Not till I read the charge no.
Procurator Fiscal	It is alleged further that on 6 April 1984 in the Fifti Ices premises at 250 Blairtumnock Road, Glasgow a Martin Stewart was threatened that he would be cut from ear to ear and that persons were going up to Castlemilk to blow every van to fuck and everybody that's in it. Have you anything to say with regard to that allegation?
Accused	Didn't know nothing about it till I read the charge.
Procurator Fiscal	Charge 11 narrates that on 9 April in Tattershall Road persons struck a Marchetti ice cream van being driven by Andrew Doyle. Have you anything to say with regard to the allegation that this was done in furtherance of a conspiracy involving you?

Accused	If it was done it wasn't done in a conspiracy involving me. I know nothing about it.
Procurator Fiscal	The twelfth charge is that on the same date in Porchester Street a brick was thrown at a Marchetti ice cream van being driven by Kathleen Mitchell. Have you anything to say with regard to that?
Accused	Nothing to say about it because I know nothing about it.
Procurator Fiscal	The thirteenth charge alleges that on the 29 February 1984 in Balvennie Street in Glasgow Andrew Doyle and Ann Wilson were both assaulted. Have you anything to say with regard to the allegation that you conspired to have this done or indeed that you were personally in Balvennie Street on that day involved in that assault?
Accused	The only thing the first thing I knew about it was when the police told me there was a rumour that I was suppose to have done it and again they told me that I was suppose to have loaned the car that was involved. I deny this and I denied it at the time. I know nothing at all about it.
Procurator Fiscal	So you deny being involved personally or conspiring to have them assaulted?
Accused	Personally, indirectly or in any other way.
Procurator Fiscal	Do you know where you were on 29 February 1984?
Accused	Yes I was – Do you want me to tell you that?
Procurator Fiscal	Yes.
Accused	I started in Duke Street, went to Duke Street – my wife goes to her mother's on a Wednesday afternoon. Spent the day in my wife's mother's house.
Procurator Fiscal	What is the address in Duke Street?
Accused	2 Dunragit Street, Duke Street.

Procurator Fiscal	Is it off Duke Street?
Accused	Off Duke Street yes.
Procurator Fiscal	When did you go there?
Accused	Went down there about 11 o'clock in the morning.
Procurator Fiscal	11 a.m.
Accused	Left about 3.
Procurator Fiscal	Who was in the house between 11 and 3?
Accused	Mrs Donaldson, Mr Donaldson, my wife, Maureen . . .
Procurator Fiscal	Who is Maureen?
Accused	Maureen Mitchell, my wife's sister and her 2 children and my son Stephen.
Procurator Fiscal	You left there about 3?
Accused	Left there about 3 yes.
Procurator Fiscal	Where did you go?
Accused	Home to the house at 38 Barlanark Road.
Procurator Fiscal	When did you arrive there?
Accused	About half past 3.
Procurator Fiscal	How long did you stay there?
Accused	I stayed there for the rest of the night. My wife left to go to work.
Procurator Fiscal	For the rest of the night, do you mean right through till the following morning?
Accused	Yes. Right through till the following morning.
Procurator Fiscal	Who was in the house with you from . . . ?
Accused	My wife left about 5 o'clock to go to work.
Procurator Fiscal	Who would be in the house then?
Accused	Only me and my son. A few people would have come to the house within that time.
Procurator Fiscal	Do you know who came to the house during that evening?
Accused	One of the girls that rents videos – to change videos tapes – a wee lassie next close.
Procurator Fiscal	Before you go further is that a girl from a video library company or something of that nature?

Accused	Yes it's a girl, I don't know the company, it's a girl that just does video tapes.
Procurator Fiscal	Do you know which company she works with?
Accused	I don't know.
Procurator Fiscal	Do you know her name?
Accused	There's two girls I don't exactly know which one it was that night that came.
Procurator Fiscal	Do you know the name of either of them?
Accused	I know the first name but I can't remember right now.
Procurator Fiscal	You indicate that somebody else may have been in the house that day?
Accused	Michelle, it's the wee girl from next door that comes to play with my son.
Procurator Fiscal	What age is she?
Accused	13 or 14. As far as I can remember that's all that arrived at the house that night.
Procurator Fiscal	Until your wife got home?
Accused	Until my wife got home just after 11 o'clock.
Procurator Fiscal	You have received a written record of an extra judicial confession allegedly made by you in the house at 38 Barlanark Road, Glasgow on 12 May 1984 to or in the hearing of Detective Inspector McCafferty, Detective Sergeant Hyslop and Detective Constables Cargill and Geddes, is that correct?
Accused	I deny that. I've got it here in front of me. I deny that emphatically.
Procurator Fiscal	You have received a copy?
Accused	I have received a copy yes.
Procurator Fiscal	I understand you deny having said to or in their hearing 'I only wanted the van windaes shot up'?
Accused	I deny that emphatically. I have no reason to say that. It wouldnae be in my interest for such a thing to occur.

Procurator Fiscal   Thank you.

I hereby Certify that the foregoing transcript is a complete and accurate record, as provided for in paragraphs 2(7) and 2(8) of the Act of Adjournal (Procedures under Criminal Justice (Scotland) Act 1980 No 4) 1981, of all questions to and answers by the said THOMAS CAMPBELL under Examination.

Shorthand Typist. CASE No. C4745/84

Next appearance in court from Wednesday 16th was Tuesday 22nd, after ten days in custody for bail application. I was feeling well and confident that the charges would be dropped at this stage, that I'd be going home from the court that day, but I was in for another surprise.

As we reached the cellblock area of the old Sheriff Court, I was huckled into a wee side interview room by four detectives. The two I remember so well we'll call Furlice and one we nicknamed Goldilox. One of the bigger lumps stood in the open doorway blocking it like a guard at ease on parade. Furlice was in charge of this posse. He held a clipboard with some kind of document or statement attached. Presenting a casual, friendly demeanour like he was only too pleased to be doing me the favour. He was sorry it had come to this, he told me, but at least I still had the chance to walk out the door. He'd met my wife outside, she was pregnant wasn't she? Congratulations and all that. She was expecting you home today. No doubt you're expecting that yourself and you will be, or at least you could be, if you play your cards right. It's all down to you. It's your choice.

'Just get on with it will ye. What do you want with me? What am I here for?'

'Well what I have here is a charge and a statement. I've been given instructions from the PF that it's either one or the other for you. The charge is murder of the Doyle family. I'm sorry. I warned you that you were the perfect target unless you cooperated and you still have that chance here at least. Your last chance. My instructions are clear – either you cooperate now or you're to be charged with the fire.'

'That's crap. You've already said that yous know I didn't do it,' I said. He agreed and said that still remained the case. However, the pressure was coming down from

Olympus to proffer charges otherwise they would all be back in woolly suits. They needed a body and I remained one of the best options.

'Naw,' I said, 'Yous are going too far here. You're going too far. Y'canny do this. It's out of order.' That's as it may well be, nevertheless those were the instructions he'd been given and he would carry them out. 'So what exactly do you want from me? What d'you expect I can do?' I asked.

The polis man looked relieved, letting out a long blow of air. Then got down to business. What he had was a statement for me to sign. Once I sign it I'm out the door today and will be used as a witness in the Doyle fire case. I glanced through the statement. It was supposed to be me saying that young Shadda had asked me for money to go on the run down south because he'd lit the fire but hadn't expected anybody to be killed. Blah! Blah! Pure crap. I handed it back to him without a word.

'Well?' he asked, handing me the pen.

'Stick it up your arse,' I told him, pure ragin. They wanted me to help them fit up my nephew just as they'd tried with me so many times and failed. No, better that they fit me up instead, I thought. At least I'd some experience of dealing with it whereas Thomas was so naïve he would take a fall for it. Yet I still didn't believe that they would actually charge me. They soon convinced me otherwise.

'Right!' he said. 'That's it,' he seemed to be psyching himself up. 'You have thirty seconds, count it down,' he said, gesturing with his hand to one of the others who started, 'Twenty-nine.'

'Sign.'

'Fuck off.'

'Twenty-eight.'

'Sign the fuckin thing, man.'

'Twenty-seven.'

'Go and take a fuck tae yersel.'

'Twenty-six.'

'I'm serious.'

'Twenty-five.'

'So am I.'

'Twenty-four.'

'We're no kiddin here.'

'Twenty-three.'

'Neither am I.'

'Don't be daft, man.'

'Twenty-two.'

'You know I never done it.'

'Twenty-one.'

'There's nae choices anymore.'

'Twenty.' And so it went on right to the end.

'Four.'

'C'mon, TC, wake up.'

'Three.'

'Yous are going too far here.'

'Please, it's only a bit o fuckin paper.'

'Two.'

'Last chance.'

'Stuff it.'

'One.'

'Right, that's it. Fuck it. Bring that other bastard in here.'

They brought in young Thomas Lafferty and charged the two of us together. He read out the charge that Thomas and I had murdered the Doyle family by setting fire to their house.

MMcW

COPY FOR THOMAS CAMPBELL

SECOND PETITION   PF Ref . . C4145/84 . .

UNTO THE HONOURABLE THE SHERIFF OF Glasgow and
Strathkelvin at
Glasgow

........................22 May ....1984...

THE PETITION OF

PROCURATOR FISCAL of Court for the Public Interest

HUMBLY SHEWETH

That from information received by the petitioner, it appears
he/she accordingly charges that

THOMAS CAMPBELL, Born 4.11.52 and THOMAS LAFFERTY,
Born 28.5.65 both now in custody, did on 16 April 1984 wilfully
set fire to a cupboard door and the entrance door of the house
at 29 Bankend Street Glasgow and the fire took effect on said
house and James Doyle, Christine Doyle or Halleron, James
Doyle Jnr, Anthony Doyle, aged 14 years, Mark Halleron aged
18 months, and Andrew Doyle, all residing at said house and
then occupying said house died as result of said fire and they
did murder them.

Procurator Fiscal Depute.

THOMAS CAMPBELL
THOMAS LAFFERTY

'You don't have to say anything, but anything you do say will be taken down as evidence and may be used in evidence against you. Have you anything to say?'

'No reply,' I said it out loud to warn Thomas not to say anything.

'Naw,' he said.

Furlice had psyched himself right up. Scribbling furiously on a piece of paper on the clip board, 'No reply, eh! I'll give you no fuckin reply.'

Shit, he was scribbling down our verbals, making them up. I was being fucking verballed for six fucking murders, I realised glancing round in panic. Thomas still hadn't tippled what he was writing. The copper on guard at the door changed his weight from one foot to another and I charged for his off balance side barging past before he could stop me. A bizzie, we'll call him Wildly, holding onto my jacket tail, was dragged with me under the momentum of the charge. Right through the door and across the corridor to the sergeant's bar. We were inside the cellblock so it was obvious I wasn't trying to escape. There was nowhere to go. I reached over the sergeant's desk and gripped the inner rim. This nut case Wildly still playing tug o war with my jacket trying to pull me back in.

'Sergeant,' I gasped, heart pounding. 'I've just been charged with murder and I want it noted that I made no reply. No reply right? Two of us.'

'Right y'are then,' said he. 'A Mr Campbell isn't it? A Mr TC Campbell.' Looking at his watch he noted down my name, the time, and the charge, CC, for Capital Crime, and No Reply. 'I'll have your solicitor informed right away,' he said.

Daft Wildly was still tugging at my tail. I turned in a rage.

'Gerraff ae me ya fuckin idiot ye,' I said knocking his

hands loose from my jacket, storming towards him as he backed away suddenly realising he'd had a tiger by the tail and it wasn't too pleased. Then I noticed big Joe Beltrami, Thomas's lawyer, and shouted to him. 'They've just charged young Thomas with murder and they're trying to verbal him.' I pointed to the room and big Joe actually ran to get in there. I doubt if we will ever see the likes of him again. A rare diamond and a brilliant lawyer. I thought there was no fucking way they could get off with verballing us now. Not with the sergeant and big Joe Beltrami to back us. I was wrong. They simply backdated the verbal to another time and place. Remember, I'd already been verballed for the shooting at the 16th May judicial examination.

'I only wanted the van windaes shot up,' backdated to the time of my arrest at home. What they did now was simply add to that, adjust it to suit the new charge. Ten days after my arrest and seven days since I was first judicially examined. So why hadn't it been mentioned then? Was it a secret? Was it supposed to be kept as a surprise? To me? The person who is supposed to have said it? They took me into the judicial examination a matter of minutes after being charged. I was handed the new verbal confession on the way in.

CASE No. C4745/84

UNDER THE CRIMINAL PROCEDURE (SCOTLAND) ACT 1975

as amended by the

CRIMINAL JUSTICE (SCOTLAND) ACT 1980

and relative Act of Adjournal

TRANSCRIPT OF PROCEEDINGS AT JUDICIAL EXAMINATION

WITHIN THE SHERIFF COURT OF GLASGOW AND STRATHKELVIN AT GLASGOW

RELATING TO

the questions asked and answers given, including declining to answer, under section 20A in the Petition of

Procurator Fiscal Glasgow and Strathkelvin	
against	THOMAS CAMPBELL and
	THOMAS LAFFERTY
DATE	Tuesday, 22 May 1984
SHERIFF	Stone
NAME OF ACCUSED	
APPEARING	Thomas Campbell
FOR THE PETITIONER	Mr D Spiers Procurator Fiscal Depute
FOR THE ACCUSED	Mr R McCormack,
	54 Gordon Street, Glasgow
SHERIFF CLERK	Mrs Gillian Sweeney Sheriff Clerk Dpt

Sheriff	Thomas Campbell, do you have before you a petition containing a charge against you?
Accused	Yes.
Sheriff	Have you read it and do you understand it?
Accused	I understand it, yes.
Sheriff	This is a judicial examination. You will be asked questions by the prosecutor. You may consult

	your solicitor before answering. You have the right to refuse to answer any question. If you do that however it may be commented on at your trial. The proceedings will be taken down in shorthand and recorded on tape and may be used in evidence at your trial. Do you understand all that?
Accused	Yes.
Procurator Fiscal	Your name is Thomas Campbell?
Accused	Yes.
Procurator Fiscal	And your date of birth is 4 November 1952?
Accused	That's correct, yes.
Procurator Fiscal	Now you have indicated I believe that you have received and you understand the contents of a petition containing a charge of murder related to you? Is that correct?
Accused	I understand it yes, I don't understand why I'm charged with it.
Procurator Fiscal	Have you also received a written record of an extra-judicial confession alleged to have been made by you?
Accused	Yes, I've seen this. I would like to deny that at the moment. At no time did I say this to anybody at all, at no time did I say it. The police said this to me and they also asked me if I knew a man called Doyle and I said no and they said, do you know him as Fat Boy? and I said I'd heard Tony mentioning the name Fat Boy and that was all I said. I made no reply to the charge.
Procurator Fiscal	I'll come on to that in a moment Mr Campbell. If I can refer you meantime to the petition itself. You will see that it it is alleged that you and Thomas Lafferty were both at the house at 29 Bankend Street, Glasgow, on 16 April 1984 where you wilfully set fire to a cupboard door and the

	entrance door of the house. Have you anything to say with regard to the allegation that you and Thomas Lafferty were both there?
Accused	We weren't there, no way was I there anyway.
Procurator Fiscal	Are you in a position to tell the court where you were – I would be interested in the period from say about midnight until say about 3 a.m.–4 a.m. on 16 April?
Accused	Midnight? I went to bed at midnight with my wife Elizabeth.
Procurator Fiscal	Where were you?
Accused	38 Barlanark Road, Barlanark. And that was me until half past seven, 8 o'clock the following morning.
Procurator Fiscal	How long had you been in your house with your wife prior to going to bed at night?
Accused	All day.
Procurator Fiscal	Had you left your house prior to this?
Accused	No, The only time I left the house was to go up the stair to decorate the house we've got up the stair that we're suppose to be moving into.
Procurator Fiscal	Is this the house which is just immediately above where your present home is?
Accused	It's a house that we've just been given by the corporation and I was decorating the living room.
Procurator Fiscal	When did you do that?
Accused	My wife left to work on the van about 5 o'clock and I would say about half past six I went up the stair. There was a couple of young boys up, more getting in my way than helping me, but they were there to do something for me.
Procurator Fiscal	How long were you in this house?
Accused	I would say about 9 o'clock.
Procurator Fiscal	From 6.30 to 9 p.m. on the evening of 15 April?

Procurator Fiscal	That's correct, yes. I can't remember his name. He's next door, oh next close, and his two friends.
Procurator Fiscal	What age are these boys?
Accused	About 14.
Procurator Fiscal	When you left there you went back to your own house?
Accused	Yes, down the stair to my own house.
Procurator Fiscal	Was your wife in?
Accused	She didn't come till about ten past eleven, quarter past eleven.
Procurator Fiscal	That evening?
Accused	Yes.
Procurator Fiscal	And are you indicating that you were in the house then with your wife and family?
Accused	Yes.
Procurator Fiscal	What family is that?
Accused	My wife and my son Stephen, aged 2.
Procurator Fiscal	From what time?
Accused	From when my wife came home till I went to bed around 12 o'clock.
Procurator Fiscal	When did you next leave the house?
Accused	About half seven, 8 o'clock in the morning.
Procurator Fiscal	Monday morning?
Accused	Yes.
Procurator Fiscal	You will see it is alleged that you in fact were at this house and that you and Thomas Lafferty wilfully set fire to a cupboard door and the entrance door of the house at 29 Bankend St Glasgow, and that the fire took effect on the house. Is there anything further you wish to say by way of defence relative to the charge, I'm thinking for instance of whether you might wish to incriminate anyone else?
Accused	There is no reason or no motive or anything

	behind why I would want to do this. I can't understand why I'm charged with it.
Procurator Fiscal	Did you understand what I just said to you though, I was particularly asking you whether you wanted to take advantage of a defence of incrimination?
Accused	Well, if I knew who done it . . . I would like to know who done it so's I could say. The police have been saying to me that if I telt them who done it all charges against me would be dropped, that they knew I didn't do it, but I would be charged anyway, if I didn't tell them who did it. They seem to believe that I do know who did it.
Procurator Fiscal	I take it then that you are denying murdering James Doyle, Christine Doyle or Halleron, James Doyle jnr, Andrew Doyle, Anthony Doyle and Mark Halleron?
Accused	I emphatically deny that, yes.
Procurator Fiscal	You have received a written record of extra-judicial confession allegedly made by you. If I can refer you to that for the moment.
Accused	Well, as I said, I didn't say this but in the police station the police said this to me. That they believed this.
Procurator Fiscal	Well firstly can I draw your attention to the fact that it is alleged that this was said on 12 May at the house at 38 Barlanark Road, Glasgow. Is that your house?
Accused	That's my house, yes.
Procurator Fiscal	It is alleged that you said this on 12 May 1984 at 38 Barlanark Road Glasgow, to or in the hearing of Detective inspector McCafferty, Detective Sergeant Hyslop, Detective Constable Cargill and Detective Constable Geddes, of Strathclyde Police and it's alleged that you said: 'The fire at Fat Boy's was

only meant to be a frightener which went too
far.' Do you admit or deny saying that?

Accused I deny saying that, as I said at the police station
they said these words to me and asked me if
I knew a man called Doyle and I said no. And
they said what about Fat Boy and I said I know
the name Fat Boy through Tony having used the
name. In the house in Barlanark the only thing I
said was when told there was a warrant for my
arrest on a conspiracy charge I asked them if
they were kidding and then I made a complaint
about the police taking money belonging to my
wife, and that was all I said. Present with me
were my wife and my niece's fiance and they
will testify to the fact that I didn't say any of
these words.

Procurator Fiscal Thank you.

Defence Nothing my Lord.

I hereby Certify that the foregoing transcript is a complete and accurate record, as provided for in paragraph 2(7) and 2(8) of the Act of Adjournal (Procedures under Criminal Justice (Scotland) Act 1980 No 4) Sect 81 of all questions to and answers by the said THOMAS CAMPBELL under Examination.

Signed . . . .

Shirley A Morrison

CASE NO. C4745/84

'The fire at Fat Boy's was only meant to be a frightener which went too far.'

Good and proper English. If I wanted to say such a thing I would not have used the word 'frightener' I would have used the word 'threatener'. Nor would I have used the proper English word 'which' because I don't speak in proper English. Many years later, someone pointed out to me that on relating the verbal evidence against myself, I always get it wrong, 'Only meant to be a frightener th'went too far.' Not realising that I'd unconsciously replaced the proper English 'which' with my natural 'that'. Not that it matters. It still stands as verbal confession evidence regardless. Thus providing the sufficiency of necessary corroboration in support of the witness Love to take the charge to a court and to a jury. As Furlice had warned, prejudice would do the rest.

Sheriff Court Cells

The cells in the old Sheriff Court are but blue-black steel plates welded together to form rows of six by three foot boxes. Each with a steel door and small hatch. Each containing a stainless steel urinal which doesn't flush but simply drains. Each with a steel flat bar grill bench. Each cell usually holds between eight to ten prisoners with standing room only throughout the day, sometimes every day for a week if you have a trial there. Mostly it is just day-trippers down on petition warrant, judicial examination or seeking bail. There are no windows and no air ventilation systems other than the four by four inch hatch on the door through which a sandwich and plastic mug of tea are handed in to each prisoner for lunch before being shut again. Prisoners take turns standing by the door hatch, for even though closed, it provides a weak breeze of fresh air from the corridor to help keep one's groggy brain alive and alert before appearance in court. Naturally, as in all such inhuman extremes, Charles Darwin's theory on survival of the fittest comes into play and the biggest or meanest gets the lion's share of air. They say that a society's civilisation can be measured by how it treats its prisoners. By this measure then, Scotland is somewhere in the sub-barbarism bracket.

It was back to this then from judicial examination, and charged with the murders of the Doyle family. Seems I wasn't to be going home today after all. The turnkey opened the cell door in the row and out poured a flood of putrid urine in a wave from the cell floor into the corridor. Someone had vomited into the urinal drain, blocking it and, for the rest of the day, the piss from eight men just overflowed, flooding the cell. The prisoners inside, crammed there like sardines in a tin, stared out numb brained and blank eyed as the turnkey motioned for me to enter.

'Gerr oot o there ya shower o ejits ye's, whit's wrang wi ye? Fuckin daft or somethin? That fuckin cell's condemned. Come on, out!'

And instead of me stepping in, they all trooped out at the voice of command like so many zombies, now voicing their complaints to me as if I was the fuckin lavvy inspector or something. Meanwhile the turnkey in a panic, his name-to-cell-number rota all screwed up, rushed about opening cell doors and pushing people in at random, and I walked down the row opening the hatches and choosing the cell with the fewest occupants. Those poor souls inside, stuck glued to the walls as if on some horror funfair ride as I paced, ranting and raving, 'Bastards! Bastards! Dirty fuckin fit-up bastards.'

Then on to C Hall Barlinnie untried.

C Hall Bar-L

C Hall Barlinnie untried is just a dirty smelly midden for dumping society's trash. The cells are filthy, the beds and bedding are filthy, the piss pots are filthy thick with barnacles. The only thing for cleaning up is water. Barlinnie is one of those jails that belongs to the screws as a community industry. Things like soap, disinfectant, shampoo and toothpaste are rare and seldom seen in the prison but could be found in abundance in the prison officers' quarters. It is a thieves' jail. Everything and anything not bolted down will take legs and walk and the screws are the worst of them all.

A total hierarchical system, the only way anybody gets any due or comforts at all is by being a name or with bundles of cally dosh. The average ordinary mug gets nothing but the daily crap handed out to him for twenty-three hours a day behind his door. The whole system is rotten and corrupt to the core. Rat race, dog eat dog and that's just the screws. They create the regime that suits them best and they revel in it – a microcosm of the criminal underworld but without the risk.

It is also, therefore, a hotbed of the underworld grapevine. The right cons in C Hall can tell you the news on every major crime in the west of Scotland almost immediately it occurs and often even before. Every major and minor active criminal in the west of Scotland passes through there. Even those not inside have relatives and associates to visit there. As a result, the place is constantly buzzing with the latest news and scandal. Who's hot on the trot for what? Or if you want to know who screwed your auntie's lassie's wee pal's brother-in-law's car, house, or stole their washing from the line – visit someone in C Hall and the info is easily gleaned. All they have to do there, all day every day, is to gossip and swap stories of their feats of daring do. You can well imagine then, what kind of source of information it is for the police. Information is tradable for reduction in charges and for cash.

It was from here that we began to gather the information on Love from the many others who had been offered the same and similar deals from the polis.

Love is . . . the Deceiver

William (Billy) Love could be described as the typical wee Glesca flyman, always on his toes and checking out the angles. Though he and his cronies, including Ronny Carlton (who later married Love's sister, Aggie) mostly dealt in scrap, they were opportunists and not averse to any wee turn that might come their way.

Such was the case of the scrap merchant's robbery. It resulted simply from their frequent visits there for payouts on the odds and ends that they'd begged, borrowed or stolen in the course of their daily activities. They'd gathered odd scraps of information regarding the days and times at which the proprietor of the premises would unload his heavy burden of cash onto the scales down at the bank. From there, it seemed the natural and obvious next step would be to nip in there first, when the time was right, and relieve him of his burden before the bank did.

Towards that end then, the tallest was selected to play the part of the bizzie rapping on the office door announcing the arrival of Strathclyde Police. Once the door was opened the other two would barge in masked and armed with a shotgun, tie up the proprietor and make off with the cash. A cakewalk!

Of course, it didn't quite turn out that way, as if it ever does. Although all went well and according to plan, there was just one minor hitch – the money wasn't there. They had been just too late, the proprietor had explained, for he'd only just converted the cash into a truck load of alternators from which he would expect to double his money via a contact of his down south.

After a thorough search, they exited the premises empty handed, leaving the owner gagged and bound and, as their 'logical' process seemed to dictate, they stole the truckload of alternators. Love, now assuming that this haul was his own by virtue of a good night's hard graft, parked the truck outside his home in Garthamlock and went to bed. The police, on their regular patrol, upon a routine check of the truck half blocking the road confirmed that it was that vehicle referred to in earlier robbery reports. Assuming it had simply been used as a convenient getaway, they had it towed to the police compound for forensics and fingerprint testing. Love, upon awakening to discover that his haul of stolen scrap had itself been stolen by the polis, promptly hiked down to the police compound and stole it back – once again parking it outside his house until he could finish off his breakfast and make a few calls for a buyer. He was quickly dragged off to the compound himself and charged with armed robbery, theft and assault. He was later further charged with attempting to pervert the course of justice by putting someone else's name up front for these offences. Of course, his accomplices were soon dragged in too.

As an untried prisoner in C Hall, HMP Barlinnie, Love was refused bail on his final appeal to the High Court in Edinburgh due to his previous bad record, including three prior attempts at perverting the course of justice. It was wisely deemed by the High Court that he was a 'menace to society' and his bail was refused. This was the court of last resort – the highest court in the land. There could be no way out now and no escaping the consequences of his illegal actions. He would be held in for trial and could expect up to ten years. But Billy the Kid was not finished yet. All the angles had yet to be fully explored.

Around the time of his bail refusal, after three weeks untried, number 29 Bankend Street went up in flames. All the press and media were full of the reports of the horrendous arson attack upon an innocent family. It seemed that people were dying day by day for weeks. In fact, six people had died in what became known as the Doyle family fire murders and, Glasgow's 'ice cream war'.

As the Daily Record exclusives from the Mitchells of Marchetti unfolded the story of ice cream wars was fast becoming the accepted theory. These reports had gone on to publicise how gangsters had moved in on the trade in the past two years. 'Relatives of the rivals of Marchetti in Garthamlock,' which could, of course, only be one person. Agnes Lafferty's brother, the TC fullah himself, had served a ten stretch for gang related offences as a teenager. Quotes from the police were saying that Andrew Doyle had been attacked on a number of occasions. Once with a shotgun while he served in his van and if they could find the culprit for that dastardly attack then they would have the perpetrator of the fire. This put Love in deep shit, but at least he had an alibi for the fire.

Death Row – New Faces

Gary Moore, Cammy, Tamby and I would walk the exercise yard together and they'd put me in the picture as to who was who from Garthamlock in relation to the various charges. At that time, Gary was charged with car offences and had only been a vague acquaintance from the time when he'd tried to trade in his non-negotiable giro. During these times in the yard, amid the masses of speculations as to what the fuck was going on, being the only accused of the fire murders there, I would rant on and on in my confusion and outrage about 'dirty fit-up bastards' and how I couldn't get it into my head that this was happening to ME. 'Why me? Why are they doing this to me?' and so on.

About a month into this long lie in Gary and Tamby just didn't show up in the yard. The assumption was that they must be over seeing lawyers or something. In fact they'd been shanghaied down to Baird Street polis station and charged with the murder of the Doyle family along with Joe Steele. I didn't get the news about it until I saw them the next day in the yard, Gary ranting on in his hyper agitation about 'dirty fit-up bastards' and how he couldn't figure out 'Why me?' Why would they do this to him? And so on.

'Fuck sake, Gary, you're no the only wan. Ah've been sayin the same thing to ye for the last month noo, it's nothin new,' I said.

'Aye!' he says, clutching his hands to his head. 'But I didnae fuckin believe ye.'

'Exactly, but now ye know how it feels. Hell slap it in t'ye.'

Yeah, it's true. There's just no words to describe how it feels to be wrongfully accused of such a horrendous crime and realise that no one believes you. The accusation itself is enough to bury you alive. The idea that those accused may be innocent just doesn't enter people's heads. It doesn't matter how much you may protest your innocence, you waste your breath. Like Gary had done with me, they just say, 'Aye Right! Yeah! Yeah! Heard it.' It isn't possible to get an insight into the horror until it happens to you and you are all in the same boat. It is no consolation. From the personal point of view of the innocent accused, nothing is any consolation. You find yourself up against an impenetrable wall of prejudice, an automatic presumption of guilt. To find any consolation in another's similar demise is the first seed of pariah syndrome.

I still hadn't got the full story of the new accused when I saw Joe Steele in the yard at the same time his name came into it. 'He's charged with WHO? Charged with WHAT?' I must have said it too loud cos he came over. 'What the fuck's going on here?' I said, beginning to think that they knew more than they were saying, falling for the same psychological trap against them as had been sprung on myself. Everybody suspects that everybody else must know more than they are letting on, otherwise, why would they be charged?

One minute I'm charged in one capacity with young Thomas Lafferty and, just when I am beginning to get my head around that, I find that I'm charged in a completely different capacity with three new co-accused? How am I supposed to figure out what it is I am supposed to have done when the prosecution and the polis don't know themselves and keep on changing it? In fact, I had a few more surprises. There was to be yet another accused added, Joe Granger, before they would change their minds again – but that was yet to come.

The Bear never ever said much. He seemed withdrawn into himself but was always there quietly in the background listening, trying to pick up any telltale signs that might give him some insight into who was responsible for what and why the fuck he'd been dragged into all this – just as everybody else was doing. Tamby the Bear was beyond suspicion in my eyes. To know him was to know this beyond any doubt or question.

Gary Moore was obviously innocent. His stunned shock was absolute and genuine. He became really over the top paranoid about the polis fit-up, believing this had happened to him because of our association at exercise time. He may even be right there, as there is no other explanation. 'If they could do this to me, they could do any fuckin thing they wanted,' was his viewpoint.

Joe Steele was the same. There was never any doubt about his innocence. He oozed ignorance from every pore as only he could. Right from the day he arrived in the untried he got himself into hot water with everyone, rubbing people up the wrong way in his ignorant presumptions of their guilt – as if he was the only innocent accused and everybody owed him a confession to get him his just due acquittal. Like everybody else not associated with the charge he had that unconscious prejudice that those accused must be guilty – except himself. I saw it in him and I understood it and it wasn't an attitude which could be faked. It was unconscious and genuine ignorance. In fact, if any jury could have seen or known these guys during that period they would never have been charged far less tried for the murders of the Doyle family. I believe the polis knew this.

Which only leaves me. What can I say?

Isn't it such an added tragedy and travesty that all accused are innocent in this case? I mean, if one or some were guilty there would be something to hold onto, something to grasp and to work on but when all are innocent there is nothing. We are no better off and still left in ignorance and in the dark of confusion. It is more difficult to defend yourself against a fit-up than it is against a crime you have committed. At least the guilty have an idea of where it is coming from while the innocent are left without a clue.

There were many accused of murder on death row. The remorseful don't deny their crime. There were many more guilty than others but there are none more innocent than the ignorant. Here they all were now on death row with me and looking towards me – the first and original accused whom they hadn't believed until it had happened to them – for guidance and for answers as to why it had happened to them. But there was nothing I could say to make it any easier to cope with.

I approached the entire ordeal from the perspective of a psychological war. A massive mind game being played against us. Knowing that the police and their fellow travellers knew we were innocent, I didn't waste my time trying to get my head round what had led to their mistake in my case. So, while the others struggled in the confusion of that psychological mind trap, I concentrated on trying to fathom the depth of their nasty tactics in an attempt to counter them. I never did much of a good job of it. There were too many surprises yet to come, sufficient to keep us all guessing for many a long year.

Aftermath – The Craw

The two witnesses, the girl from the all-night service station and Reg R, were never cited as witnesses and were not listed on any police or crown lists of witnesses. The two junkies had not yet come forward, so the only real lead was the old Escort Popular. The description had rung a bell with me. If it was the same one I was thinking about, I knew the young team who used it. I have an excellent memory but am hopeless on the mundane abstract such as labels and folk's names. People take this as a bad memory, but they are mistaken, for the fact is that I do not forget. I just cannot recall things at will. I didn't know exactly which of this crew actually owned the Escort Popular, just that they used it to get about thieving pieces off cars and the like. They were neighbours of the Craw, the Bar-L Young Team. I was sure that the Craw could help me out with the names, that was something he never forgot, and I knew they were doing work for him unloading their various hauls to him at cut price rates, so I got him up at visit. 'Who owns yon wee L reg Escort in your street?' I asked.

'Naw, you're on the wrong track there, it's an old Volvo they've got. It wasn't them,' he said emphatically.

Well, isn't life strange? This is someone who thinks he's talking to a guy with a bad memory. Sure enough, I did remember clearly that one of the brothers had an old Volvo which also sat there at the close but that was besides the point. The main point for me was that he'd just said something which told me that he knew a lot more than he was prepared to say. I mean, here I was asking about an old Escort and he was saying, 'No, you're wrong. It's a Volvo they have.' Like, who have? For if 'they' do not have an Escort (which I know they did) then how the fuck did he know who I was talking about? And with his attempted sideline remark about the Volvo, pinpoint them accurately in relation to a reference to an Escort? Elementary logic was leading me to suspicions and to the recalibration of former conclusions. That strange memory of mine flashing me back to a point in time when we were both in C Hall together.

Bombed Out & Bewildered on Death Row

Death row HMP Barlinnie on capital charge. We had just received a preliminary list of productions, witnesses and precognitions for the Crown case. This included a witness statement from a Mrs Degnan, my sister Agnes' next door neighbour from Dudhope Street. This mad woman was saying that on the night Tommy Cooper died on TV (Sunday 15th April, 1984) she'd seen me arriving in a black XR3I with the Craw at my sister Agnes' house. We'd come back out again with my sister Sadie carrying bags and what could've been a gallon of petrol. Aye right and we'd driven offski into the blazin' sunset. I was alarmed. This was garbage but significant for the fact that it would counter my alibi. So I had to get it sorted out, like sharpish.

As it had actually happened it was Saturday night 14th April. The only night that Liz didn't work on the van and so I had to go to the garage up at Fifti's to collect the night's takings for stocking up in the morning. The van was late in and it was worrying. Our schedules and routes were tightly adhered to as part of a system of early warning. Someone had said that they had seen 'Lizzy II' going up Stepps Road from Edy Road. To stray from the route was a sackable offence and I was onto it with trepidation. Chris was there with his silver Mark 5 Cortina waiting to pick up the Craw. He was acting as chauffeur till the Craw's ban was up in the next few

days. I asked Chris to take me down around Edy Road
and up Stepps Road to check out where the fuck the van
had gone. He radioed it in as a fare. Up Stepps and then
to the right into Garthamlock where my sister Agnes had
her run.

Sure enough, there was the van sitting at my sister's
close. I stormed in there, ragin, ready to sack my brother-
in-law Alex but was soon put in my place by his wife,
my big sister, Patsy. The buses had been on strike that day
and Patsy had told Alex to pick her up at her work at the
Granada Bingo in Parkhead adjoining the run and to drop
her at oor Agnes' near to Fifti's. I couldn't argue with that so
I had a wee blether and exited with Chris. Later Mrs Degnan
was to say that that was my sister Sadie (who sometimes
worked in Agnes' van) and that it was Agnes' van at
the close on the Sunday not the Saturday. The vans looked
the same, only people involved in the trade would know the
differences at a glance. Patsy and Alex had got a local taxi
(Tillicairn Taxis) from the scheme home to Easterhouse.

So I needed the Craw to trace Chris. I needed his
record of the call-in fare with East-End taxis and I needed
Tillicairn Taxis' record of the fare from Dudhope Street
to Easterhouse. I needed Patsy and Sadie to prove that it
had been the Saturday night and not the Sunday, Chris
and not the Craw. Later Mrs Degnan's evidence was
discredited when she admitted that the polis pestered her
about thirty times to say that it had been the night Tommy
Cooper had died on TV and she finally agreed because she
didn't really know and didn't see what difference it made
– but that was later. Meantime I was in a bit of a jam.
Alibi bombed out of the water and fucking bewildered as
to why this woman would say that.

The Craw came to my cell door on death row pleading
with me not to cite Chris. I'd already had strong words
with him for not giving me Chris's name and contact

information. He was nervous and expected me to do him there on the spot but he had a deal for me.

It turned out that he didn't want me to cite Chris because if the bizzies pulled him in, being a shite bag, he would open up and grass the Craw for everything. He knew too much about the Craw and would bury him, deep style. So, like what? Well Chris was an undercover paid informer who moved arms from the UDA and passed the information onto the serious faces. 'Well hard shit,' I said. 'He's your fuckin chauffeur.' But it gets deeper. Undercover as a grass he moved the bulk of the city's smack all over town. If I didn't bring his name into it not only would he provide the serial number of the shotgun on the preliminary list (we had recently discovered this was being alleged as found in my house during search on arrest) but also, through Detective Protector Jimmy of the Mob, would provide the production label number and date of the last trial it was used in. That was of Watty Norval, the Govan Godfather and the XYY gang. Fuck sake, whit next?

I gave this information to my lawyer, then Bob McCormack. This was a bombshell on the Crown case. It could be used to discredit the police who also said they'd found a map with a ring around the words 'Bankend Street'. The lawyer ran straight to the Crown Office demanding, he said, on 'my' behalf that this shotgun be removed from the evidence against me. Which it promptly was, thus fucking up a good line of defence.

It also turned out, and this is true, that although the Craw had bought the XR3I before the Doyle fire he hadn't actually taken it out of the showroom until his ban was up, a day or so after it. He was released, regardless of all the other charges. Tillicairn Taxis was bombed out. The garage burned down and Chris was off at Plompton. And I, bewildered and bemused, still hadn't tippled.

It wasn't till ten years later the first witness confessed in tears of regret for not coming forward sooner about Chris and his silver Mark 5 with the Craw in Bankend Street on Sunday 15th April, 1984. The night his brother-in-law Snadz's van was landed on its side on the grass verge by Andrew Doyle. The night before the early morning of the fire which tragically killed six members of his family. And for which I would be crucified.

BOOK FOUR

Indictment Series

Charge 1 – George Reid

George Reid modelled himself on the upwardly mobile young businessman of the early to mid-Thatcherite eighties. Open top sports cars, designer wear, private number plates, Filofax and all that palaver. A mechanic to trade, now he would never be seen dead with dirty hands – bad for the image y'see. The guy is a poser of the first degree.

A worshipper of Mammon, his god above all else is Cally Dosh and his loyalties will always lie wherever that flows fastest into his bank account. No harm in that, it was the prime directive of the Thatcherite era for so many millions per same. Once you realise this and expect no more or less he won't disappoint you. For although tight-fisted to the point of neurotic misery still, you find that he is a nice enough wee guy.

It was apparent to everyone apart from wee George that he was the second choice candidate for the role he would be given to play at the trial. A bad second choice trade in for the Craw at that. After the Craw was released by the Crown prosecutor from Barlinnie C Hall untried wing, wee George was dragged in to replace him.

At that time, the Crown were trying to build the illusion of an ice cream war conspiracy and needed a figurehead, a moneyman so to speak, to fill the void left by the Craw as the Moriarty figure manipulating from behind the scenes. Wee George was definitely the wrong man for this particular role. Inoffensive, non-aggressive, soft spoken Boy George was far too naïve to have the kind of ambition which might lead to any kind of confrontation, never mind a violent confrontation, with anyone any bigger than Winnie the Pooh.

Sure enough, he had associated with the Craw during business hours and they were partners in some enterprises. From picking him up at the depot where he too stocked and garaged his van, to buzzing about all over town on whatever business of the day. The Craw was a banned driver so this arrangement would be to mutual advantage. Sometimes George would run me down to the bank and maybe stop by for lunch at one of those fancy poser pitches he liked to be seen in. This was in his interest too. He'd stood as a signatory to my loan for the purchase of the new van and, therefore, it was in his interest to see the payments being made. Don't ever expect this guy to do anything that's not to some personal advantage but, in those days, if there was ever any conspiracy beyond a wee turn in snout here and there, I never heard any of it from either of them. Though George and the Craw did tend to spout a load of crap most of the time, that is just my opinion and it is not a criminal offence.

One of their mutual business interests was the mobile video libraries in the schemes at that time. They'd taken old school buses and converted them into video libraries, halving the rental fees in places like Castlemilk and Haghill. In fact, it was this enterprise which led to wee George's demise in both of those areas and accounted for his star appearance on the indictment.

On the times mentioned in Charge 1, George had been scouting the run in Haghill backwards as y'do when looking for the van. As it happens, his video van, which should have been on the job, had gone for diesel. He had noticed the ice cream van half blocking the narrow street and, being an ice cream man himself, that it was facing the wrong way for the side of the road where it was parked. This meant the serving hatch faced out into the road putting the kids at risk from traffic. Each time he passed the van, he had had to slow down to squeeze between it and the cars parked on the other side. This actually led to George being grafted onto the indictment under Charge 1.

> *Charge 1.* On various occasions between 1st April and 31st August, 1983, both dates inclusive, in various streets in the Haghill area of Glasgow, the exact dates and streets being to the prosecutor unknown, you GEORGE REID did, while acting along with others to the prosecutor unknown, conduct yourself in a disorderly manner, persistently follow in a motor car, registered number MDS 820Y, Graham Robertson and Donna Jaconelli, both care of Baird Street Police Station, Glasgow, who were both then trading from an ice cream van, take observations of their movements and this you did with intent to intimidate them and place them in a state of fear and alarm for their safety and commit a breach of the peace.

In fact, in the event, the evidence showed that there was only one street mentioned and only on one occasion – not following but passing them as they sat parked by the side of the road. This charge was a piece of pure and utter nonsense and designed solely to create a false and unfounded impression of sinister goings on. Implications of conspiracy, gangsterism and ice cream wars. According to the evidence of the witnesses, this charge should never have been made, for it appeared that George Reid was being accused as a result of someone else's paranoia. The evidence was as follows:

'He drove past us about two or three times, slowed down and kept looking at us.'

'Did he threaten you in any way?'

'No he slowed down and was watching us.'

'Did he say anything?'

'No it was just the way he looked at us.'

'Did he make any gestures?'

'No.'

'Any threatening gestures at all?'

'Yes, he slowed down in his car and passed us about three times.'

'And what was your reaction to that?'

'I was scared, he scared me.'

'Why? What did he do to scare you?'

'It just seemed that he was watching us.'

'He looked at you?'

'Yes.'

'Was there something about that look? Did he sneer at you?'

'No.'

'Is it, perhaps, that he didn't smile?'

'Yes! It scared me.'

'That he didn't smile?'

'Yes.'

'Tell me, how wide are these roads?'

'About ten or twelve feet I think.'

'And you were parked on one side is that correct?'

'Yes.'

'And how wide is your vehicle?'

'About six or seven feet or something.'

'And were there other cars? On the other side perhaps?'

'Yes, along the street.'

'Is it possible that he may have slowed down to manoeuvre?'

'Yes, he probably did but . . .'
'But he looked at you?'
'Yes.'
'And didn't smile?'
'Yes.'
'And that alarmed you?'
'Yes.'

That George Reid was found guilty as charged based upon this kind of evidence goes some way to illustrate the depth of prejudice against all the accused in this case. For him to be convicted by a jury on this charge left little hope for anybody else otherwise accused.

Charges 11 and 12 – George Reid & Joe Steele

Once the quick change was made, the Craw out and George in, it was discovered that a receipt for the Craw's Bowie knife had mysteriously found its way into wee George's top pocket. George swears he has no idea how it got there and, in reality, was too naïve to fathom it out for himself. The whereabouts of the actual Bowie knife, however, was even more significant. It was found planted in the back of the head of a Viking ice cream van driver in Castlemilk as a result of an incident following on from another similar one for which Snadz, the Craw's brother-in-law, had been charged before the Doyle fire had occurred.

Charge 11. On 30th March, 1984 in Croftfoot Quadrant, Glasgow, with faces masked, you GEORGE REID and JOSEPH STEELE did, while acting along with others to the prosecutor unknown, assault John Shepherd, care of Baird Street Police Station aforesaid, and did strike him on the head with a knife or similar instrument to his severe injury.

Charge 12. Date and place last above libelled, you GEORGE REID and JOSEPH STEELE did, while acting along with others to the prosecutor unknown, wilfully and maliciously damage ice cream van registered number VGD 23W and did repeatedly strike it with sticks and knives and similar instruments and did smash all the windows of said ice cream van and damage the bodywork thereof.

In fact, it had been common knowledge to everyone concerned at the time, even the police knew that the Bowie had been planted in John Shepherd's head by Billy McPhee, one of the young Bar-L. He was a car thief who made a wage by selling off the parts but was open to suggestions and adaptable to anything where the making of a few sheckles was concerned. He then worked for the Craw. Given the routes, plans, tools and transport for a target job, he and his crew would carry it out and unload their haul of stolen snout and other goodies, cash in hand at cut price rates to the boss.

He was one of the team who had attacked the van in Croftfoot Quad, personally planting the blade in Shepherd's head. Possibly, wee George may have had some wind of this beforehand, I don't know. Certainly Joe Steele hadn't a clue. Yet it was these two who were charged with this incident on the indictment.

The run under dispute was an old and well established Fifti's run controlled by the Drummonds of Bar-L who had recently gone out of business handing it over to Mudsy Mullin, also from Bar-L and financed by the Craw. Marchetti had also had a go at moving in to fill the gap, but had been promptly deterred by the incident for which Snadz had been separately charged. Now, with Snadz untried in C Hall, Viking were having a go.

The main evidence came from the two girls on the Viking van both called Angela. They had recognised George Reid as the good-looking wee guy in the blue XR3I, registration number GR 65, who owned the mobile video library in that area. They'd seen him driving past, chuffed that he'd given them a wave.

Next time they'd seen him that night he was driving

the Fifti's van and had pulled up parallel to them facing the other way. Both were keen for a sight of him and the opportunity of a chat. Just then, as he drove away again, their van was attacked by a gang of men wearing masks and wielding baseball bats and knives. They both recognised one of their attackers as Billy McPhee whom they knew from when he worked for his uncle Frank McPhee at Viking's. He had spoken directly to them during the attack, demanding his knife back, but it had been stuck in John's head and they couldn't get it out at the time. The van was being smashed to pieces with glass flying everywhere, so they'd lain down on the floor and covered their faces and heads with their arms. 'No!' they said. 'No way could George Reid have been part of that attack.' They'd seen him drive away just before it started.

They testified that they'd given the police full statements identifying Billy McPhee as one of their attackers, the one who had stuck the knife in John's head. Months later, they attended an identification parade where they'd seen this wee guy with the same hair style and highlights as Billy McPhee and had pointed this out to the police by way of identifying McPhee's hair style but saying that he wasn't McPhee who was much taller. They had both identified Joe Steele as the man in court whom they'd pointed to as having the same hair style as McPhee but who was not one of their attackers. They had explained this to the police at the time. When told that this man, Joe Steele, was there in court, charged with that attack as a direct result of their identification, they both said, 'No that's wrong. That's a mistake. We were only trying to point out what Billy McPhee's hair looked like. It was Billy McPhee.'

Billy McPhee was never charged. Joe Steele should never have been charged and was acquitted. The only other remaining evidence was the Bowie knife and the receipt found in George Reid's top pocket. His denial of ever having owned a Bowie and lack of knowledge as to why the receipt was in the pocket of his jacket in the wardrobe, looked suspicious. All he would have had to do in his defence was produce another Bowie in court to account for the receipt and thus refute that the receipt and the knife in the guy's head were necessarily related. He wouldn't do that, naïvely believing that the truth would set him free. Well, maybe in an ideal world, but certainly not at Glasgow High Court in a trial such as this.

George was found guilty and sentenced to three years when the Crown prosecutor pointed out to the jury that the alternative implicated the police as guilty of perverting the course of justice by planting evidence. Dearie me! Shock Horror! What horrendous vistas that would open up eh! Who could consider such a thing?

It was obvious by the evidence that Joe had no connection with George Reid or the Castlemilk incident and that the police and prosecution were well aware that it had been McPhee. The trumped up charges against Joe, however, had yet another, more sinister motive behind it.

They accounted for, and allowed Reid's presence on the indictment. Without this, evidence could not have been brought regarding a bank statement confirming that both he and the Craw were good for the £250,000 which they had offered for the purchase of Fifti Ices cash and carry and ice cream depot. Without Reid on the indictment, this evidence couldn't come out since the Craw was no longer an accused.

Under examination on this issue Renzo Sieki, the owner of Fifti Ices, confirmed that George Reid had made a bid to buy his business. Documents were produced to show an audit assessment had been undertaken on his behalf valuing the property at £250,000. In fact, the normal pre-purchase arrangements. Further evidence of bank statements showed that this sum was within the financial range of both Reid and the Craw. The latter was referred to orally as 'Another' because he was not then an accused.

'Who was the man behind George Reid?'
'I don't follow . . .'
'Who was the man behind the scenes?'
'I . . . I don't understand.'
'Who was the man behind the man so to speak?'
'What do you mean?'
'Who was the man who was really trying to buy your premises?'
'George Reid.'
'But who shall we say was his sleeping partner?'
'Eh! Missus Reid?'
'Who was the man behind the scenes, the man who was the driving force behind his enterprise?'
'To buy?'
'Yes.'
'George Reid.'
'Mr Sieki, there is more than one person named on Production 120 before you. What I want you to tell the court is, who was the man, the hidden partner behind this . . . this enterprise? Who was really trying to buy?'
'To buy my premises?'
' Yes.'
'George Reid.'
'Who was George Reid's partner?'
'Oh! I see, that would be Thomas . . . (He pauses then names the Craw.)

A big loud Ooh! sighed from the jury. It wasn't until then that I realised that they didn't have the documents before them and hadn't known that the Craw had been named as the second man. They had in fact expected it to be me. I hadn't had any clue about who'd tried to buy what from who until it had gone to trial. Nor would I have been expected to have. It was none of my business whatever these two had been up to. Besides, where the fuck would I get two hundred and fifty grand? All my financial statements showed that I was in debt, paying off a bank loan for eight grand. I didn't see what relevance this could have to the Doyle fire.

There then followed a long, drawn out, dreary rigmarole regarding who owned how many vans at Fifti's. About thirty vans had garaged there, all privately owned by thirty different owners. It was established that only one of these belonged to myself and Liz, one belonged to George Reid and one to the Craw. Also, although my two sisters had a van each there, that they belonged to their own business and not mine.

The coachbuilder from Scotts of Belshill was brought in to establish just how many vans had been purchased over the past two years and by whom. George Reid had purchased one, the Craw had purchased one on a trade-in deal and I had purchased one per same. Mine was noted as a cash sale. The manager explained that it had actually been a banker's draft for £8,000 but because I hadn't used their usual finance company it was put through the books as a cash purchase. Evidence was produced regarding my loan from the bank and the rate of interest. Scotts' manager, a Mr Cowie, was then asked about the premises called Fifti Ices and how many vans they had purchased over the past two or three years. The answer was none, that the business was a cash and carry and didn't operate its own vans. But from the people who operate from those premises, how many had been purchased? The answer was about twelve individual sales. This was all long, drawn out and boring detail about nothing and the jury were falling asleep. The Press had gone off for their liquid lunch and no one was paying any attention to this, or so it seemed.

Yet the Press had a lot to say on this matter.

'TC Campbell Buys 12 Ice cream Vans Cash . . .'

'TC Campbell Gives Renzo an Offer he Couldn't Refuse, Sell Up or Else'

'In his bid to take over Glasgow's ice cream trade, TC Campbell tried to purchase Fifti's Ices for £250,000 from a terrified Renzo Seiki . . .' On television, Barry Norman on Film 84's review of the movie Comfort and Joy made himself famous and won awards for the quote, 'Life emulating art' in his reference to, 'Where at present at the High Court in Glasgow, ice cream baron, TC Campbell, murdered six people in a bloody ice cream war . . .'

Was this the same trial? Was I hearing the same evidence? It seemed that there was a separate trial going on between the Crown and the Press in the court lobby or Hangman's Rest bar, other than that in court. The bleary-eyed jury over their tea and toast in the morning would be saying to themselves, 'Christ! I must have nodded off at that bit . . .' But none of it, not one fraction of any part of it could ever have been done if George Reid hadn't been welded onto the indictment as co-accused of Joe Steele to replace the Craw. The Crown tactics were always nasty but this kind of thing takes them beyond the pale.

Of course, George Reid appealed against conviction on all charges, but was sent packing by the Appeal Court. Maggie's hard lines sucker policies on law and new order regimes were well and truly set and would not be shifted by something as simple as mere justice and equality for all.

Charges 2 & 16 – Joe Steele

Gordon Ness, Joe Steele's accomplice in the attempted raid on Sammy McBride's van was, according to the evidence, a junkie police informer. It was also said that he was a child abuser and had been charged with assaulting and breaking the bones of a two-year-old baby. Naturally, therefore, as per the nature of the beast, he'd struck a deal for immunity from prosecution, trading wee Joe in for the raid on Sammy's against his own charges. According to inside info, Ness had actually told the truth in court but for one significant addition. He said Cammy had been present, sitting in the back seat of the getaway car, as Joe made his blundering but seemingly hilarious attempt on Sammy's van. Cammy swears that this wasn't true, that he wasn't there, but had been simply fitted in to discredit him in other more important areas regarding Charges 9 and 15 where he was proof that the witness Love was lying. But we will get back to that later.

Ness's information on the shotgun led the police directly to Goofy's stash. Goofy was unaware of the existence of Ness and of his part in the raid on said stash along with Joe. Under threat of being roped in to the Big Ice Cream War Conspiracy and believing the informant could only have been Joe, Goofy admitted buying the gun and losing it again. Thereby confirming Ness's story about thieving it back he was cited as a witness but failed to appear on the day.

Meanwhile, Joe was arrested in an attempted break-in to a disused farmhouse out Airdrie way, no doubt trying to thieve a shotgun to replace the one stolen back from Goofy. Yet he is so short-sighted that he failed to notice that the building had no roof and was a condemned shell. While in custody, confronted with the evidence of his pals, Love and Ness, and under threat of the Big Ice Cream War Conspiracy he too allegedly struck a deal for immunity and bail. Allegedly, Joe traded in young Thomas Lafferty as having admitted to him he was responsible for the fire at the Doyle family home. He, Joe, was then released, according to police evidence, to glean further information as an informant but had gone straight to a lawyer claiming that the police had been trying to put words into his mouth. By all accounts, it did appear that the Myopic Mole had just roped himself into the Big Ice Cream War Conspiracy for short-term gain.

For his failure to cooperate further, Joe Steele was arrested and charged with myriad crimes around mid-July 1984, some weeks after the arrest of the original accused. Gary Moore and Tamby the Bear were also charged with him at the same time, with the murder of the Doyle family. Young Thomas Lafferty, his mother Agnes and the Craw were released. Straight three for three swap.

Up on death row the indictment comes through. Among other charges Joe the Mole is charged with the attempted raid on Sammy's van (Charge 2) and attempting to pervert the course of justice (Charge 16).

Charge 2. On 29th September, 1983 in Milncroft Road, Glasgow, you JOSEPH STEELE and JOHN CAMPBELL did, while acting along with Gordon Ness, care of Baird Street Police Office, Glasgow, with faces masked, assault John Clifford and John Brady, both care of Baird Street Police Office aforesaid, who were both then trading from an ice cream van registered number LDS 999Y and did present a shotgun or similar instrument at them, smash a window of said ice cream van and did attempt to rob them of a sum of money.

Charge 16. On 9th and 10th May, 1984 at Airdrie Police Station, Anderson Street, Airdrie, Lanarkshire, you JOSEPH STEELE did, with intent to pervert the course of justice and to avoid prosecution in respect of Charge 15 above, falsely state to Detective Superintendent Norman Walker, Detective Inspector John Sharkey and Detective Chief Superintendent Charles Craig, all Strathclyde Police, that you knew a person responsible for the wilful fire raising at 29 Bankend Street, Glasgow, on 16th April, 1984, and on 10th May, 1984 at Airdrie Police Station aforesaid, you did falsely state that Thomas Lafferty junior, 20 Dudhope Street, Glasgow had admitted to you that he was responsible for said fire, and you did thus render Thomas Lafferty liable to suspicion, accusation and arrest for said wilful fire-raising and you did thus attempt to pervert the course of justice.

'Hey look, they've been recording us on tape,' Joe points t'the indictment. 'Aye? What makes y'say that then, Joe?' enquires the Bear, puzzled.

'There it's there,' Joe points to an item on the production list. 'Three invoices,' he declares, proving his point.

'Fuck sake! Can ye get myopia of the fuckin brain, Joe?' exclaims the Bear, shaking his head in exasperation. In fact, the Bear had just made an astute observation for the Myopic Mole is indeed short-sighted in many respects.

Joe was convicted on Charge 2 and was sentenced to one year's jail. He was acquitted on Charge 16 when it was pointed out at the close of evidence that the prosecution hadn't even bothered to ask Thomas Lafferty jnr whether he had in fact said that to Joe Steele. That then should have been the end of it for Joe but, no, he still remained charged with Charges 6, conspiracy to rob, Charges 11 and 12 with Reid, Charge 13 with myself, Tamby and Gary for assault on Andrew Doyle and Charge 15 with those same accused of the murder of the Doyle family by wilful fire-raising. Seems that he wasn't doing very well out of his immunity from prosecution deal and bail for burgling a ruin.

Charges 3, 4, 5, 6b, 7, 10, 14, 14a, 14b – Shadda

Shadda is the Glasgow pronunciation of the word shadow. One of the romantic yarns about the name attributes it to the amazing ability to appear and disappear silently from the shadows at opportune moments – but there are many.

Otherwise known as wee Tommy Lafferty he is married to my sister Agnes. Shadda has been a local legend in his own time, sadly, that day is long gone. Throughout the troubled times of 1983–4 he was an alcoholic and drunk all the time. A wee baldy, bunneted, bow-leggit Glesca wino wido. Wide as the Clyde and drinks as much, as we'd say. A wee flyman, but that was in his younger days before the booze took its toll on his befuddled brain.

A chronic alcoholic not allowed home whilst on a bender is effectively homeless. Dossing from one boozing buddy's house to another, wherever the flow takes him between garden parties round the back of somewhere or other where the polis never go. Yet he was never without a bed or couch to flop on mostly due to the fact that he is such a likable wee rogue. Always with some good stories or funny anecdotes to tell, he also has that Cryin Shame yodel of Hank Williams' songs down to the proverbial T, sufficient to break your heart. This guy has shakes on the shakes of his shattered nerves and couldn't conspire to light a cigarette on his lonesome blue without someone to hold his hand, or a bottle to suck on to start his brain of a morning.

This then was the numero uno. The principal accused.

Number one on the indictment. The alleged instigator. The conspirator and the link. The Big Daddy of dread and deception according to the Crown prosecution case and, sure enough, he was so clever that even he didn't have a clue what he was up to.

Charged with myriad crimes, amongst which:

- Breach of the peace and drunk and disorderly. Found Not Guilty.
- Attempted instigation to have someone throw a stone. Found Not Guilty.
- Instigation to have someone throw a bottle. Found Not Guilty.
- Conspiracy to rob. Found Not Guilty.
- Instigation to throw a bottle. Found Not Guilty.
- Instigation to shoot a van. Found Guilty on the evidence of Love.
- Push someone out of a queue. Found Not Guilty.

When asked if he actually did any of these things, his off the record reply refers to that well known Glasgow Italian by the name of Fucktiv Anno (aka I don't recall).

Charge 3. On or about 30th September, 1983, in various streets in the Garthamlock area of Glasgow, the exact date and streets being to the Prosecutor unknown, you THOMAS GAVIN LAFFERTY did conduct yourself in a disorderly manner, persistently follow in a motor vehicle James Lockhart, care of Baird Street Police Office aforesaid, and Andrew Doyle, formerly of 29 Bankend Street, Glasgow, now deceased, who were then trading from an ice cream van there and in Redcastle Square, Glasgow, shout and swear at them with intent to intimidate them and commit a breach of the peace.

Charge 4. On 2nd December, 1983, in Inverlochy

Street, Glasgow, you THOMAS GAVIN LAFFERTY did instigate William Hamilton, care of Green, 934 Gartloch Road, Glasgow, to damage an ice cream van owned by Marchetti Brothers, 40 Glentanar Road, Balmore Industrial Estate, Glasgow, and did offer to give him a reward for said act, whereby on said date in Tattershall Road, Glasgow, said William Hamilton, while acting along with William Early, 18 Inverlochy Street, Glasgow, and Paul Devlin, 98 Tillicairn Road, Glasgow and other persons to the Prosecutor unknown did wilfully and maliciously damage ice cream van registered number KHS 311Y then being driven by Irene Mitchell, 72 Cumbernauld Road, Muirhead, Glasgow and did smash the rear window of said ice cream van and you did wilfully and maliciously damage said ice cream van.

Charge 5. On 6th December, 1983 in Tattershall Road, aforesaid, you THOMAS GAVIN LAFFERTY did instigate said William Hamilton to damage an ice cream van belonging to said Marchetti Brothers and did offer to give him a reward for said act, whereby on the said date in Tattershall Road aforesaid said William Hamilton did while acting along others to the Prosecutor unknown wilfully and maliciously damage an ice cream van register number VGD 26W, then being driven by said Andrew Doyle, now deceased, and did smash a window, of said ice cream van, and you did wilfully and maliciously damage said van.

Charge 7. On 21st January, 1984 in Porchester Street, Glasgow, near Tattershall Road, you THOMAS GAVIN LAFFERTY did instigate said William Hamilton to damage an ice cream van belonging to said Marchetti Brothers, and did offer to give him a reward for said act, whereby on said date in Tattershall Road aforesaid, said William Hamilton, while acting along with others to the Prosecutor unknown did damage said ice cream van register number KHS 311Y then being driven by Irene Mitchell and did throw a bottle through the window of said ice cream van and you did wilfully and maliciously damage said ice cream van.

Charge 6b. And you THOMAS CAMPBELL had in your possession at the said house at 38 Barlanark Road, aforesaid, a quantity of pick axe handles, baseball bats and similar objects, and masks.

Charge 14. On 11th April, 1984 at the house at 38 Barlanark Road, aforesaid, you THOMAS CAMPBELL did instigate Antonio Romano Capuano, 39 Kincardine Square, Glasgow and Alan Thomas Todd, 42 Porchester Street, Glasgow to damage said ice cream van, registered number KHS 311Y, and to assault the occupants thereof, and did supply said Antonio Romano Capuano with pickaxe handles, mallets and similar instruments whereby:

a. On 11th April, 1984 said Antonio Romano Capuano and Alan Thomas Todd did in Tattershall Road, aforesaid, near Porchester Street, while acting along with other persons to the Prosecutor unknown, wilfully and maliciously damage the bodywork and light fittings of said ice cream van then under the charge of said Irene Mitchell with sticks, a mallet, an iron bar, bottles or similar instruments; and

b. On 12th April, 1984 in Knockhall Street, Glasgow, near Kincardine Square, said Antonio Romane Capuano and Alan Thomas Todd while

acting along with David Douglas, 1003 Gartloch Road, Glasgow did assault said Irene
Mitchell and Douglas Cardle, care of Baird
Street Police Office, Glasgow, then in her company throw bricks and stones and similar instruments at a motor car, registered number ULS
840, then being driven by said Douglas Cardle
whereby the windscreen of said motor car was
smashed and said Irene Mitchell was struck on
the head with a brick to her severe injury.

Shafted

If the witness Hamilton was a surprise to me, he was a bombshell to the Crown prosecution case against me on charges 6b, 14, 14a and 14b. He'd been called by the Crown as a witness against wee Shadda on charges 4, 5 and 7 for instigation to smash van windows. I was charged with instigating the Tony Capuano incident on charges 14, 14a and 14b. I hadn't realised that Hamilton had played a part in the incident and, while not named on the charge against me, was intended to be the chief witness of that particular event.

Hamilton had been granted immunity from prosecution in return for his cooperation and evidence against others in another, separate trial. This was referred to as the Capuano trial and he went on to repeat that evidence again at our trial but with just one significant little addition that rocked the Crown case against us to its very foundations.

He told how he and the four accused in the Capuano trial, all members of the GYTO (Garthamlock Young Team), had had an exchange of insults with Dougie Cardle, Irene Mitchell's boyfriend who sometimes drove her van. Though it had apparently started with Dougie's refusal to provide credit, it had escalated to the point where Cardle had swerved his moving vehicle in attempt to dunt one of his tormentors – something he'd been known to do quite frequently. Insults turned to threats but the final lines had been drawn when Cardle had threatened to bring the Milton Tongs up to sort out the GYTO once and for all. This was neither acceptable nor tolerable to the local Young Team who took it as a declaration of war. Cardle had just made his first big mistake.

Hamilton went on to tell how he and the four accused in the Capuano trial had gathered baseball bats, batons and pick shafts, some of them from their own homes and some from the local corporation dump. They then tore the sleeves from old pullovers, tied one end and made eyeholes to form masks. The five of them, including Hamilton and Capuano, set about wrecking Cardle's van, smashing all the windows and fittings while the occupants cowered in terror and alarm.

Later that evening Cardle made his second big mistake when he and Irene arrived with three war wagonloads of Milton Tongs to inflict their just reprisals on the Young Team – slap bang into a set ambush. All vehicles were wrecked under a hail of flying masonry, bottles and boulders aimed by a mass turnout of the GYTO to repel the invading forces. The Milton Tongs beat a hasty retreat to the cop shop to complain about the unfairness of it all. Many were seriously injured but most didn't turn up at the station to explain what they'd been doing there in the first place. Irene, however, had been driving one of the war wagons and had copped a dull yin with a brick on the face, to her severe injury and disfigurement.

All of this had nothing to do with any of the accused presently on trial, of course. Yet Shadda was charged with instigating Hamilton on three occasions and I was charged with instigating Capuano and of possession and supply of the pick shafts. Hamilton was supposed to have supplied the evidence of all this.

John Smith, MP QC, defence counsel for Shadda,

established how it had come to be that Hamilton was used as a witness, with immunity, in the earlier trial and was not accused with Capuano & Co. Hamilton explained that he'd been arrested as Cardle's principal antagonist. The police had taken him into custody and had severely beaten him, until he finally confessed and grassed Capuano and the others involved with him in the attack. When asked if he was saying that he'd been bullied into a confession and into saying things against others that might not be the truth, Hamilton insisted that, regardless of the beating he had received, his confessions were the truth.

'At that stage,' he said, 'they hadn't even mentioned wee Shadda because the Doyle fire hadn't happened yet.' He explained that it wasn't until some weeks later, after the fire, they'd kept taking him back into custody, beating him up and trying to get him to say that Shadda had put him up to the attack. Although he had continued to deny this because it wasn't true, finally he had had to admit that Shadda had given him the change from his pocket to buy a bottle of wine one day when he'd been begging outside the pub. Although he'd stated that this had nothing to do with and wasn't related to his attacks upon the van, the police had leapt upon it as evidence of instigation, as had the prosecutor. 'I mean, whose statement is this anyway?'

It was Donald MacAulay QC, now Lord MacAulay of Bragar, in my own defence who had taken the witness beyond the incident with the van. Hamilton described how they had all, 'duked through the closes at the tap end and belted along the back paths tae the water tower at the Barge Bar'. How they had 'slung the gear up', the batons, bats, pick shafts and masks, onto the wee low roof of the power station there before scarpering. The next time he'd seen them was after he'd told the police about this, they'd taken him in a car and driven him to the scene and punted him up him onto the roof. He had handed the items down to the police waiting below as production evidence in the Capuano trial. When shown those items as produced in court in support of the Crown case in the Doyle family murder trial, he confirmed that they were the items they'd used and which he'd handed over to the police. When asked if he could identify the production labels attached, sure enough, he confirmed that they were the labels which the police in the Capuano case had asked him to sign and date as proof of their origin in that case.

Uproar in court, for in fact these were the very same items which Serious Crime Squad officers had previously testified they'd found in the cellar of my home some five weeks later and which formed the basis of the charges 6b, possession of; and 14, supply of these items to Capuano & Co. Hamilton couldn't have known this and wouldn't know that he'd just provided the irrefutable evidence that the police had planted false evidence against me and made up their testimony accordingly. This was as much of a surprise to me as it was to anyone else. I knew the police evidence was false but had never expected it to be proven as such.

One of the officers who testified to having found those items in my cellar was examined by the Advocate Depute for the Crown, Michael Bruce QC, now Lord Marnoch, 'And when did you first see these items?'

'In the station.'

'PARDON!' roared the AD, shocking the cop to his senses.

'Eh um ah! Ah think I first seen them in the car?' he queried making the AD livid.

'ARE YOU SURE?' he shouted, shaking his head.

'Eh! Ah ahm no sure but I think I seen them in

the boot of the car ... or ... Campbell's cellar?' The AD nodded enthusiastically. 'Aye, Campbell's cellar,' the officer mumbled, embarrassed, for the other three officers had all stated that the four of them had found these items at the same time, thus leaving the prisoner unattended. It's possible that this cop had forgotten his lines but I like to think that, as he was as yet too young to be fully corrupted, he was, in his own way, letting it be known that he was stuck with a script that he wasn't entirely comfortable with. I'd like to think that, for the thought leaves me some hope for the future of my children, trapped in this screwed-up system.

Later in the trial the judge would make a decision in his charge to the jury, 'Now, I have decided, ladies and gentlemen, that there is not sufficient evidence to entitle you to convict Thomas Campbell on Charges 14, 14a or b. It is quite simple as far as 14b is concerned, because this is an attack with bricks, if I remember rightly, and there is no evidence that Thomas Campbell supplied Capuano with bricks. However, be that as it may, there is insufficient evidence in law to justify a conviction of Thomas Campbell ... So, I direct you to find him Not Guilty on both those charges. But you must draw no inference at all from that decision of mine. It doesn't mean that the pickaxe handles and the other articles were not found in Thomas Campbell's cellar; that is still part of the evidence given by the police. It doesn't mean that the police evidence is untrue; it doesn't mean that Capuano was not in fact instigated; it just means that there is insufficiency of evidence in law to justify a conviction and it is my duty, if that is the situation, so to decide and to give you direction. As I say, you draw no inference from what I have decided. A mere technicality, ladies and gentlemen, that is all ...'

I was found to be Not Guilty, with no case to answer

and was entitled to the presumption of innocence which was glaringly omitted. The real fact of the matter is that the judge had to say that, to let the coppers off the hook, otherwise the evidence in the murder case fell. For these were the self-same officers who'd provided the Crown prosecution case with the vital corroboration of the witness Love by saying that, besides the pick shafts and other weapons, they'd also found a map in my gaff with a ring around the words Bankend Street and had verballed me as uttering, 'The fire at Fat Boy's was only meant to be a frightener which went too far.' This being the vital and crucial supporting corroboration of the witness Love. If their evidence was discredited on the matter of the planted pick shafts, uncovered by Hamilton, then their other evidence on the map and the verbal would've fallen leaving the murder charge without that vital corroboration. Insufficiency of evidence in law. No case to answer. Not Guilty.

In the event, Thomas G. Lafferty, Shadda, was also acquitted of all charges relating to the instigation of Hamilton (4, 5 and 7) because, as in my own case, no such thing had ever occurred and there was never any evidence to such a thing. These charges were only included in the indictment to beef it up and give the impression and illusion of some substance to the murder charge. The accusations themselves create the sinister impression of a concerted course of action by one group against another. In fact, Hamilton, Capuano & Co had never said any thing and there was no basis for the charges at all. The Mitchell/Marchettis had their own petty problems within the locus, as do all street traders to some degree or another. There is nothing sinister or unusual about that. The only thing sinister at all was the formal charging on indictment to create the illusion of substance to the so-called ice cream wars indictment. For these charges were no more than a legalistic tactic without any foundation in fact.

If it wasn't so serious it would be pathetic. All that officious nonsense about said-so-and-so-following-said-so-and-so-in-said-van-aforesaid. You'd think that it would've been obvious that a run is essentially a circle. It may sometimes be a figure of eight or something but it is, nevertheless and by design, essentially circular. So, it doesn't matter if you're in front of another while both are confined within the restrictions of the circle. It may be said that one is following the other for they're both following each other. There's no offence in this. There's nothing sinister about it. It is, after all, only the nature of the job. Yet put on an official indictment form like this it's made to appear suspicious and conspiratorial. The only thing suspicious and conspiratorial about it is that it formed the substance of a criminal charge in a High Court trial for mass murder.

The Crown tacticians were making absolutely sure to throw enough shit to make some stick. We were all well and truly, literally SHAFTED.

Charge 6

Irene Mitchell had noticed Billy Love and his cronies, Ronny Carlton and Cammy, loitering outside her dad's home out by Cumbernauld way or sometimes cruising up and down the street in their pickup truck, eyeing up the house. She'd drawn her dad's attention to this and, he too, upon confirming Love's identity and suspicious behaviour had instructed his daughter to follow them in her car to try to discover their addresses. Irene did this and, on confirming that info with her dad, he promptly contacted the police with a statement of complaint resulting in Love being taken into custody for questioning. However, Love insisted that they'd only been curious to see Penny Mitchell's Marchetti van there on the street when they'd stopped by the local garage to use the steam jenny – it appeared that no crime had been committed and there was no case for the police to pursue. Both Mitchells testified to this in court upon examination of Charge 6. Having kept his mouth shut, Love was released but was none too pleased with the Mitchells on that score. After the Doyle fire however, Love sang another song.

> *Charge 6.* On various occasions between 2nd January and 12th May, 1984, both dates inclusive, at the premises previously known as The Netherfield and now known as Scarpers public house, 1071 Duke Street, Glasgow, at the house occupied by

THOMAS CAMPBELL at 38 Barlanark Road, Glasgow, and at other places in Glasgow to the Prosecutor unknown, you THOMAS GAVIN LAFFERTY, THOMAS CAMPBELL, THOMAS CLARK GRAY, JOSEPH STEELE and GARY LANE MOORE did conspire with William McDonald Love and Joseph Granger, both care of Baird Street Police Office aforesaid, to assault and rob James Mitchell, 72 Cumbernauld Road, Muirhead, Glasgow, and in furtherance of said conspiracy you THOMAS CAMPBELL did ascertain the home address of said James Mitchell and did point out to you THOMAS CLARK GRAY, JOSEPH STEELE and GARY LANE MOORE and said William McDonald Love and Joseph Granger the house of said James Mitchell and you THOMAS GAVIN LAFFERTY, THOMAS CAMPBELL, THOMAS CLARK GRAY, JOSEPH STEELE and GARY LANE MOORE did while acting along with said William McDonald Love and Joseph Granger, take observations of the movements of said James Mitchell, persistently follow him through various streets in Glasgow, the exact streets being to the Prosecutor unknown, in a motor van registered number RUS 985R and in other motor vehicles and;

    b. you THOMAS CAMPBELL had in your possession at the said house at 38 Barlanark Road, aforesaid, a quantity of pick axe handles, baseball bats and similar objects, and masks.

All accused were found to be Not Guilty with no case to answer with the exception of Joe Steele who was found Guilty of conspiring with himself. This was a result of the police verbal alleging his admissions during the Airdrie encounter when he was supposedly recruited as an informer to glean further information against young Thomas Lafferty on the fire. According to this then, the only information Joe Steele gave them was against himself for crimes which never occurred. He was given an admonishment and no other sentence was passed by the court, probably due to the obvious and inherent difficulty being convicted of conspiring with oneself to commit crimes which never occurred.

But why were we charged to begin with? Why did the Crown prosecution disregard and dismiss the evidence of the complainers and alleged victims, the Mitchells, and pursue the claims of the alleged culprit? It was known to the prosecution at the time that Love was a serial perverter of the course of justice with a long record of putting other people's names up front for crimes which he himself had committed. In fact, he was charged with just such an offence at the very time of this allegation and at the instance of the same prosecutor.

Perhaps the protocol where the accused are not made aware of the previous record of the accuser may account for one reason why he was recruited by the Crown to do the dastardly deed. Here is an instance where Cammy, Love's co-accused on the scrap yard robbery, is evidence of Love's lies and an instance as to why he was fitted in as a co-accused in our trial to discredit his evidence in refutal of Love. But there would be many more instances of that yet to come.

Charge 8 –
The Lone Granger

Joe Granger was around twenty-one years of age and came from Carntyne. A wee guy, fast talking, witty, extrovert, always on his toes and full of something or other. He'd served a two-year sentence as a young offender for being art and part in a culpable homicide when an armed street gang battle had resulted in a teenager being beaten to death with pieces of road works equipment strewn close by. He hadn't been quite the same wee guy when he'd dropped by at Barlinnie C Hall untried to see me. I hadn't expected him and we hadn't had our indictment yet, so a pleasant surprise became a shock as his terrifying story unfolded before me.

He was to be cited as a witness for the prosecution like Hamilton and Reynolds and so many other hapless alcoholics and drug addicts in this case. He spoke about the police leaping out of doorways and dragging him into the station for questioning almost every day. Describing sessions of intense interrogation, bullying, blackmail, manipulation, and intimidation. Because of the new six-hour rule, they moved him about from station to station through the back doors and denied that he was there or had been there. He described beatings by the police in an attempt to get him to agree to things which he'd no knowledge of. Conspiracy to rob, setting fire to Marchetti's and the Doyle family fire murders. He would be lucky, they'd told him, to get out of it with twenty years for the Big Ice Cream War Conspiracy if he refused to cooperate. They had evidence, according to them, that he'd been involved in an attempt to set a fire at the Marchetti depot, saying something about some Moorov law which could convict him of the Doyle family fire murders.

He was pale, withdrawn and deeply shaken, a shadow of his usual hyperactive self. Maybe he was going through heroin withdrawal was my thought but the real reason soon became apparent.

'I've signed the statement,' he muttered, head down, close to tears. 'Wha . . . whaaa what! Whaa . . . what did it say?' I stuttered, stunned and alarmed.

'It said that we done a fire at Marchetti's.'

'Faauck sake, Joe! What did you . . .'

'And the Doyle fire,' he muttered, head in hands, unable to look at me. Silence. God knows it's difficult enough to comprehend how anybody would sign statements against themselves which weren't true but it's all the more difficult to take in when those statements likewise incriminate others too and one of those others is you. While the psychologists may smile sagely and assure you that it happens all the time, nevertheless, that is no consolation when it happens to you and no less mind boggling.

'Fuck sake, Joe, what the fuck' av y'done t'me?'

'Thay'r fitting me up all roads man!' he pleaded for my understanding. 'They keep dragging me in all the time, kicking the shit out of me. Y'don't know what it's like. They said that if I don't sign the statement I'll get a twenty stretch for conspiracy along with yous. Ah, ah just signed the fuckin thing to get out of there but ah, ah seen a lawyer and I told him everything, that they'd made me sign these statements about things ah know fuck all about. He told me that they weren't kiddin an that if I try to retract them noo, I'll be in there with yous as a co-accused and no oot here as a witness. The statements will do me, man. Ah'm all screwed up tae fuck. He said I should just sit tight and, whatever happens, that I should tell the truth in court. No matter what happens, ah should tell the truth about it when ah go to court an that's what ah'm going tae dae. Ah'm gonny dae that. That's what ah'm here tae tell you . . .'

Well, that was some consolation at least I suppose, but it would mean that the prosecution would still be able to put those statements to him for his denial and, at the end of the day, the jury would still hear it and that would be all that would be needed. All that the police wanted to impress was the jury. Prejudice would do the rest. There was no doubt about it any more. We were all in deep shit.

He told me that the polis involved were detectives we'll call Brewis and Simpleton of the Serious Crime Squad. That he had meetings with them every other night or so in various bars but seldom the same place twice. They would go over his evidence for court with him, correcting him where he got it wrong. They always had bags of what they referred to as 'medication to keep the withdrawals at bay' and were asking what cash or anything else he needed – just let them know and it would be 'sorted'. If he got the jail for anything, he was just to tell the polis in charge to phone the number on the card and he would be released immediately.

Now, this was interesting info. These cards and their numbers are the basis for the name the Licensee, for they give police informers the licence to commit any crime they fancy, within reason, but with impunity from arrest. In the case of the well-known Licensee, it is said that it gave him a licence to kill.

I asked Granger if he would agree to carry a dictaphone with him to his next meeting and, perhaps, make a few mistakes in his account, recording their reactions to that?

'Naw! Naw! Ah canny, ah canny, yer aff yer heid man.
They search me, they'll fuckin kill me, man! They'll find
it an they'll fuckin . . . Ah ah mean, they'll put a fuckin
bullet in mah fuckin heid, man. They'll do me in an put it
down to you. If they even find out that ah'v spoken to you
ah'm wan aff the fuckin numbers, man. Don't y'see?'

So plan B then, as they say in the movies. Would he
agree to tip someone off about their next meeting place?
I'd arrange for someone to be there, a stranger, who'd
maybe hang his jacket on the back of a chair as he played
pool, dictaphone in the pocket, or something like that.
Would that be okay?

'Aye,' that would be okay. So I tried to take it further.
Maybe a hidden camera? Or reporter to snap off a shot
as they handed over the happy jack?

'Naw! Naw! Man, ye canny dae that. They'll take me
away an plant me in the fuckin grun. Ye don't know what
they're like. Ye don't know what you're up against, man.
They know. Don't you see? They know. Ah keep saying
to them that it's no true. The stuff in the statement an all
that. That it's no true but they know. They know an they
don't fuckin care, man.'

We discussed various options and plans for him to
record those coppers without tipping them off as to
what he was up to. Then he disappeared off the face
of the earth. His friends, family, nobody knew where
he was. That really worried me. Though I was deeply
concerned for his safety after the tale he had to tell, I
must admit that I was more concerned for the possible
implications this might have for me than I was about the
possibility of his murder. It was just that, from my point
of view, even although I'd always thought of him as a
relatively straight, stand-up wee guy and all that – still,
he shouldn't have signed that statement. Each and every
one of us had been offered the opportunity to put someone

else in the frame and walk free and hadn't taken it. Thus my sympathy for his predicament was selfishly diverted.

My thinking was that, if the police really had done him in and buried him, it would look like I'd been involved in a conspiracy to silence a witness. I knew that his death wouldn't be to my advantage. Also, the statement would still be evidence, only now without him to refute it. I knew as well that a jury wouldn't know that I knew that the statement would still be evidence. His disappearance then would not only be evidence for the possible motive for conspiracy to silence a witness but would also provide credibility to the police case that the content of the statement must be true. Who on any jury in the land would believe otherwise? Deep shit man, and sinking fast.

Fortunately for all, it wasn't quite as bad as that. The police had discovered that he'd come to see me – something he was free to do while there was no citation or indictment in effect – and had only kidnapped him and his fiancée, Lynne Chalmers.

They both speak of being kidnapped, of being dragged from the house and kept in isolation. Not allowed to phone home to their mothers or to contact a lawyer. The police had warrants for Lynne's arrest for non-payment of fines and no money to pay them. They had used these to keep them in line.

'We took them into protective custody.'

'Did they ask for protective custody?'

'We convinced them that it would be in their best interest.'

'I put it to you that Granger was bodily removed from the house under protest. Is that correct?'

'He wasn't happy about it, no, but he left under his own steam.'

'Supported by two officers?'

'Yes, escorted by two officers.'
'Voluntarily you say?'
'Yes.'
'Tell me, did anyone have to return to the house for
any reason?'
'Go back to the house?'
'Yes, for any reason, to get something perhaps?'
'Oh aye! His shoes you mean his shoes? We had to
go back for his shoes.'
'And he left voluntarily you say?'
'Yes.'
'Without his shoes?'
'We were in a hurry.'
'So much of a hurry that Granger's feet didn't touch
the ground . . . is that right?'
'Ah don't think so.' (Witness smiles.)

Joe and Lynne were taken to an alleged safe house in
Ardrossan.

'And did they say that they wanted to leave at
any time?'
'Aye! They were always wanting to leave, always
cribbing.'
'And did you allow that request?'
'We convinced them that it would be in their best
interest to stay.'
'And did they ever try to just up and leave without
permission?'
'Aye.'
'When was that?'
'Twice, they did it twice.'
'Did what twice?'
'Escaped, they escaped from us twice.'
'And what happened?'
'They dodged us and ran away, but we caught them
and brought them back.'

At this point the judge interrupts to ask the witness if he realises, 'One cannot lawfully be held in protective custody against one's will?' and to say that he should be cautioned before answering any further questions on this matter. That his descriptions here may constitute the conditions of abduction.

Of course, like so many occasions in this and related cases, no enquiry would ever be made into these matters.

Quis custodes ipsos custodiet?
Who will guard the guards?
Police the police?
Prosecute the prosecution?
Judge the judges?'

When an administration becomes an establishment, such as this, it becomes a law unto itself. It will always close ranks and defend itself as a body, and will not prosecute any of its lower minions for reasons of internal morale – regardless of considerations of justice or morality.

Yet another instance of that in this case comes from the police's admission in court to putting Granger into a room with Lynne with orders that he was to convince her to change her statement. Their problem with her was that she was refusing to retract her support of his alibi for 15th and 16th April, 1984, the night of the Doyle family fire, and this presented a serious problem to their case. The point is that it is not for the police to dictate what goes into a witness statement such as Lynne's and what does not. Once again, the police witness was cautioned by the judge that he might be describing the conditions of the criminal act of 'subornation of perjury' but no action was taken at that time. That was yet to come. In the meantime, however, Charge 8 on the indictment read:

Charge 8. On 1st February, 1984 at the premises occupied by Marchetti Brothers Limited at 40 Glentanar Road, aforesaid, you THOMAS CAMPBELL and THOMAS CLARK GRAY did, while acting along with said Joseph Granger, wilfully set fire to said premises and the fire took effect thereon;

Joe Granger was supposed to speak to this but he said in court that he knew 'fuck all about it' and that the police, Brewis and Simpleton, had harassed him, beaten him up, blackmailed and bullied him into signing statements that he did not make.

In fact, the independent evidence supports Granger. The Marchetti fire had been investigated before the Doyle fire had occurred and, according to the fire reports, two attempts had been made on the one night. Investigators had seen immediately that this had been an arson attack. Matches, petrol and cigarette ends were strewn around the scene and still more were on the roof and the access roan pipe. The fire investigation officer had found it significant that bolts on the corrugated roofing had been undone from the inside and petrol had been poured only onto an old shell of a van which had been used for stripping for spare parts but which was, nevertheless, still covered under the Marchetti insurance policy. This shell stood apart from the other vehicles and, should the fire have taken effect, would have put them at no risk. The fire services had arrived in time to douse the flames before any significant damage could be done which meant that the wreck was still seen as a shell and not as an operational unit. It was very unusual and important that a second attempt was made almost as soon as the fire fighters had left. This might suggest that the arsonist was aware that the first attempt had failed. The only way he could have known this, and had the nerve to go back, was if the person who'd opened up the premises for the fire brigade had informed him that he had muffed the job and wasn't getting paid.

The fire report concluded that this was an inside insurance job, so what was it doing on our indictment as part of an alleged plot against Marchetti in a mythical ice cream war? Why weren't the Marchetti management in the dock for attempted insurance fraud and arson instead of as witnesses for the prosecution of others for their crimes? Just another chapter of farce in the so-called ice cream war trial.

Charge 9 – Love is . . . the Deceiver

Shadda accepts that he asked Love to escort him as he followed Agnes' van round the run after it had been attacked and smashed to ruin. Still, he insists that he only asked Love in particular because he was handy, living locally, could drive and had wheels. He swears that he never asked Love to do anything illegal but simply follow the van to give the impression that there was a team on hand to sort out any would-be assailants thus deterring further attacks.

The van was an evening job – this left Love free to roam with his own crew and cronies, scouting out scrap and any other wee earners which might come their way through the course of day. The evening patrol job was supposed to be under the pals act but both he and Shadda had their own wee fiddle. They would overcharge Agnes for the petrol money thus allowing Shadda to slink off to the pub and, at the same time, leaving Love with sufficient petrol for his scouting parties the following day. This accounts for those parts of the charges based on following the Mitchells, taking account of their movements and so forth. (As I've said, the run is a circle and everybody on it follows everybody else.) If Love took that further it was in his own time and not part of his agreement with Shadda.

Resentful at having been pulled by the police for casing the Mitchells, it appears that Love may have decided to give them something real to complain about. It is hard for me to believe that he never mentioned this to Shadda but Shadda insists that if he did then he must have been too drunk to remember. At any rate, there is no way that he, Shadda, would've told me because I would've taken any plan to shoot up the Mitchells' van with a sawn off shotgun as the ultimate in drunken folly and booted his arse for his stupidity. It was the one sure way of bringing the police down on top of you and of closing Agnes down permanently. They would have done better to have shot their own fuckin van and left the Mitchells to cope with the ensuing enquiry. So, I don't believe the Shadda fullah is that daft but I'm never sure of him while he is on a bender.

In the event then, shots were fired and the van was blasted with pellets. Various witnesses described an old Volvo with an odd registration, FUJI 5 or something, with two men inside, both masked. They'd pulled up alongside the Marchetti van and the passenger had got out. He had walked round to the front of the van, looking in the windows of the cabin area before raising a shotgun and firing two shots, shattering the windscreen before getting back into the Volvo and driving off. At least five people witnessed this, including Love's sister, Agnes. Every single witness talks about two men in the car. Strange then that later the police and prosecution would take Love's story that there were three, over and above the evidence of all others. John Campbell (Cammy) had just been fitted in again as sitting in the back seat, along for the ride.

Now, Love says, 'When that van got done, aye it was me. Me an another geezer ah'm no gonny name. The guy was driving, we drove up an ah drew out a double barrel sawn aff shotgun an fired it at the ice cream van. Ah got back intae the car an we drove away but as I've said before, it was the wrang van. It was meant to be another Marchetti van. It was the wrang wan. It was

meant to be Jimmy Mitchell's van that was fired at. Ah
made a mistake. Ah thought it was Jimmy Mitchell's van.
Ah mean, nobody was suppose to get hurt anyway, so like
it was meant to be Jimmy Mitchell's van but it turned out
to be Fat Boy Doyle's an that's how everybody jumped
on the bandwagon as if it was Fat Boy that was the bad
yin . . .'

Agnes Love or Carlton's statement to the police at the
time was suppressed and never disclosed to the defence
at the trial. This was her version of events:

> It was my brother Billy. He came into my house
> with a shotgun, a sawn off shotgun about that size.
> He said he was going to shoot up Jimmy Mitchell's
> van to give him a fright. I seen him do it from my
> window. He got out of the car with a balaclava or
> something over his head but I could see it was him
> all right. He fired two shots at the van's front windae
> and got back in the car and drove away but it was
> the wrong van. I saw Andy Doyle and a wee lassie
> jump out the side windae and run away. It was the
> wrong van.

It is significant that even Love forgot that Cammy had
been fitted in to the back seat to make him an accused
and to discredit his evidence as a witness in refutal
of Love.

Love and Cammy had lain in together in C Hall untried
along with Ronny Carlton for the scrap yard robbery.
Refused bail on the grounds of his record of perverting
the course of justice and as a menace to society, Love
was in deep shit when the story of the shotgun attack
hit the headlines after the Doyle family home went up
in flames. The Press were saying that it was part of an
ice cream war – gangsters moving in on the trade in
the past two years, orchestrated by relatives of rivals

to Marchetti in Garthamlock. That this attack was part of a concerted conspiracy against the Doyle family and if they could find the people who were responsible for the shooting they would be a big step closer to finding those responsible for the arson attack. Expecting up to ten years for the robbery, in the circumstances, he could expect another ten years on top.

In the event, Love struck a deal with the police and his prosecutor which granted him immunity from prosecution on all charges and release on bail on the armed robbery charge. His plan had been simply to agree with the terms of the deal offered just to get out of jail and then to abscond, which he did, only to be recaptured in the commission of further crimes and imprisoned again. Now he could be charged with two attempted murders by firing the gun at the van, conspiracy to rob Mitchell, armed robbery of the scrap yard, perjury as well as attempting to pervert the course of justice by making false statements and absconding, if he didn't stick to the script. Naturally, as per the nature of the beast, he stuck to the script blaming everybody else for everything and was granted total immunity from prosecution by the Crown rather than the fifteen to twenty years imprisonment which he could otherwise have expected. The escape plan was not done for yet it seemed. With a little collusion with the police and the Crown he could crack it and beat the rap.

> *Charge 9.* On 29th February, 1984 in Balvenie Street, Glasgow, you THOMAS GAVIN LAFFERTY, THOMAS CAMPBELL, THOMAS CLARK GRAY, and JOHN CAMPBELL did, while acting along with said William McDonald Love, with faces masked, assault Andrew Doyle, now deceased, and Anne Weir Wilson, aged fifteen years, care of Baird Street

Police Office aforesaid, who were both then trading from said Marchetti ice cream van, registered
number VGD 26W, and discharge two shots from
a shotgun through the windscreen of said ice cream
van to the danger of their lives, and did attempt to
murder them.

Love's evidence was to the effect that Shadda had
approached him in the street while he was walking his
dog and had asked him to do a message for TC. Love
had agreed and Shadda given him £30 and said that TC
would square him up later but never had. Shadda had then
taken him to his house where he'd put a jacket, gloves and
masks into a plastic bag before they'd gone up to the pub
to get Tamby. Tamby had got into the Volvo and they'd
gone to some dump to test fire the shotgun. They'd then
driven round to the scheme stopping the car and Cammy
had jumped into the back seat before they drove round
till they spotted the van. This time, Love said he was
driving and Tamby had jumped out and fired two shots
at Andrew Doyle's van. They then made their getaway.
When asked why John Campbell was there, Love had said
that he was there to take over the driving in the event that
there was a police chase – which is quite odd. The idea
of stopping to swap drivers in middle of a police chase
sounds more like the antics of the Keystone Cops rather
than of desperate and hardened criminals. It also makes
one wonder what then was Love doing there?

He also went on to say many other things, which I will
get back to later, but for now let's stick with Charge 9. He
said that sometime after the shooting, either days or weeks
he couldn't say, he had run into TC in the street who had
thanked him for 'the message'. When asked what he thought
was meant by that, he said he thought it referred to him
being the driver of the car that was used in the shooting.

This is the evidence which convicted all the accused on this charge. The trial judge had said that without Love's evidence on this there wasn't sufficiency of evidence in law to convict. 'It is therefore crucial that you believe him. The Crown case [in all these charges] stands or falls upon his evidence.'

In corroboration, in my case, there was the police verbal alleged when I was arrested, 'I only wanted the van windaes shot up,' and a single fingerprint found on the inside of the front passenger window of the car. This was not sufficient evidence in itself but was sufficient in corroboration of Love to allow it to go to a jury.

The Crown alleged that the fingerprint in the car was not only proof that I was the owner of the car but proof that I'd loaned it to the perpetrators of the act for that purpose. That I hadn't tried to reclaim the car after it was impounded for the police was evidence of guilt. The fact of the matter is that I had never seen the car before in my life. If I was the owner, where was the log book and who was the car registered under? Why weren't my neighbours or anyone ever cited to say if they'd seen me with this car? Surely if it had been my car it was likely that more than one fingerprint of mine would have been found on it? Why did the Crown only make this allegation in argument to the jury and not in evidence where I would have been able to bring other evidence to refute it? Why would I even think of trying to claim a car which I didn't know anything about from the police compound? Christ! I'm sure every car thief in the country would be happy to hear that a fingerprint on a car is, according to the Crown in my case, now proof of ownership of that car. Walking down the road, dum de dum, that's mine, that's mine, that's . . .

I agree that Love did give me and the wean Stephen a lift home that time from Duke Street, yet I do not believe that it was in that car. Still, I could be wrong and if I am it would explain and account for that print. If I'm not wrong and it wasn't that car then the only alternative is that the print was planted by the police. Yet what real difference does it make? It was never alleged that I was there at the scene of the crime at the time the crime was committed.

We were all fitted up and fitted into the frame, nobody more than any other. Shadda got three years, Cammy got three years and I got ten but the big Tamby fullah was planted right in the shite as the gunman and was given fourteen years. 'But why me?' he keeps saying. 'But I don't understand, why me?' We've all asked ourselves the same question at least a hundred times a day and there appears to be no fathoming and no reckoning as to why any particular individual was selected for which particular role.

The corroboration of Love in Tamby the Bear's case was, like in my case, police verbal and fingerprints. Some slight variations however make it worth the telling. On being taken into custody at Baird Street Police Station Tamby is supposed to have asked a Detective Whiley, 'What the fuck is this all about?' Which was odd for someone who was supposed already to have been cautioned and charged and should've known what it was all about from the moment the police had entered his house. Nevertheless, this was the verbal. He was apparently then told that he was under arrest for assault and responded to that allegedly saying, 'So it's no the fire? I don't give a fuck, the fire's no down to me. The shooting aye but no the fire.' This was considered as a verbal confession at the time. No matter how much or how often you strenuously deny it you are stuck with it and it will condemn you as corroborative evidence in court. Nowadays such utterances on interview are required to be recorded on tape to prevent the standard practice of false verbals but in those days it was, well, it was standard practice.

Where the Paw Print Clings

Tamby the Bear was one of the original five Thomases arrested with Agnes on 12th May, 1984. Arrested with him from the house and later to star in court as evidence was a newspaper with the headline, 'TERRIBLE TOLL OF THE FIRE RAISERS', displaying pictures of the six members of the Doyle family with the sad story of how they'd died. The prosecution were to cite this as evidence indicating an unhealthy interest in the crime on Tamby's part – that was just utter garbage. The newspaper boasted over one million readers and I'm sure their interests were not unhealthy but stemmed from genuine concern. It was just an excuse to bring a well-written newspaper article as official evidence to help influence a jury's decision. 'Ladies and gentlemen of the jury,' the judges say, 'put aside what you read in the Press and concentrate on the evidence and on the evidence alone.' And when the Press is the evidence? Aye, right! Just put the paper doon a minute, wull ye?

The second item arrested from his house was really weird – a gas meter. So what the blue blazes had a gas meter to do with anything? Maybe he used it as a hookah to toot his dope or something eh? It was never produced in court. His house had just been renovated and this gas meter had been left there by the workmen. So what's so sinister about that? The truth is that there was nothing sinister about the meter and the entire episode of arresting it was just a farce, a ploy. Their real interest was in the plastic carrier bag into which the meter was placed for the bammy Bear to carry it out to the police car. Silly Buggers Act 19-canteen. If it had been me told to carry the bag out into the polis motor as evidence I'd have told them to carry the fuckin thing themselves. I'd have been right. For it was that bag which would later show up as evidence in court, said to have been found in the car used in the shooting and with the Bear's paw prints all over it. How do you defend yourself against that? Are the polis all liars and the fingerprint people all at it? Try the truth as a defence in that case. I'll see you in the exercise yard and discuss appeals procedure.

So it transpired that, having been arrested on 12th May, a Saturday, and after a long weekend of interrogation, we were to appear at the Sheriff Court on Monday 14th May on petition warrant and for routine fingerprinting. Oddly enough, but not surprisingly, the Bear was the only one that day who was palm printed. Even less of a surprise then, at least to me, that ten finger prints and two palm prints would show up in court clinging to a plastic bag said to have been found in the car used in the shooting. 'How the fuck did that get there,' says the Bear. 'Who's been eating my porridge,' says the fairytale. But no point in trying to tell ye, 'It was Goldilox.' Ye just don't listen.

The shooting had occurred on 29th February that fateful leap year and the car used had been taken into custody that day in the possession of Reynolds & Co. Although it was then thoroughly searched on a number of occasions by ballistics and forensic experts – like the jacket (next chapter) in Shadda's case – no bag had been found. In fact, according to the evidence of the dates, the bag was not found until the car was dusted for prints on 14th March, some two weeks later. Aye, right! How many people have been in and searched the car from the time of the shooting to the printing? Maybe it was an early Fair Fortnight. Who knows.

The two weeks delay in the dusting of the car for prints and the finding of the bag, couldn't be explained until the print expert was asked to examine the evidence of the Bear's prints on the bag under magnification. It should be explained that there were tiny little number references attached to each print on the bag. Like 01432ZJ4 corresponding with the date and time of the matching print. It was to this then that the print expert's attention was drawn. He turned scarlet, stuttering, obviously embarrassed and alarmed. What on earth could he have seen to cause such a reaction? He was asked.

'This evidence has been tampered with.'

'What? In what way?'

'It has been superimposed.'

'Do you understand the very serious implications of what you are saying?' interrupted the trial judge.

'Yes I understand that the implications are very serious indeed,' answered the witness.

But we never did get to discover the exact details of what those implications entailed, the judge dismissing the witness to consider his legal position. But what we did learn was that the reference numbers corresponding to the dates themselves had been changed. Superimposed, blue ink on black, and that the witness who'd made those references and had noted the dates denied any responsibility or knowledge of making those changes to his work until he'd seen it under magnification.

Dearie me! After all those years of malpractice, either they still could not get the colour of the ink right or they were so complacent and confident that they didn't

think anybody would bother to double check the photo-
copy with the original. But, Donald Findlay QC did and
he wasn't even defending the Bear. He was defending
Joe Steele.

Isn't life strange?

Superimposition in fingerprinting simply means that,
for example, a print can be lifted from one object and
placed upon another object. Anyone can do it with the
application of Sellotape. Also, if you alter the hand-
written letter Y, for example, to the letter R it could be
said that you have superimposed the letter R onto the Y.
It appears that it may have been something of this nature
that occurred in this case. Perhaps it explained why the
dusting of the car was not noted until two weeks later
– 14th March, when it was alleged that the bag had
shown up with the Bear's 14th May paw prints all over
it, for that's when he carried the bag. It appears from
the evidence in court, that corresponding numbers to the
dates on the bag, when carried by the Bear for the police
for dusting on 14th May were altered by superimposing
the date of the dusting of the car on 14 March. Simply
backdating the bag by the altering of the letter Y in 14th
May to the letter R in 14th March and, hey presto, they
could claim that 14th March was the date of the finding
and dusting of the bag in the car used in the shooting
of 29th Feb. And the numbers readjusted in blue. See, it
was Goldilox all along. I told you but ye just wouldn't
listen, Bear. (Goldilox was the nickname given to a certain
detective constable.)

> Where the paw print clings
> in the freezin snaw
> does the paw print cling at a in law?
> Does the paw print cling at a?

Shadda

The corroboration against Shadda was . . . oh aye! Besides gloves and masks, Love also said that Shadda had placed a jacket in the bag. Dougie Cardle, Irene Mitchell's boyfriend and van driver, tried to put the mix in for the wee man by saying that the jacket found in the car was definitely Shadda's, 'He wears it all the time. He's never got it off.' However, this caused some hilarity in court when Shadda was asked to try it on for size. It was down to his knees, the shoulders to his elbows and his hands barely reached halfway down the sleeves, it could have wrapped around him twice. Well so much for that fit.

The Crown prosecution argued that this was, nevertheless, corroboration of the witness Love. He'd said that Lafferty had put items in a bag and sure enough a bag was found in the car. He'd said that one of the items in the bag had been a jacket and, sure enough a jacket had been found in the car. This should, they argued, be sufficient to corroborate Love that Lafferty was involved otherwise how could Love have known what the police had found in the car? In fact, the policeman who had found the jacket in the car some months later was not too pleased about being used as the innocent agent in the planting of the jacket.

His evidence went as follows:

'I was sitting at my desk and the boss told me to go down and search the car.'

'This would be at Easterhouse Police Station and the car FIJI 5 is that correct?'

'That's correct yes.'

'And did you see anything unusual in that request?'

'I thought it was odd, yes.'

'Why was that?'

'Because I had no part in the Doyle fire enquiry and it wasn't my job.'

'And were you aware that this car had been in custody for some time?'

'I was and I thought that too was odd.'

'And did you search the car?'

'I did, yes.'

'What then if anything did you find there?'

'I found that jacket on the back seat just laying there.'

'Were you aware that this car had already been searched in the past?'

'I was yes.'

'And that no jacket had previously been found?'

'I was.'

'What then was your impression at that time?'

'I thought the whole situation was very odd indeed.'

'Indeed, what then did you do, if anything?'

'I was told to search the jacket and I did so.'

'And what, if anything, did you find there?'

'Nothing.'

'Nothing?'

'Nothing.'

'Then what happened?'

'The boss told me to search the top pocket again and I did that.'

'And . . .'

'I found some photographs there.'

'And did you complete your search of the car?'

'No, that was all that was required of me.'
'And didn't you find that odd?'
'Very odd, I felt very unsettled by the whole thing. I felt I'd been used.'
'And if I was to tell you that this car had previously been searched no less than four times by forensic scientists and that no jacket had been found, what would you say to that?'
'I would say that I'd been put right in it.'

We never did get to see nor hear any further evidence on those photographs, though we were informed that they were intended to link Shadda to the jacket, the jacket to the car and the car to the shooting on 29th Feb 1984. But the result of this evidence was that the prosecution didn't pursue that line of evidence as it was exposed as an obvious plant.

Charge 13

Charge 13. On or about 5th April, 1984, the exact date being to the Prosecutor unknown, in the common close at 29 Bankend Street, Glasgow, you THOMAS CAMPBELL, THOMAS CLARK GRAY, JOSEPH STEELE and GARY LANE MOORE did assault said Andrew Doyle, now deceased, and did repeatedly punch and kick him about the head and body to his injury.

The evidence on this charge came from a witness, a Mrs Mills.

'I suffer from asthma and so I was out on the veranda getting some fresh air. I seen the boys who assaulted Andy Doyle, there were four of them.'
'And could you recognise any of them?'
'Aye, they were local boys. I've seen them about. He was fighting with them before that.'
'And can you identify any of the accused as the assailants?'
'Naw, they were only about fifteen to seventeen year old. I knew them.'
'And you saw four assailants is that correct?'
'Aye, but only one was fighting with him.'
'Could you see into the close below you?'
'Below me? Naw!'
'So there may have been others there whom you did not see, is that correct?'

'Naw, I don't think so.'
'But it is possible?'
'Ah don't think so. Ah was there for a wee while.'
'But you cannot say that there wasn't, is that correct?'
'Ah don't suppose ah can but ah don't think so.'
'But you could not see into the close and it is possible
that there may have been others whom you did not
see, is that correct?'
'Ah I suppose so.'

Mrs Mills under cross examination:

'You saw four boys around the age of fifteen to
seventeen years of age is that correct?'
'Aye.'
'Are any of the accused around that age?'
'Naw.'
'Have you ever identified any of the accused?'
'Naw.'
'And do you do so now?'
'Naw.'
'You were asked if there may have been others below
and you agreed that was possible is that correct?'
(Witness nods.)
'This is in reference to a level below you is that
correct?'
'Aye under the veranda.'
'That there may have been four other men there
whom you did not see?'
'Aye but I don't think so ah was there a wee while.'
'There could have been six or seven whom you did
not see, is that correct?'
'Aye, but ah don't think so.'
'In fact, Mrs Mills, put in those terms, there may
well have been an entire army which you did not
see is that correct?'

'I suppose so but I doubt it.'

'But it is as possible as any further four, is it not?'

'Putting it that way, aye, I suppose so.'

'Thank you, Mrs Mills.'

Once again, it makes you wonder what the Crown were doing by placing us on this charge. There seems to be no evidence to justify it other than to establish that Andrew Doyle was assaulted. There were four boys present at the time and four accused charged with it. If the jury were supposed to draw some adverse inference from that then the evidence of Mrs Mills put a stop to it. As a Crown eyewitness for the prosecution, she couldn't have been a better defence witness. Still, it was established that Andrew Doyle was assaulted and that the four people charged with the murder were the same four charged with this assault – though acquitted. Not Guilty.

The oddest thing that comes out of this from my perspective is that I was charged with the Doyle fire murders. Part of the evidence on that charge was that the police say that they'd found a map with a ring round the words 'Bankend Street'. This is no doubt intended to imply that I was either trying to find Bankend Street myself or that I was showing some other accused where it was for the purpose of committing an arson attack there. Yet, the fire was on 16th April. This assault of which all the accused of the fire were also accused of committing was on 5th April. If they'd been guilty of the assault as accused by the Crown case, then why would they or I have needed a map to find the address on the murder charge? According to the Crown case, we had already been there to assault Andrew Doyle on the 5th. In fact, I could see Bankend Street from the top flat of my own close at home. We were all locals to the area and none of us would ever have needed nor have thought of a map.

Charge 15 – Love

Charge 15 – so easy to say, but it entails the murders of the Doyle family and is obviously what all these charges on indictment were really all about. For although each are separate charges with separate evidence distinct from one another and no inference may legitimately be drawn from one upon another, nevertheless, the law is based purely upon good reason and does not account for emotive reaction, nor can it. In truth then, this entire indictment is based upon trumped up charges designed to inspire emotive reaction and which give some appearance of credence to it in the light and background portrayed in the story told by those charges. For at the end of the weary day, regardless of the fact that we were acquitted of those charges, the Crown prosecution's aim and their crowning achievement was to show that these crimes did in fact occur and, that they could be alleged against us on indictment alongside this single, but horrendous Charge 15 – the murder of an entire innocent family as they slept peacefully in their beds. This indictment makes the point, simply, that we are accusable of such dastardly deeds. That in itself goes a long way by way of evidence in defining the characters thus accused. Simply to be accused of such, is in itself, a devastating slur, the implications and repercussions of which there is no escape from.

Like being accused of sixteen charges of child abduction and sexual assault. If the accused were to meet a juror in the foyer and enjoy a friendly chat, that juror might be impressed by the likable chap and, even later, seeing him in the dock and not the jury box, might give him a smile, a wave or a nod. Then once the charges are read out, outlining such horrendous charges against children, does the juror's view and attitude towards the accused change? Of course it does. And when evidence is brought that he was seen leading a little girl away from the swing park by the hand, that he showed yet another how to ride a bike, that he films children at play and is in the habit of handing out sweets – it doesn't matter that there may be innocent explanations to this evidence – the nature of the charge and the fact that he is accusable in themselves inspire emotive reactions and the worst will always be suspected. He may be a film documentary producer and those children seen with him may have been his own, unbeknown to the witnesses. Yet before the defence and his side of the story are even heard, in the eyes of the jury he is a beast and deserves no consideration whatsoever for the very accusation of such deeds. What then of the horrific murders of an entire innocent family as they slept in their beds dreaming of better days ahead? And of the sixteen brutal crimes around it?

Charge 15. On 16th April, 1984 at the house at 29 Bankend Street, Glasgow, occupied by James Bernard Doyle you THOMAS CAMPBELL, THOMAS CLARK GRAY, JOSEPH STEELE and GARY LANE MOORE did, while acting along with said Joseph Granger, wilfully set fire to a cupboard door and the entrance door of said house occupied by said James Bernard Doyle and the fire took effect thereon and this you did wilfully and with criminal disregard for the safety of the occupants of said house and adjacent houses whereby Christine Doyle or Halleron, Anthony Doyle, aged fourteen years, Mark Halleron,

aged eighteen months, James Doyle junior, said
Andrew Doyle, said James Bernard Doyle, Daniel
Doyle, Stephen Bernard Doyle and Lillian Peacock
Doyle, sustained severe injuries as result of said fire
and in consequence thereof said Christine Doyle
or Halleron and said Anthony Doyle died as a
result of their injuries on 16th April, 1984 and
said Mark Halleron died at the Royal Hospital
for Sick Children, Glasgow, on 16th April, 1984,
and James Doyle junior died at the Royal Infirmary,
Glasgow, on 17th April, 1984, said Andrew Doyle
died at said Royal Infirmary on 20th April, 1984,
and said James Bernard Doyle died at said Royal
Infirmary on 24th April, 1984, and you did murder
said Christine Doyle or Halleron, Anthony Doyle,
Mark Halleron, James Doyle Junior, Andrew Doyle,
and James Bernard Doyle.

> One night as I was sleeping
> Upon my feather bed
> An angel came from heaven
> And told me mom was dead
>
> I woke up in the morning
> To see if this was true
> Yes mom had gone to heaven
> Above the sky so blue
>
> So children obey your parents
> And do as you are told
> For when you lose your mother
> You lose a heart of gold
>
> (Old children's song)

So far as Billy Love was concerned, there remained but
one small hitch before his plan B for escape could proceed smoothly. The problem was that his armed robbery

charge had two further co-accused – John Cammy and Ronny Carlton – and, for that reason, the trial had to proceed on schedule. Luckily, or perhaps more by contrivance, the Procurator Fiscal involved in that case also happened to be involved in the Doyle family murder trial and had judicially examined Love on both accounts. First, as an accused in the robbery and, secondly, as a witness in the Doyle fire case.

As the robbery trial proceeded, the two co-accused, Ronny and Cammy, were acquitted leaving only Love still to answer to a string of serious crimes including the armed robbery and an attempt to defeat the ends of justice. There was also the obvious evidence of the truckload of alternators to account for. Fortunately for Love though, the procurator fiscal had 'forgotten' to have the court production labels certified by signature as proof of their origin. Thus, in one foul stroke, rendering all material evidence in his case as inadmissible and incompetent in law. On that technicality, no material evidence meant that there was insufficient evidence in law and Love was acquitted. Lucky in Love.

Love now swears on affidavit:

> I was seen again by the police and this time there were two of them. One was called Norman Walker and the other we'll call Crippler. On that occasion there was no prison officer present. These two police came to see me the very next day.
>
> They were asking me questions about what has been called the ice cream war and I was denying any knowledge. They started getting more friendly with me and then saying how various things were supposed to have happened and going into detail about them. They then offered me bail.
>
> Almost everything that was mentioned in court

was discussed at that meeting. After that, the other meetings were to clarify what the Crown prosecution had agreed to. Various things, but they did offer to relocate me and my family and to give us money and make sure I was all right and did not want for anything. I did not provide them with a statement at that stage. I did not admit to any involvement in any shooting at that stage.

It was from the first meeting with Walker and the other that they were making hints and actually saying to me that there was a meeting in the Netherfield and they talked about a discussion that was suppose to have taken place. They actually said to me that they had heard this from somebody else and they wanted me to go along and say that. It was Norrie Walker who was doing all the talking and the other man was just nodding and saying, 'Aye, that's right.'

They came back a few days later and that's when they put their cards on the table and said that I would not be charged with anything and that I was just to do what they wanted me to do and they would look after me. They weren't hiding anything. They just came straight out and told me what they wanted me to do and they would look after me. Then, I was only able to give them information about the shooting of the van but the discussion went on to other things about the fire and they were wanting me to say that those things happened although I knew nothing about anything beyond what they were telling me.

The central and essential condition of the deal struck with the police and the prosecution was that he had to say that he had overheard TC, Steele, Granger and Gray in conversation discussing setting fire to the Doyle family household.

'But it isn't true, none of it is true. There never was any conversation in any pub nor anywhere else to discuss setting fire to anything. That was all just something that was put into my head for me to go along and say that,' Love now admits.

At the trial however he stuck to his part of the bargain and to his given court script. That TC, Tamby, Joe Steele, Granger and Dinky Moore were all sitting round a table in the pub: 'They were talking about setting fire to Fat Boy's door to give him a fright.' This evidence, according to the judge's directions in law at the end of the trial was fundamental and, 'crucial to the Crown case. There is not sufficiency of evidence to entitle you to convict without it.'

Obviously, as Love was in prison at the time of the fire, then this alleged conversation would have to have taken place before his arrest on that account. Under examination in the witness box he at first remained vague and unspecific, saying only that it was a weekend or towards the end of the week, a Friday or Saturday. He could only repeatedly insist that it was a weekend and that he didn't pay any attention to the dates. Finally, under cross-examination he was pinned down.

'You paid no attention to the dates you say?'
'No sir.'
'That surprises me. Tell me, what date were you arrested?'
'25th March, sir.'
'The day after?'
'Two days after, sir.'
'We are talking about the 23rd and 24th March then are we not?'
'Yes.'

'You were arrested on 25th March. Was that a Monday?'

'Yes, sir.'

'Is that right?'

'No, sir, it was a Sunday.'

'We are talking about Friday 23rd March then are we not?'

'Yes, sir.'

'And you still insist that you heard the conversation on that date?'

'Yes sir.'

We had no clue of it at the time but realise now that the prosecution must have been appalled by this specification of date. The Advocate Depute was back on his feet like a shot at the first opportunity, nagging away at him, trying to get him to revert back to being vague and non-specific. Yet no one but the prosecution were aware of why this specific date was so important to them. It was simply that, having previously prosecuted Love on the armed robbery charge, they were the only ones present in the court who were aware that Love had just contradicted the terms of his alibi in that case. Nor were they about to broadcast the fact that their principal and only witness had just proven his own perjury by this specification of date of the alleged overheard conversation. For he could not have been in two places at the same time as he had now stated in two separate trials. Thus, instead of trying to help the witness be specific in his evidence, as is their duty to do, here then we had a situation where the prosecution were intent on having their witness revert back to being vague and unspecific. Too late, the cat was out of the bag, so to speak, but no one had seen it nor were aware of the significance due to the fact that the terms of Love's alibi were never disclosed to the defence. The Crown would continue to hold it a closely guarded secret for a long time to come.

This in fact accounts for one of the reasons why Cammy was again fitted in to the indictment. For as a co-accused at our trial and not as a witness to Love's perjury, he was effectively prevented, now in the interests of his own defence, from advertising the fact that he too was charged with an armed robbery together with Love. Thus, by the time the information got out on Love's alibi through Cammy, it was too late to corner him on cross-examination. Still, our information was only Cammy's hearsay and not direct evidence. The Crown would continue to refuse to disclose the exact terms of Love's formal plea of alibi for many a long year to come.

It was the Crown's position that as Love had mentioned that Granger had been present during this alleged conversation this had led to the police enquiry of Granger on that score. The police had testified at the trial that Love hadn't given this information until 2nd May.

DI Crippler:

'The first meeting Mr Walker and I had with Mr Love was on Friday 20th April.'
'Was that when he said that he might be able to give information about the fire but it would depend on his position about bail?'
'That is correct.'
'Then there was a second meeting?'
'Yes the second meeting was on 2nd May.'
'And you got the information about the fire?'
'That is correct.'
'What was his position on 20th April?'
'He indicated that he knew who was involved in the shooting incident and he had information that might

well help with enquires into the fire. He did not wish to give it unless he could be promised bail, that he would be given bail.'

'Did you see Love with Detective Superintendent Walker on 2nd May?'

'I did yes, sir.'

'Did he give you further information with regard to the fire?'

'He gave a full statement yes, sir.'

'Before he did so was he given any assurance about the matter of bail or anything like that?'

'He was told that he would need to give a statement before a sheriff, be precognosced before a sheriff, and once that had been done he would undoubtedly get bail. He also asked if he did this would any charges be dropped against him and we said that we couldn't do that but that it was most likely that if he gave a statement before a sheriff then anything he said involving himself would be very unlikely to be proceeded with.'

'You were able to tell Love that he would undoubtedly get bail?'

'I was under the impression that once he had been precognosced there would be a bail hearing for him and it would be likely that he would be given bail.'

'In that the Crown would not oppose that application is that right?'

'That's correct.'

'And did he, to that end, at that time you saw him in prison, that is on 2nd May, give you further information which would be the subject of precognition on oath?'

'He did sir. He said that if he could get bail he could give us information on the shooting and possibly the murder – we got back to him on 2nd May.'

'So he would require to get bail if he gave the information?'

'Yes.'

'So, he wanted something in return for the information?'

'Yes.'

'Did you tell him he would undoubtedly get bail?'

'Yes.'

'So, Mr Love was given to understand that there wasn't much doubt about it that he was going to get bail provided he gave information is that right?'

'I would accept that is what he took, yes.'

'So the thing Love had wanted from the outset was that he should be released from prison?'

'He wanted bail, yes.'

'And that's what he got?'

'Yes.'

DCS Norman Walker

'When Love was interviewed . . . I think on 20th April and on 2nd May?'

'The 2nd May that's correct, sir, he said he did not want to give me too much because he wanted bail.'

'When you went back to see him on 2nd May did you get fuller information?'

'I did, sir, yes.'

'And what, if anything, was said to him on the subject of bail?'

'I said, told him, I said, well I can't see you being charged if you give a statement before a sheriff. I think at the time I told him he would get bail provided he was prepared to go before a sheriff and get us this statement.'

DCS Walker cross-examined by Donald Findlay QC:

'That last observation, Mr Walker, that you couldn't see Mr Love being charged if he gave evidence before a sheriff, this would give, might reasonably give Mr Love the impression that he was getting immunity from involvement.'

'Yes.'

'And there would be no further proceedings?'

'Yes.'

'So he was getting two things, bail and immunity from prosecution?'

'Well that was my opinion of it yes.'

Walker cross-examined by Donald MacAulay QC:

'Did you take him before a sheriff?'

'That was on 8th May.'

'What did he say?'

'I asked him what he told me to tell him about the fire – what he could tell me . . .'

'His account in this court was that the conversation took place about mid-March and certain people started talking about setting the Fat Boy's door on fire to give him a fright . . .'

'I didn't get that! That must have come out in precognition. I didn't hear that.'

'Did you write down the questions?'

'I can't remember some of the questions. I didn't have to write them down – the answers give you the key to the questions.'

'Would it be fair to say that he gave some information to attract your interest and then set out what he wanted in return before giving any more?'

'Yes, but he wasn't going to give any information at all unless he was not in Barlinnie when these people were arrested.'

'He wanted out? He wasn't going to give any information?'
'Yes he wanted this.'
'Before he gave any information? Is that right?'
'Yes!'

If Love hadn't given the information about the fire, according to the police evidence in court, until 2nd May and, as Walker said, that the answers give you the key to the questions – odd then that, according to the Crown case, that Love's information on the conversation given on 2nd May would then lead them to the examination of Granger on that topic. For later a statement of Granger's, not disclosed at the trial and dated 23rd April, some nine days before, Love is alleged, at best, to have first mentioned the conversation according to Crippler (though Walker said not until precognition on 8th May). Yet Granger's statement of 23rd April is clearly denying that any such conversation had ever taken place. Before Love is alleged to have first said it, which led the police to question Granger, according to Crippler on 2nd May, and according to Walker on 8th May – Granger states on 23 April that yes, he does know TC. His wife's mother is a friend of his mother and he has sometimes seen him in the Netherfield with her. Yes, he does know Tamby, another older guy with a beard who sometimes plays dominoes there. Yes, he thinks he knows a guy called Joe Steele whom he may have met in the Barge Bar in Garthamlock. Yes, he does know a guy called Gary Moore from the YO in Glenochil. Yes, he (Granger) does sometimes drink in the Netherfield Bar which is now called Scarpers. He has read about the fire in the papers and has been into the bar a few times in the past months but no, he has never heard it mentioned. The statement goes on in reply to questions about TC for some time before at page 8 he states, 'I'll tell yous again, I know nothing about the fire and have never been in (their) company when it was discussed. I didn't know the Doyle family and didn't know one of them was called Fat Boy.'

Odd then that Granger is saying No to Love's evidence in court in a statement dated before Love is alleged to have first said it in his statement of 2nd May. This statement of Granger's shows that all the information which Love would have required was being transmitted to Granger in the questions before Love is alleged to have first said it. It was Walker who said that 'the answers give you the key to the questions'. This statement, if disclosed at the trial, would have been a bombshell, blowing Love and the police version right out of orbit by showing that the alleged conversation in that named bar by those named accused was being put to other witnesses by the police before the witness Love is alleged to have first given them the information. We, the accused, had already known that the police had been asking everyone with regard to overheard conversations linked to deals on immunity but we had never expected that evidence would emerge in proof of it. Just a pity that it didn't emerge until after the trial, due to the Crown prosecution's denial of its existence until Granger's lawyer, John Carroll, took legal action forcing the Crown to hand over all relevant documents concerning Granger. If the prosecution were not aware of Love's perjury, then why would they think to keep such a statement secret and lie about its existence? Why would they repeatedly refuse to hand over the terms of Love's formal plea of alibi? These and many other questions have never been answered as result of the massive cover-up that then ensued and which is still in effect to this day. Why did DCS Norrie Walker commit suicide?

Charge 15 – Joe Granger

Joe Granger was alleged to have made yet another statement a month after this first. This one on 23rd May, 1984 and which later, in court, he denied having made. In this latter version, the day after I was charged with murder, the police have Granger as saying that a conversation took place at the end of the month of March, around 27th or 29th. These were not the same police involved with Love and, though they were aware of Love's statement on that matter, weren't aware of Love's personal circumstances. They could not know that Love was in prison for the robbery from the 25th and couldn't have been in any pub to have overheard any conversation about anything. Nor could they have known that I had lain drunk in the police cells from Friday 16th till release on Monday 19th. Love was well and truly pinned down to the Friday night of 23rd March and this did not sit well with his alibi.

'Ha well! Ah can tell ye right now,' Love grins, beaming with pride. 'Ah must have had a lot o hours in my day eh! Like ah'm suppose to be in a pub in Duke Street with Tommy Campbell an all that. Ah'm suppose to be doin' a robbery doon by the new sheriff court way with the lads an ah'm suppose to be at hame with my alibi an all at the same time eh! Aye, well let me tell ye this ... through all that time o the van gettin' its windaes shot an all that carry-on, Tommy Campbell never spoke two words t'me, no even wance.

In all that time the man never even spoke wan word t'me . . .'

At the trial Joe Granger told the truth in the witness box and, although it was a nightmare for all concerned, nevertheless, it was good to see him somewhere back on the road to being his usual self: 'Ah know fuck all about that fire an ah'm no gonny stan here an say that ah do.'

'But you said you did in your statement didn't you?'

'Ah never said that, they did.' Granger pointed out.

'Are you implying that police officers . . . ?'

'Aye the polis, Brewis an Simpleton, they said it an made me sign but ah know fuck all about it, it's no true.'

He was arrested and charged with perjury, where downstairs in the cells, Love looked on with trepidation at the lesson of what would happen to those who don't stick to the script. Lynne Chalmers backed Joe Granger's evidence to the hilt, 'They wrote the statements for Joe to sign and eventually he signed them. They wrote the statement for me to sign and I wouldn't sign it,' she said. 'You signed the statement,' demanded the Advocate Depute.

'Naw, ah wouldn't sign it because it wasn't true. Joe was with me and we never left the house. Anything else is a lie.' Many years later she did admit that she signed a second statement but still swears that she didn't say and has never said anything other than what she said in court.

Joe Granger was found Guilty of signing a false statement to the police dated 23rd May with regard to the Doyle family fire murders but Not Guilty of lying in court in that respect when he said that the statement wasn't true. He was acquitted of signing a false statement regarding the Marchetti depot fire when the jury accepted that he'd only done so under extreme pressure, assault, and blackmail. He was acquitted of lying in court by his denial that the contents of the statement were true. The evidence at our trial supports this verdict that the fire at Marchetti's was an inside job.

He appealed against conviction on a number of points of law and of fact, one of which was 'unreasonable verdict and misdirection in law' – that any reasonable jury, properly directed, could not find him Not Guilty on one charge due to duress whilst not carrying that duress on as likewise applicable in the second instance. It does seem ambiguous and appears that the jury have not taken full or sufficient account of the psychological effect of the ill-treatment which they accept that he had received in the first instance, with regard to the second signing. It should have nullified his culpability on all counts.

He also appealed against conviction and the five-year sentence on the very technically complex legal point that the second alleged statement, that of 23rd May, 1984, upon which he was convicted was not legally a statement at all but was, in accordance to law, a precognition and that, according to law, a person cannot be caused to suffer for changing, altering, or scrapping a precognition for they cannot be held to it in a court of law. The distinctions between statements and precognitions are technical and legalistic. In effect, a precognition is described as an outline of what someone who is already of designated witness status is likely to say. Usually taken from someone with prior knowledge of the case and who could possibly, either intentionally or unwittingly, transmit that knowledge to the witness in their questions or incorporate it into their interpretation of what they thought the witness may have meant. One of the main milestones, therefore, in defining a precognition is as to whether at the time it was taken the accused was then charged with the crime and the officer noting it was aware of this. For that entails sufficient knowledge to warrant caution against possible contamination of that which is then stated. Granger's was dated 23rd May, 1984 upon a witness statement form and I had been charged with the murder of the Doyle family on 22nd May, 1984, ten days after my arrest on the original petition warrant. Therefore, his was, as legally defined, a precognition not a statement and as such did not hold the same power as a police statement. It is, in fact, inadmissible in law. Granger then was serving five years for retracting the terms of a precognition. Something which was not against the law.

Of course, the average man is not aware of the finer intricacies of the law in this field which have evolved over hundreds of years of trial and error and by precedent. They exist for the safeguard of the citizen and to ensure that fairness is built into the system of justice. We ignore and disregard them at our peril, for that is the route to the fruit of the poison tree and the man's fall from grace.

Though Joe Granger's points were made and typed out by his solicitor, John Carroll, for Granger's appeal, legal aid for counsel was refused as a direct result of the cut-backs from Thatcherite hard lines sucker policies on law and new order. Thus, like me, Granger was abandoned and thrown to the wolves because John Carroll wasn't allowed to represent him in the appeal court. Not just any old wolves. The Solicitor General himself, no less than Lord Fraser of Carmyllie QC, with a full entourage of senior and junior Queens Counsel, Procurators Fiscal and Deputes in opposition. His appeal was thrown out.

This however threw the administration of justice in Scotland into turmoil and confusion. Was it now the case, after hundreds of years of precedent and procedure that a citizen could be thrown into jail for retracting a precognition? The Lord Advocate, head of prosecution services in Scotland, then took up Granger's point of law under Lord Advocate's reference to the High Court seeking a definitive ruling on the state of the law. This went before a full bench of five judges, the equivalent of the House of Lords in Scotland. They threw out the Solicitor General's arguments and returned the law to where it had been before Granger. This meant that Granger was still serving five years for something which was not against the law on the precognition issue.

The European Court of Human Rights ruled that Granger had not received a fair trial in accordance to law and thus was innocent until or unless proven otherwise by a fair trial. He still seeks a rehearing of his appeal here in Scotland.

Alex Reynolds

Alex Reynolds' alibi had checked out. He was processed through the court and bailed in the meantime until, six weeks later the house at 29 Bankend Street went up in flames and the Doyle family died. As there had only ever been one suspect with any connection to the car used in the shooting, which was obviously connected to the fire, Alex was hauled back in again and again for intense grilling and close scrutiny of his alibi. He still had the banned driving charge to go up for and the warrant for his arrest had been for a more serious charge of assault and robbery. These, among other things, were to be used to bring pressure to bear.

He testified that the police had kept on taking him into custody and, like so many others had said before and after him, that they kept beating him up. Trying to get him to say things which, on the one hand, weren't true and on the other, he didn't know anything about. They beat him around the body so brutally that at one point he was choking on his blood from the internal damage. The Crown Prosecution AD tore into him. He was a Crown witness but the AD called him for everything, not least a liar. But, calmly and with quiet humble apology, Alex gave him the answer. The police had had to take him into hospital, coughing up blood. The details of when he'd been taken into custody and the time he was taken into hospital would be on their records. He'd been taken back into custody and the torment continued. They'd make sure he'd get put away for a long, long time on the charges pending. His sister, his alibi on the shooting, would be charged with perjury and conspiracy. Or he could sign up for immunity and walk out the door a free man, all charges dropped. Finally, exhausted and disorientated, he had signed the statement which the police had written and presented to him and was allowed to go home. He said he didn't know what was in the statement but assumed that it was some or all of the things the police had been trying to get him to say. At that stage, he said, 'I would've signed anything to get out of that police station. I was scared.'

He testified that Gary Moore had taken him to a house in Reynolds' own car. He couldn't actually remember any more whether it had been Gary who'd said that it was TC's house or whether it was the police who'd said that Gary said that it was TC's house. But it didn't matter, because he hadn't gone into the house but sat in the car outside so couldn't identify anyone nor whose house it had actually been. Whatever, Gary had said that he owed this guy a car because he'd got this guy's car taken off the road and had wanted to give Reynolds' car to this guy as a replacement.

This was obviously the carry-on with Gary Moore, Cammy and the three-wheeler belonging to Marion's mother's neighbour at the other side of the city from my house, and Reynolds was so confused by intense interrogation that he could no longer distinguish who had said what to him from who said what to him. The wife of the owner of the car had given very clear evidence on this. She was not my wife. I'd never seen her or Reynolds for that matter before in my life. Gary I'd met briefly about twice, Cammy never. But here they were my co-accused on mass murder and shooting.

Alex Reynolds was taken away, charged with perjury for not sticking to the given script, for not testifying to the statement he'd signed. Next day he was brought back into the court on the understanding that he would retract his retraction of the previous day.

'No!' he said and went on to tell again how it had all happened. He'd been taken from court to prison and was visited by the court prosecutor there. He had been told that he was in for five years for perjury and the same for the robbery charge if he didn't retract his retraction. If he did, he would walk free with all charges withdrawn. But he had to withdraw his allegation against the police. He said in court, 'I just said yes to everything, like I said before. I'll agree on anythin' if they promise to let me out of prison but now that I'm here on oath I will tell the truth. Everything I've said is the truth.' He was taken into custody, charged with perjury and got five years for signing the statement.

However, it didn't end there. On summing up the evidence to the jury, the AD for the Crown prosecution service, Michael Bruce QC, managed to bring it round again. He said that Reynolds had said that he and Gary Moore had driven to Thomas Campbell's house. They had both gone into the house and Reynolds had heard Campbell tell Moore that he owed him a car because his, Campbell's car, the Volvo used in the shooting, had been taken off the road. Though this wasn't anything like what the actual evidence had been, that minor detail appeared to be of no consequence. For the judge, in HIS summation of the evidence, referred to what the AD had said about Reynolds' evidence, repeating the AD's version again in detail instead of quoting the actual witness direct. This little anomaly was pointed out at my appeal in my own defence without a lawyer. The Appeal Court, on their review of the evidence, withdrew it as evidence but it was to pop up again fourteen years later via the back door on the next appeal. Maybe some day we will get it right.

On the Spoor of the Silver Fox

Foxy Ferguson (aka the Silver Fox) was an old hawker. Nothing particularly bad or nasty about him. A bit of an old Grandpa grump, bow-leggit with a swathe of sweeping silver hair but sly, sly like the fox. Y'don't make the mistake of thinking that you could take the micky out of this old fox, he'd run rings round Roger, the proverbial dodger.

Up in Shit Street C Hall untried on death row for the Doyle family fire murders we kept getting these reports of statements, apparently emanating from Old Foxy but, something was up. Something wasn't right. The Fox was afoot and the hunt was on. Find the Fox.

His statements were saying that he'd been in the Netherfield Bar in Duke Street one afternoon. He owned an old fruit and veg mobile shop and had been going round all the scrap yards in the area looking for tyres for it. He'd dropped by the Netherfield for a quick refresher when he'd overheard these two big guys talking. One big guy was apparently called Tamby and he was talking to another big guy with a beard called TC. (In fact Tamby has a beard.) They were talking about a shotgun he said, 'something to do with a shotgun'.

Besides being untrue, this was more than merely odd, for Foxy's next statement was exactly the same but with one difference. The location was changed to the Ballochmile Bar, also in Duke Street. His third, but not last, location was changed again to a pub in Parkhead.

The next was located up in Fifti's Ices in Queenslie. His last statement was yet to be heard. Odd? Because known as the Fox as he is, no one could see him putting his head on the block for a charge of perjury like this. He was up to something. There must be a sly move afoot somewhere, but what? And why would he get involved?

He was finally tracked down by my brother-in-law, Billy, who, as it turns out was related to the Fergusons in some way (I hadn't known that). Billy came to see me up in the Bar-L and passed on the gist of it. Foxy had been asked what the fuck he was up to as all those conflicting statements were bound to get him the nick for perjury. Foxy had apologised and asked that his apology be passed on to me. He explained that the coppers had him over a barrel and were trying to get him to fit up some guy called TC. It had been his son Charlie who'd first said it and he'd just gone along with it but hadn't realised that this TC fullah and Tommy Campbell were the same person. But I was not to worry, the Fox said with a wink, because old Foxy was going to take one of his heart attacks before they could get him into court. No way would they get him into Court to say THAT crap . . .

Enquiries around C Hall untried confirmed that his son Charles, Charlie Farlie, was indeed there for a heavy consignment of drugs. Sure enough, he also confirmed that the polis had offered him a deal to verbal TC in return for a reduction in charges, but he had refused. Knowing well that the offer of deals on serious charges was the order of the day, this then seemed plausible. After all, had he accepted the deal he wouldn't still be there.

So, it was left at that. It wasn't 'til Charlie Farlie did disappear from the Hall, his charges reduced from major to minor, that we started to worry again. What was the old Fox up to and what would he do on the day?

Come the trial, the trail of the Silver Fox ended in classic farce – a pure pantomime in full regalia worthy of Jackanory. The scene opened with a dramatic announcement by the devil's advocate for the Crown. The public, the court, the Press and the jury on the edges of their seats. Only the drum roll was missing.

They had a witness, a vital and crucial witness who was dying, was expected to die at any moment now and it was vital that his evidence be heard before this tragic event. Begging the court's indulgence to extend the normal hours to allow this on the grounds of vital urgency before this crucial evidence was lost for evermore. The court graciously granted the indulgence. Hmm, so Foxy has taken one of his heart attacks right enough then? But there was obviously more than one bushy tail in the field. The AD was onto him and was turning it around to his advantage. One call is all.

Hence it was that the Silver Fox was literally strapped down and wheeled into court, the epitome of the reluctant witness. Ah, but what drama. Ambulance attendants strategically placed throughout the court like so many spear carriers, directed by the AD, only now clutching oxygen masks and cylinders. Nurse in attendance. Old Foxy was wheeled in to the show looking scared and bewildered, peering around the packed court and the jury, all on the edges of their seats, waiting on this poor old fart dropping dead. So what would the Silver Fox do now? Something old? Something new?

This time it was something new. It was the Barge Bar in Garthamlock. Well I hadn't heard that one before. This might yet prove to be interesting. He went on to say how he had overheard these two guys talking there.

'But who were they and what were they saying?' prompted the AD.

'It was GGG . . .'

'Gray?'

'No! It was Gary Moore and Joe Steele.' Uproar in court. This wasn't in the script.

'Where the fuck did that come from?' muttered Joe Steele in astonishment.

'They were talking about that fire.'

'Who said what to whom?'

'That Gary Moore wan said it tae Joe Steele'

'Said what?'

'It whiz an easy three hunner poun' they got fur torchin' a cellar.'

'Who got?'

'Thaim.'

'Who are they?'

'Thaim thit torched the cellar.'

'Who torched the cellar?'

'Thaim that got the three hunner poun.'

'Who got the three hundred pounds?'

'Thaim that torched the cellar, did ah no say that?'

'Do you understand, Mr Ferguson, that you may be using your own words and that you should repeat what was verbatim, so to speak, do you understand that?'

'Aye.'

'So what exactly was said and by whom?'

'Gary Moore said tae Joe Steele that it wiz an easy three hunner poun' they got fur torchin' a cellar . . .'

'But . . . who are THEY, who were they talking about?'

'THAIM that torched the cellar . . .'

On and on and on around the magic roundabout Foxy led them a merry dance, knowing well what the problem was but playing it dumb. He was simply repeating the script verbatim in the grammatical context as he'd been given it, but it was this context which made it inadmissible as evidence against anyone. They had to get him to say 'you got', 'we got', 'I got', anything but 'they got'. For as it was, it was the same as A saying to B that it was an 'easy ten grand they got for that bank robbery'. Which does not incriminate either A or B in anything. Also, Steele being B and not alleged to have said anything, nor even alleged to have nodded nor confirmed that he had even heard A, was totally in the clear. Obviously this would not do. So the AD hammered away at him. On and on, round and round the rugged rock the rugged rascal ran. So much then for the poor, old, desperately dying soul, for the old Fox wouldn't budge. An adjournment was called for and granted. Man! Whatever happened to the vital urgency trip?

The Serious Crime Squad swarmed round the Silver Fox like flies around shite and, as sure as shit would stick, I knew we were in it, deep style.

They wheeled him back into court. Pale and drawn. Scared. He didn't waste time waiting to be asked anything. Without any prompting, he blurted out, 'And TC will see them all right with the three hunner poun.'

'Eh! What?' The AD looked like he'd just caught the chicken.

'TC'll see them all right with the three hunner poun. That Gary Moore wan, he sniffs the glue.'

'Excuse me, but who will see who all right?'

'Thaim.'

'Who are they? The "them" to whom you refer?'

'Wiznae me! Ah didn't say it . . .' The AD's grin faded as once again it all went round. Do dloo do dloo do roo'd loo. Boing. 'Time for bed,' said Zebedee.

Of course this evidence was still not admissible against anyone. The law on that score being that it is not admissible evidence while that third party referred to is not there present at the time to agree or confirm, deny or refute when their name is uttered by another party. It's called hearsay and gossip and is not allowed as evidence, for good reason. Nevertheless, it portrayed a picture prejudicial to my interests in the eyes of the jury and made good sensational copy for the Press. Sure enough, throw enough shit.

On gentle cross-examination by Donald Findlay QC for Joe Steele, Foxy testified and continued to insist that this alleged conversation took place about three months after the fire. When it was pointed out to him that Gary Moore was in prison within weeks of the fire (for a car offence) and that Joe Steele was in prison within weeks of that – suddenly and dramatically, Foxy clutched at his chest, groaned, slumped and slid down his chair, twitching and kicking the proverbial bucket.

The court erupted. Panicking, the wee judge was on his feet banging away with his gavel, trying to be heard over the babble of the rabble. 'Get a doctor. Get a doctor. Why isn't there a doctor?' he yelled. Astute question, thought I. All the accused looked round at each other quietly raising eyebrows with sideways sardonic smirks as the hullabaloo ensued, but they were not the only ones in the court who knew the score. The wee nurse was trying to get herself heard over the mad babble. I watched her there in the well of the court. She stood there, a pretty wee thing, her petite body rigid in her outrage. Hands clenched tightly into fists clamped firmly by her sides and stamping her neat little smartly shod foot on the floor, more and more firmly as her little tantrum mounted in righteous outrage. Stamping out the words to the beat she shouted in her frustration at being ignored, 'THERE IS NOTHING WHATEVER WRONG WITH HIM.' Right at that exact moment when the court fell to a sudden hush and her wee sweet voice resounded clear as a bell vibrating throughout the entire building. God bless that little angel. The entire court looked towards Foxy, slumped there, apparently dead. The silence went on until, finally, the Silver Fox opened one eye. Peering around the court in the deadly silence. He coughed, 'Ah Hmmm!' sat up and smiled sweetly, making himself comfortable he settled himself upright without as much as a blush.

'No further questions, m'Lord.'

Enough said!

No Case to Answer

Upon the close of the prosecution case there were long legal arguments put forward on behalf of all the accused and for the prosecution. All the defence counsel argued that there was no case to answer, insufficiency of evidence in law to allow it to go to a jury.

Shadda was defended by the late John Smith, MP QC and his argument in summation of the evidence led to Thomas Lafferty snr being acquitted of Charges 4, 5, 6, 7, and 10, but he would go to the jury on the two charges – 3 (drunk and disorderly) and 9 (shooting Andrew Doyle's van).

George Reid's plea was rejected and he would go to the jury on all of his charges – 1, 11, and 12, the Haghill and Castlemilk incidents.

Donald MacAulay QC, now Lord MacAulay of Bragar, submitted an excellent argument in law for acquittal on all charges on my behalf and I was acquitted on Charges 6 (conspiracy to rob Mitchell), 8 (Marchetti fire), 13 (assaulting Andrew Doyle), 6b (possession of pick shafts), 14 (the supply of pick shafts), 14a (instigation), 14b (instigation) but would remain charged with Charge 9 (shooting) and Charge 15 (fire murders). The judge, Lord Kincraig, could make no decision and abstained from judgement on the question of whether there was legally sufficient evidence to go to a jury or not. It would thus be for the jury to say.

Tamby the Bear, defended by the late great Hamish Stirling QC, would be acquitted on Charges 6, 8, 13 and, most importantly, the fire murders at 15. Insufficient evidence in law, no case to answer. It is significant that Tamby was on all the same charges with me on all the same evidence and we were acquitted of those charges, no case to answer, with the one exception of charge 15. Tamby was acquitted and I was sent to the jury on the same evidence because the judge could not say whether in my case that was sufficient or not. However Tamby, like me, would still have to face a jury on charge 9 on the strength of the evidence of the witness Love.

Joe Steele was brilliantly defended by Donald Findlay QC and his arguments resulted in Joe the Mole being acquitted on Charges 11, 12, 13 and 16 but remaining on Charges 2 (attempted raid on Sammy's van), 6 (conspiring with himself) and 15 (the fire murders).

Cammy would go to the jury on both charges 2 and 9 where he was fitted in to Sammy's and the shooting. Here the Moorov principle was used to say that although there was only one witness in each case and without corroboration, nevertheless, the similarities – both being close to each other, both were shotgun attacks on vans and that on both occasions he'd sat in the back seat – showed sufficient similarity to allow the application of the principles as first applied in the case of Moorov.

Briefly, Moorov was a tailor who employed girls as sewers. Each night he would tell one girl to stay back for overtime and refusal would mean they would be sacked. He would then have sex with them against their will, refusing at pain of losing their job. This was around the 1930s when work was a precious commodity. Each girl was only one witness without corroboration on any attack and Moorov just claimed that each was willing. For the first time it was allowed for all the incidents to be considered as one charge so that the witnesses in each separate incident could corroborate the evidence of each other. Same place, same time, same circumstances in allegation. The principles as established in Moorov would usually require a minimum of three incidents. Of bag snatching, for example, that the bag strap was cut with a razor on Maryhill Road on three nights or three weeks in a row by the same person identified. Each may be separate incidents without corroboration but each show such similarity in time, place and mode that each witness may now support the evidence of the others in all three cases as the one charge. Common sense really but should it have applied in Cammy's case? Only two incidents, six months apart, one an attempted robbery on a Fifti van with Joe Steele and Cammy allegedly in the back seat, the other a shooting on a Fifti rival, Marchetti, in a different area and by other people? In fact, it should not have applied but it gave the prosecution the opportunity to impress upon the jury that it could be. Simply because, you may recall, there were also two fires alleged in this case. Nobody then told the jury that Moorov principles could not be applied to that or to all these charges of attacking ice cream vans.

Gary Moore would be acquitted on all charges, 6, 13 and 15, but he would be forced to sit through to the final verdicts to prevent him being cited as a witness. Charges withdrawn then, Not Guilty, no case to answer were 4, 5, 6, 6b, 7, 8, 10, 11, 12, 13, 14, 14a, 14b and 16. This left Charges 1 (breach of the peace against George Reid), 2 (raid on Sammy's van by Joe Steele and Cammy), 3 (drunk and disorderly against Shadda). Charges 11 and 12 were now alleged against George Reid alone. Thus leaving Charges 9 and 15 alleged on the evidence of Billy Love against Shadda, Tamby, myself, Cammy on Charge 9 (shooting), me and Joe alone on Charge 15, Tamby,

Gary and Granger being acquitted on that one. Seemed there was not much left of the ice cream war indictment going into the defence case.

Now that Joe Steele's imaginary link with George Reid is severed we can take George Reid out of the equation as being charged on his own in this indictment with crimes not connected nor associated with the others. That then leaves Joe and Cammy on Charge 2 on the evidence of Gordon Ness, Joe's pal, whom I'd never met and who had traded Joe in with the truth and lied about Cammy. Yet still no connection with the Doyle murders, at least on this indictment, other than the fact that Joe was charged with that too. Yet the judge admits to the jury that there is no evidence to say that either Joe Steele or I were near or at the scene of the fire at the time the fire was started. He may as well have said, 'nor at any time', for that too is a fact. Joe's alibi remains unchallenged by any evidence in rebuttal. This then leaves the evidence of Joe's other pal, Billy Love, and of old Foxy Ferguson regarding overheard conversations in pubs. Neither of these witnesses ever alleged that Joe Steele had uttered a word in either instance. There can be no conviction in Joe's case without either Love or Foxy Ferguson. The absence of Ferguson would put him in the same position as Tamby, no case to answer. As would the absence of Love against him have a likewise effect. Also, I was already in the same position as Tamby the Bear so far as the evidence was concerned but he was Not Guilty and I had no judgement by the court. Without Love in my case, there would be no argument about it. There would, as the trial judge agreed, be insufficiency of evidence in law against me on the remaining two charges, the shooting and the fire murders. That leaves Cammy, Shadda and Tamby on the shooting of Andrew Doyle's van, again solely on the evidence of Love and police evidence of verbal. And again, without the evidence of Love there is not sufficiency of evidence in law to convict anyone of anything except for Joe Steele on Sammy's van through Ness, which has nothing to do with anybody else.

In the event then, the main two charges, the shooting and the fire murders, alleged against six accused, rely entirely on the evidence of the witness Love. Take him out of the equation and you are left with George Reid charged with breach of the peace in Haghill, assault in Castlemilk and with no connection to any other accused. Joe and Cammy on the attempted raid on Sammy's van, again with no connection to the other accused. And Shadda charged with drunk and disorderly on Charge 3. Thus, without the evidence of Love, there is no place for me or Tamby or Gary Moore on this indictment. Nor is there a place for Joe on the fire murders or for Cammy or Shadda on the shooting. This indictment stands or falls on the evidence of Billy Love. And everything else is an illusion.

In Defence

All the accused then took the stand and called evidence of their alibi and defence with the exception of Gary who was effectively acquitted of all charges but just not released yet.

Shadda's point of view was that he was 'an alcoholic not a fuckin cowboy' and had nothing to do with any of the crap he was accused of. He had never asked Love to do anything regarding the shooting and that the whole thing was a lie and a fit-up.

George Reid just quietly denied all accusations and stated there was never a receipt for a Bowie knife in any of his pockets. He didn't know how it had gotten there. In fact, a great part of his evidence was in answer to questions about me – how much the van had cost me, where I bought it, where the run was, how much I earned and so on. This was info that had already come out during the course of the trial and anyone in the court could have answered these questions. It was annoying and frustrating for me to watch this. George was treating it like a challenge to a schoolboy, testing to see how much he had been paying attention but the Advocate Depute was simply establishing that George knew a hell of a lot about my personal business even though, by that time, so did the entire country. It would have been more sensible to have said 'you better ask him that' but George couldn't be sensible while there was a chance to be smart. When anybody ever asks me about somebody else's business, I always say, 'You better ask them about that.' But that's just the way I am.

My own cross-examination, they tell me, was the worst of them all. I never noticed as it was all just the usual for me. I do recall though that my QC stopped it no less than three times to strongly object, threatening to make a motion for mistrial if it didn't stop. It was simply that I would be asked one question by the judge and another by the Crown's Advocate Depute, Michael Bruce QC, now Lord Marnoch. The answers to each would be conflicting so that when I answered one the other would take that as their answer and when I answered that again the other would take it as their answer. Mutt and Jeff. They seemed to me to be working together as a team in an attempt to stitch me up, trip me up and make me look bad. I was used to this treatment and it didn't faze me at all but it's how it looks to the jury that counts. My QC, Donald MacAulay, commented that it was the most unfair cross-examination he had ever witnessed in his entire career and 'deplorable conduct'. I thought I had handled myself well, though obviously not. When accused of being at the scene of the fire at the time it was set and of thus killing the Doyle family, I answered with anger.

'You have no right to say that, no right! There has been no evidence given in this court which entitles you to say that. It is simply not true . . .'

'Well perhaps you weren't there then, Campbell,' he conceded. 'But you must have got someone else to do it then didn't you, Campbell?'

'No I did no such thing.'

'Just as you got someone else to assault Andrew Doyle at his close.'

'It's not true.'

'Just as you planned to have someone assault Mitchell, didn't you?'

'No.'

'Just as you got someone else to set fire to Marchetti's factory.'

'I have been acquitted of these charges you have no right to . . .'

'Just as you got someone else to smash up these ice cream vans . . .'

'No, I . . .'

'Just as you got someone else to shoot at Andrew Doyle's van with a gun you got someone else to set fire to the Doyle family household, didn't you, CAMPBELL?' He roared. 'DIDN'T YOU, CAMPBELL? You got someone else to do all of these things, didn't you?'

'Well? Do you deny it?' says the trial judge.

'Yes,' I reply to him.

'SO YOU ADMIT IT THEN?' roars the prosecuting Depute.

'No I don't,' I turn to answer him.

'So you don't deny it then?' responds the judge.

On and on it would go like this until, 'OBJECTION.' Donald MacAulay would give the judge a telling off but he would just keep doing it again and again till the threat of trial abandonment shut him up. It didn't matter to me but what I hadn't realised was that although I was turning toward the person I was answering a turning towards is not noted in the transcripts. It would not be noted in the record who I was answering at what time and the judge's comments and questions to me may not even be noted at all. It would look like admissions on record. Only my counsel's objections and notices for the record were keeping them from stitching me up right there in the court and on transcript. I'm told that the only gain that the Advocate Depute made from our encounter was that of impression. That of all the accused to testify, I was the one who came across as the most intelligent, articulate, least intimidated but most dominant and, by inference therefore, the leader. In fact, that was his closing argument.

I was closely examined regarding the night I'd gone to Garthamlock to find the van and my sister Patsy with her man Alex, the driver. Explaining that it could only have been a Saturday night as that was the only night Liz had her day off and accounted for why I was up at the garage to collect the takings for the following day's stock. The van hadn't appeared on time and I'd found it with my sister Patsy and Alex at Agnes' in Garthamlock where Alex had taken Patsy after her work at Parkhead. That it had been Patsy and Alex on a Saturday night and not Sadie and the Craw on a Sunday night as Mrs Bruce or Degnan had said. Though she'd finally conceded that she hadn't known which day it had been but only agreed to the police assertion that it had been the night Tommy Cooper had died after they'd pestered her about thirty times and she'd finally only agreed because she didn't really know and didn't see what it mattered anyway.

Sadie's original statement had some confusion as to where she'd been the night Tommy Cooper had died. She hadn't seen it on TV, hadn't been at home but had been out at the Blessed John Ogilvie's social club.

'If they'd just given me the date I would have remembered and been able to tell them but they kept asking about the night Tommy Cooper died and I didn't know what night that was.' In fact that day had been her daughter's birthday and she remembered trying to get the strap fixed for the watch she had got her. About ninety people from the club had confirmed that she'd been there. Sadie had also mentioned her van driver arriving as the club was coming out. He too was called to confirm or refute this. He confirmed he'd arrived as the club was coming out, met Sadie and handed over the takings for the following day's stock. He spoke of the police slapping him about in an attempt to have him change this piece of his statement but he wouldn't do it.

It was confirmed then that Mrs Bruce or Degnan had confused my two sisters, Patsy and Sadie, and that she'd seen Patsy on a Saturday night. Mrs Bruce's admission that she didn't really know which day it had been meant that there was no evidence to refute my alibi. I mean, if Mrs Bruce had been right then that would have been my alibi. There is no crime in visiting one's sister and it would have been a better alibi than the one I had. As it was, she had mistaken the days under police pressure and I was at home with Liz and the wean on the Sunday.

Gary Moore pled alibi that he was with his fiancée, Marion Reynolds, at her mother's house in the north of the city. They'd watched TV and gone to bed at around 2.30 a.m. but didn't sleep until much later into the wee hours of the morning of Monday 16th April. There had been about nine people in the house, including Marion's mother and brother Alex, two other adults and three school children. There was no way that he could have left the house without the rest of the household being aware of it. He would have had to pass Marion's mother and the rest of the people to have done so and hadn't. Nor could he have gone out the window, as had been suggested, for the window didn't open due to some safety device fitted while the windows were being renewed. There were other detailed explanations of his position which were not called upon to be proven when the statement extracted from Alex Reynolds, as per the same situation and circumstances as Granger, was retracted and he reverted to the truth under oath in court. Gary Moore's alibi was accepted by the Crown prosecution and he was acquitted without contest. No case to answer. Not Guilty.

Tamby the Bear's alibi was that he was at home with his common-law wife Margaret and her two school-aged children. This alibi too was accepted by the prosecution without contest or any evidence in refutal. Tamby the Bear was acquitted. No case to answer. Not Guilty.

Joe Granger's alibi that he was with his fiancée, Lynne Chalmers, which was supported by her in evidence, was also eventually accepted without contest or any evidence in refutal. No case to answer. Not Guilty.

Joe Steele's alibi was that he'd been at home in bed suffering from flu. His mother and grandmother were the only two people at home with him during the actual time of the fire but he called various witnesses who had come and gone to the house throughout that day and night to testify that he had been in bed ill with the flu. There was no evidence brought to refute this alibi but the nature of the charge would be changed and he remained accused.

By the close of the Crown prosecution case there was no evidence produced in refutal of any alibis and they remained unchallenged by any evidence. In these circumstances we could normally expect to be acquitted but these were not normal circumstances. The prosecution didn't simply move the goal posts, they changed the name of the game, making up the rules ad hoc as they went along. After all, they are the Crown and this is their court . . .

'Perhaps you weren't there then, Campbell but . . . You must have got someone else to do it then. DIDN'T YOU, CAMPBELL.'

Changes the nature of the charge rendering, at least, my alibi as irrelevant. Yet you would assume that, even in these circumstances, Joe being the only accused, they would still require to refute <u>his</u> alibi to sustain that new allegation. Common sense says so and, in fact, the law says so but such considerations were irrelevant in this case.

Tamby Gray was Not Guilty, Gary Moore was Not Guilty, Joe Granger was Not Guilty. All those alibis of our own were unchallenged by any evidence. That left the allegation that I must have got someone else to do it and the only remaining co-accused being Joe Steele, they should have had to refute his alibi having circumnavigated mine. The law on that score being that A cannot be convicted in art and part capacity along with B, C and D whilst B, C and D are acquitted. Thus it became imperative to convict Joe Steele to convict me . . . the primary target.

All very well but the only remaining evidence against Joe Steele, besides police verbal 'I'm no the wan that lit the match' was none other than the illustrious Foxy Ferguson, the Silver Fox himself. His evidence was ruled as inadmissible against myself and Gary Moore so how, therefore, could it be admissible against wee Joe who was not even alleged to have uttered a word or even to have nodded in response?

Some quick and fancy foot work would have to be done on behalf of the Crown case against Joe before the entire trial collapsed around their ears. There was more than one bushy tail in the field. Thus it was in his summing-up to the jury the devil's advocate slipped in those subtle little adjustments required to do the dirty deed. He simply told the jury to take their pencils in their hands as he dictated the new and authorised version of Foxy's evidence according to the Crown, 'It was an easy . . . It was an easy . . . an easy three hundred pounds . . . an easy three hundred pounds . . . For torching . . . for torching . . . a cellar. TC will see . . . TC will see you all right . . . All right . . . with the three hundred pounds . . . with the three hundred pounds . . .'

Missing out the key words 'They got' and 'them' on the grounds that the witness was obviously confused and that this is what he had actually meant. He had simply confused his grammatical tenses. Thus, regardless of what the witness had actually said, this new official version could now be deemed as admissible against Joe Steele who is not even alleged to have acknowledged that he heard anyone say anything:

'Did he nod?'
'Naw.'
'Did he say anything at all?'
'Naw.'
'Did he give any indication that he had even heard Moore?'
'Naw.'

This evidence of remarks allegedly made in his presence in a pub months after he was in prison would now be sufficient to take him to a jury on a mass murder charge. Yet his alibi still remained unrefuted.

As they say in the back streets of Glasgow where they play the game called the Meegie, 'Looks like you're het, Joe.'

The judge directed the jury, 'Now both of these accused plead alibi but the Crown do not say they were there at the scene of the crime.' (Eh? Who was that, 'Someone else' then?) 'They say that they are guilty because they were part of a plan, a common plan, so the question of alibi does not come into it.

'There is no evidence to say that these accused were near, or at the scene of the fire at the time the fire was started.' (Eh? Who was that 'Someone else to do it' then?) 'And so the evidence is that of inference from the evidence which is before you and which is that of the witness Love's overheard conversation in a public house. The Crown case stands or falls upon his evidence. It is therefore crucial that you believe him.'

Wee Joe also cited two prisoners from C Hall. A guy called Caff or something who I didn't know and a big fullah called Dougie T who I knew from as far back as Approved School when I was fifteen. They both told of how Love had boasted of how he had blasted this ice cream van. Caff's evidence was straightforward and even though called a liar he came away from it relatively unscathed. The Big Dougie T fullah though took absolute pelters and gave back as good as he got. The difference with him was that, besides giving Love's description of how he had blasted the van, Dougie T went on to explain that he was a prison pass man. This meant that his cell door was mostly left open during the day to allow him to carry out his cleaning duties. Being out and about, he was able to pay attention to what was going on in the Hall. These cleaners are called pass men for a good reason. He could keep an eye on the staff activity board on the landing. This included the numbers out of their cells or off the landing. 'One Off so and so to surgery.' 'Two Off for solicitor's visit.' 'One Off police interview' and so on. He had noticed that Love was having a hell of a lot of police interviews and had not been declaring them or explaining them to anyone. Dougie T had then thought to engage Love in conversation to try to glean whether he was acting as an informer. They became friendly. During these conversations Love had not only told Dougie T all about how he had blasted the van that was in the newspapers but all about the armed robbery he was charged with. It wasn't odd that he should tell him these things. No, they weren't confessions but conversations where a prisoner states his form, usually exaggerating, to try to gain a step up in the pecking order. He had also told Dougie T about his charges of attempting to pervert justice and his previous record of it – this in an attempt to get an opinion from an old lag as to what kind of sentence might be due if found Guilty. Dougie T did not go into this, however, until he himself was called a liar under cross-examination.

The devil's advocate had pointed out Dougie T's long list of previous convictions.

'Aye,' said Dougie T, 'but that doesn't make me out a liar.'

'It makes you dishonest,' responded the Advocate Depute.

'But it doesn't make me a liar. I pled guilty to those previous. It's your witness, Love, who has the previous history of perverting justice not me,' Dougie T responded. The Depute was absolutely livid. His feet coming up off the ground as he shouted, 'WHO TOLD YOU TO SAY THAT? WHO TOLD YOU TO SAY THAT? WAS IT HIM?' He ran over pointing his finger in my face. 'WAS IT CAMPBELL WHO TOLD YOU TO SAY THAT?' he roared. But it was the first I'd heard of it myself.

Dougie T and Caff were disregarded as unreliable witnesses because they were prisoners. But then so was Love at the time and he was held up as a courageous and honest witness. So why the double standards? What is good for the goose and all that. Ah, but they are the Crown y'see and this is their court. They will do whatever they damn well like. They will not only have their cake and eat it they will have it and eat ours as well.

Just the way the cookie crumbles. Hard lines (sucker) on law and new order means that hypocrisy and double standards are the new order of the era.

The Trouble with Jaki . . . and the Issue of Support

Joe Steele also brought evidence to show that he was never in the Netherfield Bar in the company of Billy Love and, typical of the Myopic Mole's shortsightedness, that he had only ever been there in conspiracy with another love. In fact, in secret liaison with a girlfriend, wee Jaki. His wife Dolly wouldn't be too pleased about this.

Jaki was in her teens. I'd known her and her family well. I'd seen her grow up and, up until that point, still looked upon her as a child. She was a very pretty wee thing, small and petite, shy and nervous in the witness box, yet sexily coy. The problem with Jaki's nervousness was, as some people are, she was giggly with it and for such a petite little thing, she had these huge mammaries which would jiggle and dance as she giggled. Which of course meant that all the dickheads in the court were not paying any attention to one word she had to say. Jaki is not a tart. She was a home grown girl who mostly looked after her dad. The problem was with her nerves and her girlish giggles. On top of that, she had a habit of chewing on her tongue and licking her lips between replies, totally unconsciously and totally oblivious to the fact that she was oozing with erotic undertones to the point where even the wee judge seemed mesmerised by her natural charms – turning around on his seat and sitting forward beside her on the bench for closer examination. Only because I'd never seen her before in this light, could I see that it was all unconscious on her part and that she'd no clue of the effect that she was having, effectively mesmerising every dickhead within half a mile of her scent and her smile, endearing all to her erotic girlishness.

Her evidence was that she was a local to the pub, was there most days and most nights because there was nowhere else to go. The only time that Joe Steele was ever there was when he had arranged to see her. And she had never been in the company of Billy Love who she had never met nor heard of. Nor TC nor Tamby and the rest who she knew but didn't associate with. When asked about being in the pub most nights and the suggestion made that perhaps she drank too much, giggling nervously, she explained that she only had a wee drink at the weekends but that she sometimes helped out there.

'Most of the time,' she said, 'I sit with my dad and his pals.'

'Do you prefer the company of older men?' interjected the wee judge, smiling sweetly.

'Oh yes, sir,' she breathed huskily, giggling a jiggle, fiddling with her tongue, causing the wee judge to beam brightly and start on a follow-up line. 'Ahmm,' interrupted the Advocate Depute, breaking the spell, causing the judge to start and turn away with his head down, suddenly intensely interested in his notes.

Yet another witness on this theme was Helen Wetheral Welch, Crown prosecution witness number 230 and the manageress of the Netherfield Bar. I knew this woman from when I'd been a regular to her pub. However, the reason I was no longer a regular was due to her. She'd stood as witness against me in an earlier trial in this very court and had tried her damnedest to put the mix in against me on an attempted murder charge, a stabbing, but it had been self defence and I'd been acquitted in spite of her nasty efforts. She didn't like me one iota, nor was there any love lost in reciprocation. She was brought in as the attempt at supporting the evidence of Love. I dreaded this. She hated me so much for embarrassing her publicly once before that she might just say anything to get back at me.

'Thomas Gray and Thomas Campbell were close associates?' she was asked.

'No they used to always be pals but they fell oot.'

'But they would still sit and have a chat from time to time?'

'Naw y'would never see them th'gether after that.'

'Surely they would stop for a chat?'

'Naw if TC came into the lounge, Tamby would go into the bar away fae'm or leave th'pub altogether. Y'wouldn't see them in the same room th'gether.'

'But surely they would say something?'

'Naw they weren't talking. Ah don't know what it was about. Nobody does.'

'Not even a hello?'

'Well in passing maybe once in a blue moon they'd maybe nod in passing.'

'Not a word? Not a single word?'

'Well maybe one would say, "Alright big yin" and the other would say, "Aye no too bad, big man" or something like that, know what I mean?'

'BIG MAN?'

'Aye! big man, big fullah, like that y'know?'

'Who was the BIG MAN?'

'Well they are both big but I suppose TC would say "Alright, big yin" and Tamby would say "No bad, big man".'

'So TC, Thomas Campbell, was the BIG MAN?'

'Well, as I say, they were both big, but aye! I suppose so.'

'Take a note of that ladies and gentlemen. TC is the BIG MAN. The BIG MAN, ladies and gentlemen.'

Down in the cells after that, I turned to Tamby saying, 'Maybe I should have cited Billy Connolly or Jock Stein?'

'Naw, no Jock Stein,' he says. 'He's fuckin deid.' Shaking his head saying, 'That could just as easily have gone either way,' he paused for effect, 'Big Man,' and howls with laughter. And, in truth, I had to smile.

CHAAARGE

'It is important in a case of this kind that I have your undivided attention,' said the judge and he had mine. For the next two days the judge gave his charge to the jury, telling them what the law is and isn't in relation to the trial before they went off to make their decisions, their verdicts. Two days are a lot of words, here are some of the most pressing points.

Point 5a: Now persons involved directly or indirectly in blasting off a shotgun at an ice cream van in a public street during the hours of darkness are villains of the first degree; and those who set fire to a top flat in a tenement at a time when the house is occupied and the occupants are liable to be asleep, where there are no available means of escape except through the very place where the fire is started, and who, as a result, cause the death of six persons, mostly young, are wicked and depraved persons, inhuman and evil; they merit no sympathy nor consideration. No decent person could be other than appalled at such dastardly deeds. These thoughts and these emotions, however, are not for you to entertain when considering your verdict . . .

Points 13c, 14a and 17b: Ladies and gentlemen, it probably has not escaped your notice that some of the accused are charged with committing a crime and the evidence does not put them at the locus of the crime and, therefore, the evidence does not show they were committing it directly. For example, in Charge 9, the evidence is that there was only one person who shot at the ice cream van and yet we find four persons accused of that shooting; and also on Charges 11 and 12, the assault on Shepherd and the damage to the ice cream van in Croftfoot Quadrant . . .

. . . two people were originally charged with that offence but only one is now left in it – George Reid – and yet the evidence was that Reid had left the scene of the attack on the van and the assault before it happened; so you might have thought at one time it was strange to find people charged with committing a crime when they were not even there. Well, I have to explain to you how this is so. An accused person may be guilty of a crime committed directly by another because of the concept of law which we call art & part . . .

The Crown do not have to prove that any particular member of those engaged in the crime actually perpetrated it; what the Crown has to prove is that one member did it and the others were associated with him in the way I have explained. You have to look at each accused separately to determine whether there was a common purpose and whether that accused was involved in it . . .

Points 26c, 27 and 28: Now, in this case an attack has been made by counsel on the credibility of Love and Ness and many of the detective officers involved in investigating these crimes. I have already given you directions upon the evidence of Love; you have to consider whether you are to accept Love's evidence which incriminates some of the accused.

So far as the detectives are concerned, Mr Macaulay delivered a vehement and sustained attack upon a number of detective officers involved in this case, some of considerable experience and in superior positions, some with less experience and in lower positions. He used such words as 'rotten', 'Strathclyde Police rotten' and you will remember he used such expressions as 'there are good policemen, bad policemen' and then reference was made to 'the ugly'; and they have been submitted to be liars and bullies. Well, of course, you appreciate that this attack was made on behalf of Thomas Campbell; Mr MacAulay is acting on the instructions of his client, either expressly or impliedly because counsel do not hold any views on these matters; Mr MacAulay said this to you himself. So what this attack amounted to was Mr MacAulay on behalf of Thomas Campbell alleging that the police were liars and bullies. Now, the force or validity of any attack of this kind must be judged on the evidence in the case not on evidence in other cases, what other policemen may have done in other cases or on anything else. You have to ask yourself, 'What is the evidence on which this attack is based that the police are liars and bullies? What is it based on?' So far as I can gather from the evidence which you have heard it is based upon the evidence of the accused, Mrs Campbell and on the young man, Hamilton, who said he was bullied by the police into making a statement which he says is not true. Joseph Granger, who said also that he was bullied, or definitely said he had his hair pulled in order to be forced to make this statement or to sign a place on a plan. The witness, Reynolds, who said a thirteen-page statement was put before him and he was told to sign it and it was made up by the police. There may be others. Now, against that body of testimony you have the evidence of the detectives themselves to whom these allegations were put and who denied them. You have to choose. It is only if you accept the evidence of the accused and the others to whom I have referred that you could agree with Mr MacAulay's submission. If you do, you must consider what follows. What follows is that you are saying that not one or two or four but a large number of detectives have deliberately come here to perjure themselves, to build up a false case against an accused person, and they have carried this through right to the end; a conspiracy of the most sinister and serious kind. They have formed this conspiracy to saddle the accused wrongly with the crimes of murder of a horrendous nature. If so, it involves their making up and persisting in a concocted story, concocted statements attributed wrongly, falsely to the accused. Now, what do you prefer, ladies and gentlemen? It is up to you . . .

Points 61c, 62c and 63: This is the background against which you have to consider the evidence of Love. If he is untruthful, if this is a concocted story, a false story, then it follows, doesn't it, that he has played a gigantic confidence trick on the police, senior officers, the Procurator Fiscal and, indeed, the Crown authorities because they accepted his story, allowed him out on bail and have proferred him as a witness before you. They, according to the submissions of the defence, have swallowed hook, line and sinker Love's story, which they say is false.

Well, you have to consider this submission, ladies

and gentlemen, because it is the foundation of this charge; because, if he is lying, he has played a colossal deceit on you; but if he is telling the truth, whatever may have been his motive for not remaining silent, then his evidence is powerful and damning against the accused . . .

Ask yourselves, was he capable of hoodwinking the police and the Crown and you with an utterly false and concocted story? Could he have conceived of such a story in the first place with no foundation in fact to work on? Could he have persisted in it successfully, so far as the Crown is concerned and now before you without being tripped up, without being shown up as a liar or as a complete inventor of the account which he gave . . .

Something, however, ladies and gentlemen, was said about there being a basic lack of check on Love. I have already referred you to the plastic bag. Did he know that was the one found in the Volvo car before he spilled the beans to the police? If he did, the police are also involved with a conspiracy with Love to do down the accused. Having put up Love to concoct a story, having told him, 'We found a plastic bag in the car.' Would the police have plotted with Love to concoct a story to that end do you think? That is a matter for you. If you think Love has concocted a story, your verdict would be in favour of the accused; if not, but you accept his evidence, you must look for corroboration of it . . .

Of course, ladies and gentlemen, Love has made himself immune from prosecution on this charge, that is the law I referred to earlier. It may be that having given a statement on oath he was also immune, that is not quite so clear. As a statement given on oath before a sheriff, if it was untrue, then he would be guilty of perjury; and having given evidence . . .

Point 71: Now, again, all three of these accused put forward alibis and they impeach Mr Love. Of course, the Crown do not say that Thomas Campbell was there or Thomas Lafferty; they say they were guilty because they were taking part in a plan, a common plan, so the question of alibi does not come into it in relation to these accused.

Point 93b: Now I deal with Charges 14, 14a and b. I have considered the evidence on this charge which is one of instigating the young man Capuano to attack an ice cream van and also to attack Irene Mitchell and Douglas Cardle in their car, and to instigate Capuano and supply him with pickaxe handles, mallets and similar instruments whereby he could commit these crimes. Now, I have decided, ladies and gentlemen, that there is not sufficient evidence to entitle you to convict Thomas Campbell on Charges 14, 14a or b. It is quite simple as far as 14b is concerned, because this is an attack with bricks, if I remember rightly, and there is no evidence that Thomas Campbell supplied Capuano with bricks. However, be that as it may, there is insufficient evidence in law to justify a conviction of Thomas Campbell . . . So, I direct you to find him Not Guilty on both those charges. But you must draw no inference at all from that decision of mine. It doesn't mean that the pickaxe handles and the other articles were not found in Thomas Campbell's cellar; that is still part of the evidence given by the police. It doesn't mean that the police evidence is untrue; it doesn't mean that Capuano was not in fact instigated; it just means that there is insufficiency of evidence in law to justify a conviction and it is my duty, if that is the situation, so

Tommy at home in 1983: before the storm

(L – R) Brothers Locky and Rab, and friend George with 8 year old Tommy on the far right

A family celebration: Helen 'Nellie' Campbell with TC's brother George and sister Helen

Right: Bobby Campbell,
TC's father, with sister
Sadie on her wedding day
Below: Agnes Lafferty,
TC's sister, and one of
the original co-accused in
connection with the
Doyle murders

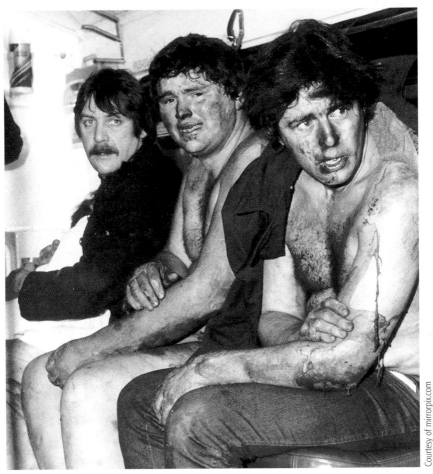

Above: Andrew 'Fatboy' Doyle sits between brother Daniel and a fireman cradling 18 month old nephew Mark. Four days later, both Andrew and Mark had died

Opposite page: The Doyle house, 29 Bankend Street, Ruchazie, April 17th, 1984, after the fire

Courtesy of Scottish Television

Above: Young Thomas McGraw circa 1983, one of the original co-accused

Right: William Love, key witness against TC Campbell

Below left: Joe Steele, convicted for the Doyle murders along with TC

Below right: Tamby Gray, one of TC Campbell's co-accused in the Doyle murders

Courtesy of News International

Courtesy of Scottish Media Newspapers

TC Campbell and Joe Steele leaving High Court in Glasgow on October 10th, 1984

Above left: Michael Bruce QC, now Lord Marnoch, prosecutor in the Doyle murder trial
Above right: Detective Superintendent Norrie Walker, senior officer in charge of the investigation. He committed suicide four years after the trial

The price we pay: TC Campbell from his prison cell, nine years after being convicted for the Doyle murders

to decide and to give you direction. As I say, you draw no inference from I have decided. A mere technicality, ladies and gentlemen, that is all . . .

Points 96 and 97: Now, as I said earlier, you cannot see into the minds of the perpetrators of this appalling act; and, to discover the intent behind it, you have to look at all the circumstances which have been proven before you and draw from them such inferences as to intent that these circumstances can bear; and that is your province. The circumstances proved – and there is no dispute about this so far as I can recollect from hearing the witnesses – that it was not an accidental fire; it was started deliberately. It was started by petrol being applied to part of the house, the door and/or the cellar outside, and ignited. Possibly petrol was poured through the letterbox. There was a rapid spread of flame and fire and this was done at a time when people would be expected to be in the house and to be asleep and, therefore, not immediately alerted to fire in their dwelling house. The only means of escape . . . was through the very opening where the fire started and would be expected to burn earliest and perhaps most intensely. The question is, was it therefore a likely consequence that the occupants would not escape death? Do these circumstances indicate on the part of the fire-raisers an utter criminal disregard for the consequences of their actions? If you think so, then you would hold that the crime of murder has been proved. Whatever you hold, it would be wilful fire-raising, which is, as I have said, a crime and because death resulted from that crime, the crime would be one of culpable homicide, culpable homicide being the crime of killing a human being as a result of a criminal act. Now, it is a matter of admission in this case that the six persons who died in the Doyle family died as a result of the fire; and so if the fire was started deliberately and the crime of wilful fire-raising committed, the crime also of culpable homicide was committed. Even if it was intended originally as a 'frightener' and not intended to cause death, it would still be murder as I have defined it.

Points 104 and 105: Now, on Charge 9, if you hold that it was not attempted murder then you will say so in your verdict and say so whether it was assault to or . . . not to the danger of life. So far as Charge 15 is concerned, if you do not say murder has been proved you will indicate that in your verdict by returning a verdict of culpable homicide, assuming you hold proved that the fire was caused wilfully . . .

Then, suddenly, it was all over and the jury out.

BOOK FIVE
Guilty!

Guilty!

Guilty . . . It is more than a mere word. It is a verdict, a verdict in condemnation of a life and which strikes at the very heart of all that you stand for or have ever stood for. It is a judgement upon you that you are deemed capable of . . .

It struck me like a physical blow, a bullet to the heart, staggering me back, stunned, 'Did I miss a word there? Like the word "not" perhaps?' People screaming, wailing, crying, fainting in the court all around me. No then, I hadn't misheard it! This was for real, but how? How was it possible? How could it be? How could they?

Nothing else mattered, the sentence was passed in a haze. What the fuck did it matter? Life or death, it was irrelevant. For no greater sentence could possibly be passed than this 'Guilty' verdict. Everything else was just humdrum garbage. 'Life, recommended twenty years.' So is that it? Is that all? It was nothing compared to the utterance of that word 'Guilty'. I felt violated to the deepest recesses of my soul. Soiled, fouled, abused, no one word could describe this deepest of violations to the person and nothing on this earth could have hurt me more than the utterance of that single word. It seemed that the whole world had gone topsy-turvy, upside down, back to front, inside out. I'm on the outside looking in. Outside this world I've known. Somewhere beyond it now. They have violated me to the very essence of my being, soiled my very soul. They have thrown enough shit that some has stuck, enough to stitch me up. They have played out their stupid games to their ends and have crucified me in their lies . . .

The storms and turmoil rising, raging throughout my entire being as I clung desperately to a fragment of self-control. I stood there, so they say, appearing proud and apparently undaunted, while shock waves of horror shook me to the very foundations of my soul.

'Plea of mitigation,' someone said.

'Fuck your mitigation, I never did this crime and that's all I have to say.'

As the shock waves churned into fury and the pain in my heart burned like a flame of righteous outrage, inside I screamed. I screamed a wail of mourning for life and for justice lost. I screamed a silent scream in outrage from somewhere through and beyond me. Yet still, they say . . . I stood proud, apparently undaunted. No! I stood in defiant outrage against the evil of their corruption and against the darkness into which I am cast.

'And what of the Doyle Family? Ya bastards! What justice for them?'

Downstairs in the dungeons below, twenty years was nothing. It meant nothing. An irrelevance. The bastards who did this deserve more. I'd have given more so was this supposed to be some kind of bone of contention? Was I supposed to feel less violated that I was only given twenty years? Well fuck your twenty years. It means nothing in comparison with that single word GUILTY and two thousand years could not compare with the dire devastation that word wrought upon my soul.

I stand outside your world now. That world which I had once known. I stand beyond and somehow outwith. I am the stranger looking in at the window, the traveller you have cast out to die in the snow. And I think to myself . . . if this is the measure of justice in the society of your household, then I damn and defy the rule of your household as an abomination.

The outrage, which burns like the furies in my heart and soul, has never gone away, not abated. It is almost as if, by some miraculous process, I was touched or that I touched upon the spirit which rages like the flames of fury, and they rage for justice, driving me on and ever on for justice.

> If I ever thought that Jesus Christ
> would for one moment have thought it right
> that you keep me here in prison
> If I even thought that he might say
> you have the right of way . . .
> Then I'd curse him too as I curse you
> and care not for remission
> But I do not pursue the blood I'm due
> and Jesus is . . . Forgiven.

Black Maria

There is just no describing the devastation and no point in trying . . . Led back to prison in chains, convicted of the most heinous and horrendous of crimes, flash bulbs popping, bundled into a Black Maria, condemned as a mass murderer on the last draft to hell. This is a waking nightmare. Strangely, no screaming sirens any more? No wailing police cars or motorbike outriders escort anymore? I guess that there wouldn't be much point to that farce. No point to that expense now. Such dirty tactics had served their intended purpose while we were yet still only accused, there would be no expense spared to help create the impression for the jury, Press and public perceptions that herein are dangerous and desperate men. Now that we were convicted, no need any more for such dramatic illusions. Now we were just another bunch of sorry lags in a Black Maria on our way back to the nick to sup our porridge and repent. Devastation. Sighing in the shadow of the gallows.

'This is going to take fuckin MONTHS to get sorted out,' I crib irately. They all glance at me with brief and sorry smiles. Months and months in that rotten stinking jail before the appeal could get this madness sorted out and send us home – was my thought. I just couldn't get it into my head that I was convicted of the fire murders and what public perception that would necessarily entail. Shock I suppose. I just couldn't figure out how it had happened. Couldn't quite figure out what exactly it was that I was supposed to have done.

The fire murders, sure enough, but in what capacity? I knew that the charge read that I was supposed to have been there at the time and on the scene with Tam Gray, Gary Moore, Joe Granger and Joe Steele but Tamby, Gary and Granger were acquitted and the judge accepted that neither I or Joe Steele were near or at the scene of the crime at the time it was committed. There was, in fact, no evidence to the charge as alleged on indictment. The prosecution had conceded to Joe's alibi and accepted my own on cross examination agreeing that I'd been at home but then alleging that I must have got someone else to do it. Yet this was only the Advocate Depute's accusation based on old Foxy's evidence against Joe. It was not evidence against me and not what I had been charged with. Surely the jury hadn't believed Foxy? And I thought that the prosecution still had a duty to bring evidence as to my presence at the scene of the crime and to refute an alibi before the charge could be held as proven? Unless, I was convicted of a charge I wasn't accused of? How is that possible? How could that happen? It was like being wrong footed. Tricked into defending myself on one charge while in fact convicting me of another charge in a completely different capacity not alleged on the indictment?

So, whatever happened then to the presumption of innocence? Are not accused persons supposed to have prior notice of what it is exactly that they are accused of having done? Otherwise how could they be expected to know how and where to defend themselves? Only the innocent could be deceived into defending themselves in the wrong area and that is exactly what had happened here.

It may seem strange to say now, but at the time I couldn't figure out just what exactly it was that I was supposed to have done or in what capacity I was supposed to have done it. Or on what evidence I was convicted. It took some time to finally figure out that I was convicted of having put Joe Steele up to it. Even though there was no evidence of that nor that Joe had done any such thing. Nor of Thomas Lafferty as per the first accusation. Nor with Tamby, Gary or Granger as per the second accusation. Nor with Joe as per the third. But now, on the evidence of Foxy, to have been at home at the time while Joe did the damage by himself? How could that be? Besides being a lie, Foxy had never even alleged that Joe had uttered one word or given any indication that he had even heard Gary in a crowded bar room. How could I then be convicted of this when it is not even legitimate evidence against me? How, therefore, could I be convicted on the strength of Love's alleged overheard conversation in yet another pub? It seemed inconceivable, unbelievable, impossible that I could now be sitting in this Black Maria condemned in history as a mass murderer based on this evidence. This was not the Dark Ages. This was 1984 and I was entitled to expect more and better from our modern justice system.

Even the alleged corroboration was pure and utter garbage. Polis verbal.

'The fire at Fatboy's was only meant to be a frightener which went too far,' is not a confession of anything. At best, it was an expression of popular public perception at the time. Even the polis had expressed this publicly to the Press and before I was ever even questioned, never mind arrested.

The map with a ring around the words 'Bankend Street' besides being planted, at best, could have been ringed after the event and was, or should have been, discredited by Hamilton's evidence in the Shafted incident. It should have been discredited by the very fact that Charge 13, assault on Andrew Doyle at his close, even existed. For it was alleged against us as having occurred before the fire, in which case, why would anyone ever have needed a map when, according to the prosecution case, we'd already been there on that instance?

It all comes down to Foxy against Joe and Love against me and God only knows how anybody could have believed either of them. In fact, I don't believe that they did. I believe that it was simply a case that we were the only ones left still accused and there was no other theory put forward as to who else it could have been. The only option then for the jury was Guilty. Like DS Forsyth had said, 'All we have to do is charge you, prejudice will do the rest.' There was just no way that we were walking out that door with no convictions whatever on the fire murders. Someone had to go down for it and guess who's het? Donald Findlay QC was later quoted as saying, 'We were left with the impression that the Almighty himself could not have walked out that door with an acquittal, the prejudice against the accused was so great.' My own counsel, Donald MacAulay QC, is quoted as commenting, 'There is something rotten at the very core of this investigation, it stinks.' Obviously then, this was an irrational, emotional reaction by the jury and it would all soon be sorted out by the cool heads, objective and impartial reasoning of the appeal court in the next few months. In fact it would take just a little longer.

Sitting in that Black Maria in the shadow of the gallows, these thoughts were not exactly rational or logically laid out in reasonable order but chaotic, ricocheting echoes rebounding in confusion. Echoes of the Emperor's new clothes with a twist. There were twin perceptions of reality in simultaneous existence. Myself entrapped in the aura of what I knew to be true, whilst popular misconceptions had me exposed naked in the glare of the verdict. The feeling is like that of being trapped inside a glass bubble looking out. You may scream but no one can hear you. Your world, your perception, your environment, isolated and divided. Other than that beyond the invisible wall, you know one reality whilst the world believes another – the Press and Media having a field day with sensational tales of gangsterism, drug barons and the Emperor of Carntyne's struggle for control over the Lords of the Underworld. Insane sensationalism in journalistic celebration of the liberation of the written word. The creation and foundation of the establishment of alternative realities. It seemed that our convictions now allowed anyone with a pen the freedom to express whatever fantasy took their fancy in our case. You cannot defame the already ultimately defamed. Ah! but gie's a break Jimmy, we still have our appeals to go up for.

The Black Maria rumbled on through the city I had known so well. Through Geordie Street, Duke Street, Carntyne Road. A tour of my life on to the pits of hell – Barlinnie. They housed me next door to the old death cell. They tested its mechanism every Wednesday. I could hear the trapdoor fall and the sandbag strike against my wall. Alternative realities? Fuck you Jimmy, I know the truth.

In the Shadow
of the Gallows

From the shadow of the gallows I start again. My lawyer at the time, Bob McCormack, told me that I'd been refused Legal Aid for appeal. I'd never been in an appeal court in my life and didn't have a clue where to begin or what to expect. I could order one of the two law books from the prison library but had no choice of which one I got. Take what you get and be thankful you get anything at all was Governor Slasher Gallagher's attitude. Both books were out of date, in tatters and with pages missing. Procedures had long moved on since their publication. We could only view one book overnight after a two-week waiting list. Christ, this was not going to be as straightforward as I'd at first imagined. The system was geared at every step, from top to bottom, against anyone with the audacity to dissent. Right from the cell doorstep you are up against it. What a struggle and what a fuss it caused when I was forced to fight for and won the right to access to my own law books. This had never been heard of before and it was taken as an outright affront within the establishment that a prisoner had access to the rules of law. What would they expect next? The Holy Bible? Yet what a breakthrough it was at that. No wonder the authorities didn't want prisoners to have access before. These greedy bastards had been charging people cash for photocopying their grounds of appeal and for sending them to the court, for example, while the prison governor had a duty in law to ensure that the court received three copies. It was the prison's cost and duty not the prisoners'. For the first time a prisoner was aware of his rights as an appellant and law books were flooding into the jail as the hottest hits since The Carpetbaggers and the prison authorities were none too pleased at all at the foundation of a new culture beyond their control. Appellants' rights.

John Carroll, Joe Granger's solicitor, came to see me for a statement for Granger's forthcoming trial. From there he became the only source and guide I had through the labyrinths of the law in relation to the issues in this case. From my point of view, he had the qualities I needed to fight for justice in this case – honesty and integrity. The fact that he also happened to be a great lawyer was just an added bonus. Thus, without Legal Aid and without a fee, John Carroll took up the case to help me prepare myself for the appeal court. I will not waste time on the details. Let's just go right to it.
16th May 1985

EDINBURGH HIGH COURT OF APPEAL

HIGH COURT OF JUSTICIARY

TRANSCRIPT OF PROCEEDINGS

IN

NOTE OF APPEAL AGAINST

CONVICTION

BY

THOMAS CAMPBELL, Appellant

in causa

HER MAJESTY'S ADVOCATE

against

THE SAID THOMAS CAMPBELL

High Court of Appeal 16 May 1985

Lord Wheatley	Your name is Thomas Campbell?
T. Campbell	Yes.
Lord Wheatley	You appeal against conviction on both charges is that correct?
T. Campbell	Yes I . . . Could I have these handcuffs removed please I . . .
Lord Wheatley	No you can't. Well what are your grounds for appeal? What do you have to say?
T. Campbell	I have . . .
Lord Wheatley	We have a great pile of papers here, we cannot go into all that, now what exactly is your grounds? Briefly.
T. Campbell	I have . . .
Lord Wheatley	What about this? It's your update hearing grounds for appeal. Do you have a copy of this?
T. Campbell	Yes I . . .
Lord Hunter	What about this omission of the presumption of innocence? What about that?
Lord Wheatley	Let's deal with that then, read that.
T. Campbell	But I . . .
Lord Hunter	What about page 6? Can you read? Read page 6, read it out.
Lord Wheatley	Can you explain what you mean by that?
T. Campbell	This is not what I wanted to do, I have . . .
Lord Wheatley	Well what about this then? It's headed 'Grounds for appeal against Lord Cameron's decision to refuse interim liberation'. Do you have that? Read that then but . . .
T. Campbell	That's . . . What you have there is this file. There is over six hundred pages here, I have prepared a summary if I could just read . . .
Lord Hunter	Do you have a copy of the judge's charge to the jury?
T. Campbell	Yes I . . .

Lord Hunter	Read page 6, how is there an omission of the presumption of innocence?
T. Campbell	I . . .
Lord Hunter	That's ridiculous, read page 6, read it out and let us hear it.
T. Campbell	This is a direction on the presumption of innocence.
Lord Hunter	I know what it is, read it out to the court.
T. Campbell	'Put aside also any feelings of sympathy which you must undoubtedly have for the surviving members of the Doyle family. When I say you have to decide the case on the evidence, you pay no attention to anything which you may happen to have read in the newspapers; nor do you pay any attention to what you may have seen or heard on television; nor do you take into account any previous knowledge which any of you may have had of the events or of the persons who gave evidence before you. You judge on the evidence and on the evidence alone. Now the first direction in law which I have to give you is one which has been repeated on many occasions, and have had it in this court before. This is that the onus of proof of the charges against each accused is on the Crown and remains on the Crown throughout. The accused are presumed to be innocent, and they must be proved to be guilty before they can be convicted. They do not have to prove anything in order to be acquitted. An accused person in these courts is entitled to remain silent throughout and to submit at the end of the day that the Crown has failed to prove his guilt. That is a legitimate defence open to any accused in these courts.'
Lord Hunter	Well, what do you have to say about that?

T. Campbell	Well okay. I refer you to pages 52E, 54B, 55AC, 56DF, 58DF, 59AB, 64C, 66D, 67EF, 68D, 72C, 95B, 96DE, 97AE, 98AE, 104E to 105AB. These are all directions that regard either attempted murder or assault, murder or culpable homicide . . .
Lord Wheatley	Yes? Yes?
T Campbell	Thus it is my submission that the judge has not properly directed the jury that I deny the charges libelled or any charge and, may have misled the jury on a hypothesis which in effect asserts the issue to be that of murder or culpable homicide, attempted murder or assault; superseding any other issue. I do not know if this is the correct terms, but I am sure, my Lord, that the point I am making is obvious and apparent.
Lord Wheatley	Yes . . .
T. Campbell	It regards the first of my grounds for appeal under sub A. 'Although his Lordship has directed the jury on the existence of the three verdicts that remain open to the charges that remain on the indictment – page 104 – he has, however, continued in that instruction to misdirect the jury, trespass on the jury's province, by his direction to the jury on which of these verdicts they were to hold in regard to Charges 9 and 15.'
Lord Wheatley	Yes?
T. Campbell	In furtherance of my point I refer you to page 22, top of the page of the judge's report. His Lordship says that the passage referred to here could not be construed as a direction to find any accused guilty. However, if you read my point again you will note that I make no reference to any particular verdict. Thus his Lordship has anticipated my point . . .

Lord Hunter	How can you say that he doesn't direct the jury that you deny the charges? Look at page 83DE, 'Now Mr Campbell, Thomas Campbell, denies all this. He never said all these things to the police, according to him, he said that he has an alibi for this particular night, he was at home.'
T. Campbell	That's a denial of the evidence. I refer you to page 71, 'Now, all three of these accused put forward alibis and they impeach Mr Love. Of course, the Crown do not say that Thomas Campbell was there, or Thomas Lafferty; they say they were guilty because they were taking part in a plan, a common plan, so the question of alibi does not come into it in relation to these accused.' This, in effect, renders my alibi totally irrelevant.
Lord Hunter	Page 101, 'If after considering all the evidence you find yourself still in a reasonable doubt as to Thomas Campbell's guilt, then you would give him the benefit of that doubt.'
T. Campbell	Yes and find me guilty of culpable homicide instead. Sorry! Page 104 and 105, 'Now, on Charge 9 if you do not hold that it was attempted murder then you will say so in your verdict and say so whether it was assault to or not to endanger life ... So far as Charge 15 is concerned, if you do not say murder has been proved, you will indicate that in your verdict by returning a verdict of culpable homicide.' That, sir, leaves no option beyond the nature of guilt.
Lord Wheatley	'Assuming you hold proved that the fire was caused wilfully.' You understand Mr Campbell that the judge must define the alternative charges?
T. Campbell	Yes sir, but whether the fire was caused wilfully or not was not the issue. The issue was as to whom. Who did it? Page 97C, 'Whatever you hold, it

	will be wilful fire-raising.' I don't know how that is but . . .
Lord Wheatley	But it is meant in the context . . .
T. Campbell	Yes, but it goes on to say that 'it is not disputed, that it is a matter of admission that the fire was wilful' and that is correct. It is not for me to dispute. The issue is who. Look at page 68. This is important.
Lord Wheatley	Yes?
T. Campbell	This is quite a lengthy direction. It goes on for what? Three pages?
Lord Wheatley	Yes.
T. Campbell	It regards an instance. It goes on about the choice of attempted murder or assault. His Lordship makes this direction no less than fifteen times. Attempted murder or assault to the danger of life. He finishes by saying, ' This is your choice, ladies and gentlemen, I hope you understand the directions I am giving you.' Page 104E to 105A, 'Now on Charge 9 if you hold that it was not attempted murder, you will say so in your verdict and say so whether it was assault to or not to danger life. So far as Charge 15 is concerned, if you do not say murder has been proved, you will indicate that in your verdict by returning a verdict of culpable homicide, assuming you hold proved that the fire was caused wilfully.'
Lord Hunter	In its context, Mr Campbell, it defines the charges.
T. Campbell	That's what I'm saying. It is out of context. In this context it leaves no option beyond the nature of the guilt. There is no need for that, especially after fifteen repetitions this was the last word.
Lord Wheatley	Okay, Mr Campbell.
T. Campbell	But this is not what I wanted to do. This was to be my last point. I wanted to read this first.

Lord Wheatley	What is that? Do we have a copy of it here?
T. Campbell	No, sir. It's a summary of my argument and . . .
Lord Wheatley	Do you have another copy?
T. Campbell	Yes I have a . . .
Lord Wheatley	Give it here, pass it to the clerk. (Debate on bench)
	CLERK RETURNS WITH COPY FOR ALL
Lord Wheatley	Is this all of your grounds, Mr Campbell?
T. Campbell	Everything here is on my grounds yes.
Lord Wheatley	Proceed then, Mr Campbell, but please speak slowly and clearly so that the shorthand . . . you asked for your hearing to be transcripted, he has got to catch it all you know. Would you rather sit down Mr Campbell? It looks rather uncomfortable.
T. Campbell	Well it is rather awkward.
Lord Wheatley	Proceed then.
T. Campbell	My appeal is against conviction in respect of Charges 9 and 15 of the indictment. It is my impression that all of the evidence which was led at the trial and, upon which conviction was based, is referred to in the judge's charge to the jury, judge's report.
	Dealing first with Charge 9 and taking the Crown's case at its highest, my submission is that there is insufficient evidence upon which to found conviction. If we work backwards from the statement to the police, namely, 'I only wanted the windaes shot out,' we then find that the only evidence which was submitted by the prosecutor as against me is the evidence of the witness Love. Love states that some time after the incident referred to in Charge 9 I thanked him for 'the message'. He was asked what his impression was of that comment and stated that he understood

it to be related to his driving a motor vehicle
to the scene of a shooting. Whilst this may
have been his impression, formed as a result
of what other people had told him, there was no
evidence from him to indicate that this is what
it was really about. He did give evidence that said
that I would see him 'all right'. Some time after
the shooting the Volvo motorcar which was used,
was recovered by the police in the possession
of another person. One fingerprint which was
identified as mine was taken from the inside front
passenger window. The Crown submitted that this
indicated that I had control of the vehicle and had
directed the operation. With respect, I challenge
the Crown to produce any authority or argument
in logic which would justify any reasonable jury,
properly charged, to reach that conclusion. I think
it is clear from the evidence in the case that I was
not in the vehicle at the time of the shooting. At
page 70B, the trial judge gave a direction in law
that comments alleged to have been made by me
to the police, namely, wanting the van windows
shot up, could act as corroboration of Love that
I was involved. This is a misdirection as Love's
evidence deals only with statements attributed to
me after the crime. Although my argument is
that such statements could not be regarded as
confessions, even if they were, they could find
no such corroboration by further confession in
different terms to another person. I think that
it is a grave misdirection in law and very likely
to have swayed the minds of the jury. There
was other evidence from the witness Reynolds
and this is dealt with at page 82 of the charge.
However, my recollection is that he did not

identify me as the man referred to in the conversation. He did identify me in connection with another incident but in his evidence, was unable to say that the person referred to in the earlier discussion about the car was, in fact, me. In any event, even if Gary Moore did owe me a car and Reynolds did offer to give Moore his car to give to me, it is quite clear that it is only Reynolds' understanding that the car taken from him was mine. It is significant to point out that there is only one fingerprint of mine found inside the car. If the car had been mine, it would be quite reasonable to infer that there would have been numerous such fingerprints. That was all the evidence against me relating to Charge 9.

In short, the confession alleged to have been made by me to the police, finds no corroboration by the comments allegedly made to Love. The fingerprint adds nothing beyond the fact that it appears that at some stage, one of my fingerprints touched the inside front passenger window. This is important because the evidence is quite clear that I was not there at the time the crime was committed. Reynolds' evidence adds nothing to this.

Turning now to charge 15. The judge's charge and report set out in detail all the evidence against me here. If I could again work backwards from the statement alleged to have been made to the police namely, 'The fire at Fatboy's was only meant to be a frightener which went too far.' It is my assertion that this statement is not a clear unequivocal confession. The statement is alleged to have been made a number of weeks after the fire and following upon extensive publicity. It

is also important to note, and this is not mentioned
in the judge's charge but in his report, that I was
spoken to by the police on a number of occasions
before that. In any event, the alleged statement is
not a clear unequivocal admission. If we go back to
Love's in which he refers to a conversation, several
weeks before the fire, at which I was alleged to
have been present and the topic of conversation
was alleged to have been setting fire to Fatboy's
door. My submission is, that this evidence provides
little or no assistance. First of all, the witness Love
was unable to state in evidence just who said what.
He was only able to state that this was a topic of
conversation. At no point in his evidence did he
say that I instigated the setting of a fire. Even
less does it indicate that I instigated a fire at the
door of a house in which people were living. It's
quite clear, according to Love's evidence, that he
was present during the alleged conversation but
that could not render him liable to accusation in
respect of this crime. When the police searched my
house on 12th May, 1984, several weeks after the
fire, they alleged that they found a map of Glasgow
and the area of Bankend Street was circled. In the
absence of evidence that I instigated any fire and
in the absence of a clear unequivocal admission,
the presence of a map is simply not sufficient
evidence; I am not at all sure what it is the
Crown say is of importance in the evidence of
Mrs Bruce. There can surely be nothing sinister
in a man visiting his sister. It may be that the
Crown was relying upon this to undermine my
alibi but even if the alibi were to be undermined
by Mrs Bruce's evidence, this would not provide
support for the Crown case.

If I could now deal with the charge.

I do not think that there is any need to repeat what I said earlier about the misdirection in respect of an accused person being corroborated by another statement of a person to another individual. You will recall that this criticism was made in respect of the judge's charge at page 70B.

On directing the jury on how they should go about considering the evidence of Love, the trial judge gave directions to assist the jury in dealing with the evidence of an accomplice at page 19E. I make no criticism of that direction so far as it goes. However, it is my submission that the value of this direction was wholly undermined by the judge at page 61C. I think that it is wrong that the trial judge should attach a stamp of credibility upon the witness Love in the way he did. He indicates in strong terms that Love has the Crown's stamp of credibility by virtue of the Crown accepting his evidence and allowing him out on bail and thereafter proffering him as a witness at this trial. It is not a question of whether Love is capable of, as the trial judge says, hoodwinking the police and the Crown with an utterly false and concocted story. I think that this part of the judge's charge completely undermines his earlier direction on how to deal with Love's evidence. It must be wholly wrong to state in such terms, or in any terms at all, that the Crown's credibility as an investigative body stands or falls by the credibility of Love in this trial. Neither do I think it is right that the police conspired, see page 63B. The police were involved in a detailed examination of Love and information

passed in the form of questions. Genuine and
honest questions could easily have been picked
up and incorporated in Love's statement by Love
himself. There may be other explanations but it
is unfairly prejudicial to me to ask the jury to
decide on the balance between the Crown and
the police as a body and me. Love seems no
longer to figure as a witness because he is now
so closely linked to the Crown's credibility as a
body. I think the issue should have been made
plain that the matter was between the evidence
of Love and the evidence for the defence.

Page 97 seems to be the essence of the judge's
charge so far as it relates to murder. He also deals
with culpable homicide, but at section E of page
97, the two become confused when the judge says,
'Even if it was intended originally as a frightener
and not intended to cause death, it would still be
murder as I have defined it.' It seems by that
statement that he has now taken away from the
jury the option of conviction on the lesser crime of
culpable homicide. However, my appeal is against
conviction on any charge. The judge does not
warn the jury that if they do not believe the
denial they could not infer the opposite was true.
This is very important in a trial where previous
statements are put to witnesses, as there may be
a strong tendency to prejudice in the minds of
the jury by substituting the statement denied for
the denial. I believe this is particularly important
in my case because a statement implicating me
in wilful fire-raising and murder was put to a
witness Joseph Granger at my trial. Joseph
Granger denied making the statement. Although

the trial judge said that there was no evidence
given by Granger which implicated me, I think
that a warning along the lines I have stated
should have been given. This is dealt with at
page 98F of the judge's charge. It is clear that
the Crown sought conviction on Charges 9 and
15 on the basis of statements attributed to me and
which they say are corroborated by other evidence referred to in dealing with Charge 9. The
verbal statement, 'I only wanted the van windaes
shot out' can clearly be taken as a confession to
one crime or another.

However, there are two charges on the indictment
involving the use of a shotgun. Charge 2 is one of
attempted robbery although I am not named in
this charge. The statement is alleged to have been
uttered many weeks after the crime libelled at 9 of
the indictment and, of course many weeks after
the crime libelled at Charge 2. From the evidence
concerning each of these charges, it is possible
that the statement, although it was denied by me,
could have referred to the events that gave rise to
Charge 2. I do not put this forward as a strong
point, but think that some mention should have
been made of it in the judge's charge. The jury
were entitled to take the view that the statement
related to Charge 9. In Hartley v Her Majesty's
Advocate referred to in Scots Law Times 1976
the court deals with statements by an accused
person to the police while a suspect. The case
also deals with corroboration. At page 29, about
half way down the first column, it commences,
'But that brings us to the second point in
the appeal: is there corroboration?' Reference

is made to a case Sinclair v Clark where it states, 'There is a rule in our law – a somewhat archaic rule, the merit of which under modern conditions is not always obvious, at all events where the admission is beyond suspicion – that an admission of guilt by an accused person is not conclusive against him unless it is corroborated by something beyond the actual admission.' From what I can see in Hartley's case, there was no dispute that a confession was made by Hartley. Hartley's confession was quite specific and related only to the crime with which he was charged. Reading the case, there was still a number of points required to corroborate that confession. The verbal confession attributed to me is, in my submission, not quite so specific.

I do not think that corroboration of the verbal confession attributed to me can be found evidence that shots were fired at the ice cream van. It could not be said that the confession contained information which could only have been known to me by virtue of being present at the time of the offence was committed. I do not think that the Crown or the judge addressed the jury on the basis of what had been referred to as 'special knowledge' confessions. It seems to have been accepted that a great many people knew of the fact that shots had been fired at a van at some time before and knew that an attempt had been made to rob people in a van several weeks before that.

I have now presented my argument which is based on the evidence led at my trial and the judge's charge. If, having considered my argument, the court is persuaded that my appeal is sound and is prepared to find in my favour then I have no more to say. However, if on the basis of my argument the court is not prepared to find in my favour, then I would ask for leave to lead additional evidence. The existence of this evidence was not known to me at the time of my trial. Its nature is such that I could not have discovered it at that time despite due diligence.

I have now received information that the witness William Love was previously charged with armed robbery which was alleged to have been committed over the weekend during which he says he overheard a conversation at which I was alleged to have been present when the question of setting fire to Fatboy's door was discussed. My information is that, at Love's trial, he lodged a special defence of alibi, stating that he was at home for the whole of that weekend and never left the house. At the moment I do not know if Love gave evidence in support of this but I do know that he was acquitted at his trial. If this evidence had been available to the jury at my trial, it might have had a considerable influence on the jury since it would indicated that Love could not have been present at any alleged discussion. Alternatively, it would have indicated to the jury that Love, if he has given evidence at his previous trial, must have committed perjury.

Other evidence I would wish to lead is that of a statement taken by Detective Sergeant Patterson at Easterhouse police office from Joseph Granger on 23rd April, 1984. In the statement, Joseph Granger says, 'I'll tell you again I know nothing about the fire and have never been in company when it was discussed.' It is clear from the statement, taken about a week after the fire, that the police were questioning Granger about a discussion in the Netherfield bar. The police indicated at my trial that the discussion referred to was first mentioned to them by the witness Love when he gave his statement in May. If this evidence had been available at my trial it may have persuaded the jury to conclude that the police officers were not credible in a material respect in connection with their interview. Joseph Granger was, subsequent to my trial, tried and convicted of perjury. The statement of 23rd April, which was in the hands of the police, was not readily produced by them in connection with the criminal proceedings against Joseph Granger. I am told that his solicitor asked for previous statements and this statement of 23rd April was only produced when Granger applied to the High Court for an order instructing the police to produce such statements.

Lord Wheatley	Do you have anything more to add?
T. Campbell	No . . . For now.
Advocate Depute (paraphrased)	The witness Love's evidence against Lafferty that Shadda had asked Love to do the message for TC was very strong evidence against Campbell and was corroborated and verified when Love told Campbell about his role in the shooting the next day when TC had thanked him and promised to square him up with cash. Campbell had as good as admitted it under cross-examination.

That Campbell was an associate of Love's who chauffeured him about from time to time . . .

That the fingerprint on the car was very important proof of ownership of the car. Together with the very important and damning evidence of Reynolds who spoke to having a conversation with Campbell in his house. Promising to replace his Volvo which was lost to the police after he had loaned it to do the shooting, Reynolds had promised Campbell that he would give him his car as a replacement. This together with the verbal confession to the police trying to lessen the degree of his complicity in the crime. The fact that pickaxe handles were found in Campbell's cellar together with masks. Campbell had been charged with assaulting Andrew Doyle and had as good as admitted it under cross-examination. Andrew Doyle's van had been smashed up. His sister's and his wife's own ice cream vans. Doyle was the principal competitor and a minder for Irene Mitchell who had been seriously assaulted in another attack. The jury were entitled to bring back a verdict of guilty.

On Charge 15 all this could be viewed as motive and malice. The fact that Campbell was found Guilty on Charge 9 could lend weight to the evidence on Charge 15. There was the map marking out the Doyles' house with a ring round it. Together with Love's evidence that Campbell and Gray just started talking about setting fire to the Doyle's house to give him a fright. He did not say which weekend it was, so the alleged new evidence there means nothing. It was an issue at the trial and the jury rejected it.

The statement of Granger's is irrelevant and a red herring. It was available at the time and means nothing. Mrs Bruce's evidence entitled the jury to hold that Campbell was an out and out liar. Then there was his confession to the police anticipating the murder charge and trying to lessen the degree of his guilt. Campbell had called sixteen police officers liars and claimed to be fitted up and planted with false evidence. Then there was the evidence of the Marchetti fire and a conspiracy to assault Mitchell with knives. The jury were entitled to return a verdict of Guilty.

High Court of Appeal 17 May 1985

T. Campbell	I would like to dispute with the Advocate Depute.
Lord Wheatley	What?
T. Campbell	Sir, I would like to dispute with the Advocate Depute.
Lord Wheatley	Mr Campbell, you've had your say. You've had your opportunity to speak. No you can't that is the procedure.
T. Campbell	But I would like to dispute with him.
Lord Wheatley	We have our procedure Mr Campbell.
T. Campbell	But I thought I would be allowed to dispute with the Advocate Depute?
Lord Wheatley	But you had your opportunity.
T. Campbell	But I thought I would be allowed to dispute with the Advocate Depute. If I could just for a moment . . . two minutes, just two minutes. What I have to say, it won't take long. The evidence is here right in front of you in the judge's charge . . .
Lord Wheatley	But Mr Campbell . . .
T. Campbell	The new evidence then. May I just go over the new evidence?
Lord Wheatley	Okay. Shortly then.
T. Campbell	Love did specify, quite specifically refer to the

Saturday before he was arrested on the Sunday. On examination by Mr Findlay he said specifically the Saturday before he was arrested on the Sunday. Love's alibi was that he never left his sister's house from the Friday before he was arrested on the Sunday . . .

Lord Wheatley   Mr Findlay?

T. Campbell   Yes quite specifically. It will be noted in the evidence and the statement by Detective Sergeant Patterson. I have a copy of it here, it's dated 23rd April 1984. If you would like to look at it. I sent copies. I'll just read it out. 'I first heard of the fire when I read it in the papers.' Page 4, 'I haven't heard anything about the fire from anybody else. I have been in the Netherfield bar, it's now called Scarpers, a couple of times over the past week but I haven't heard it mentioned.' Page 8, 'I'll tell you again, I know nothing about the fire and have never been in company when it was discussed. I didn't know any of the family that were involved in the fire and didn't know that one of them drove an ice cream van.'

You must understand that I am not saying that the police perverted justice, what I am saying is that this is what Love said, exactly Love's evidence before Love said it. All the information required is inherent in the questions as you can see here. William Love picked up on it and incorporated it into his statement in May.

Lord Wheatley   Yes, yes.

T. Campbell   In regard to the Advocate Depute's submissions of yesterday. Perhaps I could hear from the Advocate Depute just where exactly in the judge's charge or indeed in his notes, or in the evidence in

court, is there any reference at all to William Love
having informed me of the crime he had recently,
the day before, committed? Indeed I would submit
that there was and is no such evidence. I refer
you to page 76C of the judge's charge. There can
be seen the entirety of the admissible evidence
of Love. That evidence then, damning as it is,
submitted by the Advocate Depute. 'Later he saw
Thomas Campbell who thanked him and said
he would square up with him but didn't.' Sir, I
don't know about you, but where I come from,
to 'square up' with some one actually means to
'get even' as in the context of an eye for an eye.
But no, this is not the real point. Love's evidence
is totally irrelevant here. He said, 'sometime after'
the shooting he ran into me, and who knows how
long as Love couldn't say, and I thanked him
for 'the message'. When asked what he thought
I meant by that, he said he'd taken it to refer to the
shooting. However, I cannot be held responsible
for the state of Love's distempered mind in his
presumptions from information transmitted to
him by another – outwith my knowledge and
consent. And as far as the corroborating force of
Reynolds is concerned, I refer you to page 82.

I submit that this is the submission of the
Advocate Depute, Mr Bruce QC, who is not a
competent witness in this trial. I refer you to
page 25D of his Lordship's charge to the Jury,
again, mid-way, starting with the words 'Mr Love'.
'Mr Love in his evidence said that Moore wanted
to give my car to Thomas Campbell.' Though his
actual words were TC. 'Because TC's car got
taken off the road, that would not be evidence

against Thomas Campbell.' His Lordship makes the simple mistake in a trial of this length and complexity of confusing Love with Reynolds. That then is the entirety of Reynolds' evidence on that matter. Reynolds did not say that he heard any such conversation as described on page 82. He said he said he did not pass the door. He did not identify me as the man referred to on this occasion. I would draw your attention to the fact that there are two TCs charged with this crime. Thomas Clark Gray and where also on page 25 his Lordship cont . . .

Lord Wheatley   Ho! Now hold on Mr Campbell. That is quite enough. It was a long and tiring trial. The judge is an old man. Mistakes can be made on a trial of this length and complexity. It was for the jury to say, it was for the jury to remember . . .

T. Campbell   But . . .

Lord Wheatley   This is an English law you know, this going over the evidence is an English practice. The judge isn't even supposed to go over the evidence at all, except where the jury are likely to forget . . .

T. Campbell   But . . .

Lord Wheatley   Now that's enough! We have given you a few minutes against our normal procedure to go over your new evidence and to dispute it with the Advocate. You aren't supposed to dispute . . . we've been very generous with you, that's not procedure, that's the pitfall of opting to conduct your own case without counsel.

T. Campbell   Well, can I just dispute with the Advocate Depute about Mrs Bruce then? I have so much more to say. What the Depute was saying was just . . . It was just ridiculous.

Lord Wheatley   What for? (shrug)

T. Campbell	Because I know Mrs Bruce and Mrs Bruce knows me very well. All this . . . this stuff about the state of the light and the distances involved . . .
Lord Wheatley	Yes?
T. Campbell	That was not the issue. The issue was as to when, which day, that was the issue here . . .
Lord Wheatley	It was a long trial, Mr Campbell, as I explained it's an English practice, nothing to do with Scottish . . . (inaudible)
T. Campbell	But I still feel that if his Lordship is to raise an issue he should raise the proper issue. I have . . .
Lord Wheatley	Okay, Mr Campbell, that will do. I realise it's a long time out of your life but . . .
T. Campbell	But I . . .
Lord Wheatley	We have been very generous. Try to calm down, Mr Campbell . . .
T. Campbell	There is . . .
Lord Wheatley	You will receive a written answer, Mr Campbell. That's all now.
Agnes	Tell them about . . .
T. Campbell	What?
Agnes	. . . the statement.
T. Campbell	Can't hear you, Agnes. Hold on, don't pull, she's trying to say something..
Agnes	. . . COPY OF THE STATEMENT.
T. Campbell	What is it Agnes?
Agnes	Ask them if they want a copy of the statement.
T. Campbell	Aye! They've got a copy. Here! Who do you think your pullin, ya halfwit ye?

Still the Storm

Still the storm rages like the furies, roaring in righteous
outrage through my soul. I feel its force, like searing hot
sands blasting through flesh and bone to the very core of
my being and beyond. I am the storm. At one with the
wrath of Angels. Violated in the devil's dark lair.

Anger claps
Like a thing of thunder
In righteous outrage
Strove to hold
Soul wrought pain
In molten lava
Till the raging Vulco
Simmers cold.

So the steel within
Is now finely tempered
Who now will sing
Of knights of old?

Then let the fair play
Be for the fair
Truth and justice
Are not found here
Only the dead, naïve and innocent
Slain in corruption's
Darkest lair.

What say ye now
My noble soldiers
Who died upon the battles there?
What say ye now
Proud grieving mothers
Who gave their all
In love and care?

What say ye now
Who died for justice
Equality and all that's fair?
What say ye now
My Lords and Masters
Who wrought nowt but despair?
What say ye now
You evil bastards
Thy kingdom come
But soon I swear.

'Just put'm doon Tommy. Put'm doon, he disnae know any better,' Shadda was saying through the haze of my rage. I was holding the screw I was fettered to in the air with one hand shaking him like a rag doll. I had dragged him about by the manacles, throwing him back and forward across the corridors as he had dragged me in the court. See how he liked it.

'You ever, EVER treat me like that, treat anybody like that again, mister . . . Even a fuckin animal deserves better then that, ya fuckin halfwit ye.'

The screws were all over us, releasing him from my manacles and letting him drop to the floor and duck through the throng away from me. I was still ranting in my outrage but Shadda was right. It wasn't his fault. He was just another ignoramus taught to think it's okay to abuse and drag people about just because they're prisoners and in chains. He is just another product of disposable morality without any thought of his own. A guard dog, trained to obedience without question. My rage was not with him, but with his masters.

I'd thought my appeal would be fair. I'd expected that appeals were supposed to be fair. I'd thought that I would be allowed to debate and dispute the issues like they do in a court. I'd thought the judges would be objective and impartial. I'd expected the Advocate Depute to stick to the facts and the evidence. I'd expected a fair hearing. I supposed I would be entitled to expect these things just as most of us would but that is naïve and we would be deceived. There is no justice, no equality or fairness in a self-serving, self-selecting system concerned only with the appearance of justice. That it may be seen to be done regardless of whether it is actually done beyond the superficial appearance and illusion, or not.

A legal administration primarily concerned with the maintenance of its own credibility as an authority. Like the worshippers of Moloch, they sacrifice truth and justice along the road to power under the lame excuse that the end justifies the means for the greater good of the whole. They gorge greedily upon the fruits of the poison tree and anoint themselves as blessed for their efforts.

From the precept that 'All war is terrorism and all soldiers are terrorists' by the nature of the beast. Then the fact that one side or other wears one's team colours and is condoned by whatever church or government as a so-called just cause does not alter the fact that it is no less terrorism by its very nature. Condemned while in opposition but condoned at the slightest whim of convenience.

Such blatant double standards in authority have a profound effect upon the collective psyche of society, especially the young. For they advertise and advocate hypocrisy as an acceptable standard. Advocating that truth and morality are but disposable commodities, rather than universal standards to live and to die by. The application of such double standards is to advocate that fundamental principles are adjustable to whichever is most convenient at the time. Thus, that justice may be seen to be done in its superficial appearances, regardless of whether it is actually done or not. These are the acceptable standards of an administration fallen into Babylon and they shall reap what they sow.

> Where God hath given man taketh away
> In boundless arrogant vanity
> Lords temporal dare proclaim
> God's given law as their domain
>
> Even as the songbird sings
> They don the mantle of the kings
> In their ignorance so to presume
> Crusading armies to their doom
>
> Trodding on a blade of grass
> They do not wonder so to ask
> What miracle hath created thus?
> In arrogant ignorance crushed to dust.
>
> Dead as the doormat, dare to care,
> They murder the innocent and the fair
> An administrative mincing machine
> Lost humanity in between . . .

You know when you are being railroaded. It was obvious to me in the first seconds in court. I didn't need their answer to see that. The QCs who had watched the proceedings said that I'd done well but I didn't think so. I felt that I hadn't been allowed to get started. Once again, I felt degraded, violated and abused. It was difficult to still the storm.

Tamby the Bear's hearing lasted about three minutes. They gave him that cross questions treatment. A question from each judge, each with conflicting answers, no matter which judge you reply to, the other takes it as his answer. The Bear couldn't take it. He just stood there in silence and in tears. He is not like me. The heart of a gentle giant breaks in its pain whereas mine rages in defiance.

They shipped me out to Saughton prison digger, shanghaied without my law books. Then they shipped me back to the court, sirens screaming, stopping traffic and taking me straight into court for this . . . But at least I got my law books back. The Advocate Depute had blagged them and the court clerk got them back.

<u>Court reconvened after lunch</u>

Lord Wheatley	Mr Campbell.
T. Campbell	Yes.
Lord Wheatley	What we have here is what the court calls avi . . . Do you understand?
T. Campbell	Eh! . . . I eh, yes.
Lord Wheatley	Avizandum, Mr Campbell, you will hear from us. That's all.
Clerk	There is one other matter, your Lordship. Mr Campbell has applied for interim liberation.
Lord Wheatley	Do you wish to proceed with that application, Mr Campbell?
T. Campbell	Eh! . . . Well, yes.
Lord Wheatley	Is there anything you would like to say, anything at all?
T. Campbell	My grounds for interim liberation are my grounds for appeal before you.
Lord Wheatley	Yes, yes but is there anything you would like to add?
T. Campbell	Well just that there are problems at home that require my attention.

Lord Wheatley   We find no reason at this time to overturn Lord Cameron's decision to refuse interim liberation upon the grounds of previous convictions but don't worry, Mr Campbell, it won't be long now. Perhaps a week . . . Perhaps a week or two. You will appear here. It's not long is it?

Opinion

*There now follows a mental health warning as we revisit
the surrealistic labyrinths of this living nightmare, yet again,
with commentary. Some repetition of the facts and issues are
inevitable. However, this endeavour is to clarify and inform.
Not entertain. This is my life.*

We were all taken back to court a few weeks later. I
was happy to be getting on with it. Believing that this
would be another stage in the due process that, due to
the conflicting positions as to the actual evidence, the
court would have to call for the production of transcripts
to discern the facts for themselves before the appeal
could proceed. I was still naïve and still expected that
there would be some concern for the interests of justice,
especially at this level.

The opinion of the court was mumbled. No one would
look at me. I knew then that there was something wrong.
I strained to hear what was being said but what little I
could hear didn't make any sense and I thought that I
couldn't be hearing it right – something about the Bear
having, 'the same solicitor as Love'. I mind the Crown
advocate saying something like that but it was simply not
true and I had no idea why it was mentioned here. The
whole thing was just a mumble. Later it struck me that
maybe I wasn't supposed to hear it in case I objected,
corrected or put up some dispute which I would've done
if I'd known what was happening.

Finally, I heard the word 'Dismissed'. There was no
mistake about that except that I didn't know in what
context it was intended. Was I dismissed from the court?
Free to go? Were the charges dismissed? The conviction
or what? I could only wait to see if the manacles would be

removed. They weren't – I was led away still in chains and in confusion. It hadn't sunk in yet that this had been a final judgement and not just another hearing. There would be no further enquiry. No more decisions, discussion or argument. No appeal. Full stop. End of story. Just go away now and accept whatever crap is handed down to you by your superiors.

It finally dawned on me when I saw Tamby's tears. My reaction was predictable. 'Aye that wull be fuckin right!' Do they really think that this is an end to it? That I am just going to walk away and accept this crap as justice? Do they really think that they may just decree and their word becomes law? That by some position of privilege that their pronouncements define the truth? They may be lords but they are lords temporal and they are not my lords. I dissent and I admit to contempt of any court that behaves in this manner. For in the light of reality this is not justice. This is not even an attempt at justice. This is a pretext, an attempt at the creation of a false illusion. A deception by the highest law lords in the land. Beyond perversion. The incestuous rape of justice by those grandiosely set as guardians of her purity.

I was shanghaied to Peterhead sol con dungeons and it was another few weeks before the written opinion came through the post. Only then could I see just exactly how wrong they had been. They had taken the Crown advocate's word for everything. I got that much right at least.

EDINBURGH HIGH COURT OF APPEAL

HIGH COURT OF JUSTICIARY

OPINION OF THE COURT

in

NOTE OF APPEAL AGAINST

CONVICTION

by

THOMAS CAMPBELL, Appellant

in causa

HER MAJESTY'S ADVOCATE

against

THE SAID THOMAS CAMPBELL

By unanimous verdicts the appellant was found guilty of Charges 9 and 15 in the indictment, and now appeals against these convictions.

The appellant decided to conduct his own appeal and, in preparation thereof, he compiled stacks of notes in which submissions, arguments and references to authorities were inter-mixed with what appeared to be grounds of appeal in the form of grievances and complaints. He had, however, attached to his Note of Appeal which bears the date stamp 14th January, 1985 a manuscript document headed 'Grounds for Appeal', and, while some of these are repetitious, and some are either irrelevant or lacking in specification, they at least constitute a basis on which the appeal can proceed, as it might have been difficult to have accepted these other effusions as grounds of appeal. Even with these 'Grounds for Appeal' it might have been difficult to obtain from the appellant coherent verbal submissions on the points which he wished to argue, but with commendable consideration for the Court the appellant had prepared what he described as a 'Summary of his Grounds of Appeal'. When he was called upon to make his submissions in support of his 'Grounds of Appeal' the appellant stated that they were all included in the said Summary and asked the Court's leave simply to read that document to the Court. Such leave was granted and he read the document to the Court. When he had done so he was asked if he wished to add anything to what he had already submitted and he replied in the negative. The learned Advocate Depute replied, and the appellant then sought leave to answer some of the points made by the Advocate Depute. Although this further speech is contrary to normal procedure in criminal appeals, we granted the appellant the indulgence.

The Advocate Depute stated that he proposed to deal first of all with the issue whether there was sufficient evidence in law to justify the respective two charges, since, if there was an affirmative to that, the answers to other issues became much simpler of resolution. We entirely agree with that approach, which is in harmony with the appellant's own approach in his Summary.

Note: This simply means that, taking the Crown prosecution's case and argument at best, if there is technical sufficiency of evidence in law, in their opinion, to convict then all else is out of the window thus allowing them to sidestep and ignore the 'omission of the presumption of innocence' part.

So far as Charge 9 is concerned, the Advocate Depute pointed to the following evidence, which, he said was sufficient to warrant a conviction if believed by the jury, as it clearly must have been. (1) Love deponed that he was asked by Lafferty to do 'the message' for 'TC', Lafferty gave Love £30 and said that 'TC' would square up with him (Love) once things quietened down. The appellant admitted in evidence that he became aware of the shooting on the following day (he said that he assumed that it was a grudge against the driver).

Note: Besides the fact that it was in the newspapers the following day, this is Love's verbal against Lafferty and it is inadmissible hearsay evidence against me. Why is it listed in the evidence in support of the case against me?

According to Love, when the appellant later saw Love he thanked him for 'the message' and said that he would square up with him later, which Love said he never did.

Note: Love never said how long later and only that he 'assumed' that I was supposed to be referring to the shooting. Am I to be held responsible for the state of Love's distempered mind as a result of information allegedly transmitted to him by another outwith my presence, knowledge or consent? Am I responsible for what he thinks and assumes?

(2) There was a thumb-print found in the Volvo car used in the attack. It belonged to the appellant and was found inside the front passenger door on the side of the window frame. The appellant in evidence gave an explanation of how it could have been there as a result of him having been driven home by Love on a previous occasion, but this was not put to Love during his cross-examination.

Note: This was also the Advocate Depute's submission but it is simply not true. The transcripts now show that it was put to Love.

In any event, the jury were entitled not to accept but to reject the appellant's evidence thereon. (3) There was police evidence that when the appellant was charged <u>inter alia</u> with Charge 9 he said under caution 'I only wanted the van windaes shot up'. In addition, said the Advocate Depute, the appellant had a motive for the offence. This was that the appellant was involved in the ice cream van scene both directly and indirectly. His wife and two sisters (one of whom was Mrs Lafferty) operated ice cream vans.

Note: Neither of my sisters or my wife were charged with any offences. My sister Agnes' husband, Shadda Lafferty, was acquitted of all charges related to alleged ice cream wars with the exception of this charge. Motive could only be inferred if those charges had been proven.

In our opinion the Advocate Depute was well founded in his submission that on this evidence there was sufficient to warrant the jury's verdict on Charge 9. Although most of this evidence was disputed, it was open to the jury to accept it and proceed upon it while rejecting the witnesses who disputed it.

Turning to Charge 15, the evidence on which the Advocate Depute relied to support the jury's verdict was as follows. (1) Love gave evidence to the effect that on a Friday or Saturday towards the middle or end of March 1984 he overheard the appellant and his co-accused Gray and others talking in a public house, during which there was talk about 'setting the Fat Boy's (Doyle's) door on fire to give him a fright'. Love thought that this related to the Fat Boy's competition in the ice cream van business in the Garthamlock area. (2) Police officers gave evidence to the effect that after caution and charge in relation to charge 9 the appellant said: 'I only wanted the van windaes shot up. The fire at Fat Boy's was only meant to be a frightener which went too far'. At that time the fire at Doyle's house had not been mentioned.

Note: Why was it not enquired as to why this second part of the police verbal evidence was never put to me on the first judicial examination on 16th May? Was it intended to be kept as a surprise to me on the second judicial of the 22nd? Who was supposed to have said it? According to this, there was no more evidence against me on the 22nd when I was charged than there was on the 12th upon my arrest.

(3) The police found in the appellant's house a map of the Garthamlock area with Doyles' house circled in blue. Moreover, the motive referred to previously in relation to Charge 9 was present in Charge 15 as well.

Note: See no reference is made to the Crown evidence of Hamilton and the planting of the shafts. This was Crown evidence from a Crown prosecution witness but it would render this evidence of the map, planted at the same time by the police, as discredited evidence. It was the words 'Bankend Street' circled in blue, not the house.

Although here again the Crown evidence was strongly disputed and an alibi was spoken to, the jury were entitled to reject the defence evidence and proceed on the evidence above narrated and so to convict. Once again we hold that the Crown's submission is well founded.

In the light of the foregoing we turn to consider the points raised in the appellant's Summary of the evidence. Our finding that there was evidence to warrant the convictions on Charges 9 and 15, and what that evidence was, provides the answer to many of these points. Despite the judge's clear directions on the subject, the appellant seems to think that defence evidence which contradicts or modifies the Crown evidence has to be accepted and given effect to, and this underlies many of his arguments and much of his thinking.

Note: I was entitled to think that my alibi was relevant and more especially as there was no evidence to the contrary. I did not expect that my alibi could legitimately be disregarded by the trial judge in support of the change in the nature of the charge by the Crown's acceptance that 'Well, perhaps you weren't there (at the scene of the crime) but you must have got someone else to do it then. Didn't you, Campbell.' This reverts back to the point made on the 'omission of the presumption of innocence'.

This opinion simply presumes that all the Crown evidence is valid and that the defence evidence is not. Yet Granger, Hamilton, Reynolds and the others were Crown witnesses not defence.

He asserts that the judge omitted to direct the jury on the presumption of innocence, and in doing so he chooses to ignore the clear direction given at page 6 of the judge's charge.

Note: I never asserted that the judge omitted to direct the jury on the presumption of innocence. I asserted that his directions omitted the presumption of innocence by leaving the jury no option beyond the nature of guilt. There is a clear difference that the court chooses to ignore and, in doing so, deliberately misses the point, using semantics to twist it out of context thus avoiding the issues presented in the run up to my Summary. 'It might have been difficult to obtain from the appellant coherent verbal submission on the points he wished to argue.' Allowing the excuse to ignore those points as if they were never raised.

He maintains that the judge at p 51C unfairly put the stamp of credibility on the evidence of Love who was such a damaging witness for the Crown. No such thing was done in the passage referred to in the judge's charge at p 51C. All that was said there was that evidence of what the co-accused Steele said on a certain matter would (if accepted) provide corroboration in law of Love's evidence. The judge was not dealing there with credibility only with corroboration.

Note: Once again, it appears that the court would prefer to sidestep the issues rather than address them. They address themselves to page 51C when the point was clearly referring to page 61C. Even if they could not understand me they still had the printed copy of my summary before them.

The appellant then submits that at page 97 of his charge the judge took culpable homicide away from the jury in Charge 15. What the judge did was to direct the jury on the conditions to be satisfied before a verdict of murder could be returned and the conditions which had to be satisfied before a verdict of culpable homicide could be returned. In that connection he very properly pointed out, as appears from the context of the charge as a whole at that point, that if the fire was started deliberately and the circumstances indicated that those who started the fire did so with an utter disregard of the consequences and death resulted it would be murder and not culpable homicide. He did this just after he had explained what would be culpable homicide and not murder. There is clearly no point [to be made] in this.

Note: Once again omitting to follow through with the second part of the point regarding page 105. 'If you do not say that murder is proven you will indicate that in your verdict by returning a verdict of culpable homicide.' But, of course, according to this opinion that argument did not occur.

The next point taken is that the judge misdirected the jury in that he did not warn them that if they did not believe a witness's denial of a point of evidence put to him they were not entitled to infer that the opposite was true. That was said in the context of and under reference to a denial made by the witness Granger that he had made a statement to the police implicating the appellant in the murder charge, No. 15. It was also said in relation to the evidence of the witness Reynolds. What the judge said at page 98 et sequitur of his charge was this. 'His (Granger's) evidence does not assist you at all, whatever you may think of his credibility. He did not give any evidence which implicated Steele or Thomas Campbell. The same applies to Reynolds. Whatever you may think of Reynolds' evidence, none was given by him upon which you could find in support of the Crown allegation against Thomas Campbell and Joseph Steele.' To suggest, in face of such clear directions that nothing could be taken out of the evidence of these witnesses to implicate the appellant, that a further direction in the terms desiderated was necessary to make the point clear to the jury reeks more of an insult to their intelligence than a requirement for their proper guidance. We reject this complaint out of hand.

Note: Still, the trial judge refers to their evidence given in court and does not tell the jury that the statements made to the police were not legally evidence against us either. The jury would not know this and would not know the law on that matter. There was a requirement for the judge to direct them on the law in that respect. Just because it is obvious to the appeal court judges implies that anyone else who does not know it must be stupid.

The next point taken by the appellant was, in relation to Charge 9, that the statement attributed to him by the police (which he denied) that he 'only wanted the windaes shot up' could possibly have related to Charge 2. There was no shooting libelled in Charge 2, which in any event was not laid against the appellant. This was just a nonsense.

The final matter raised by the appellant was that there was new evidence which he sought the leave of the Court to introduce. Before considering the merits of such a motion the Court has to be satisfied that the new evidence was evidence which was not known to the appellant, nor could it have been known to the appellant or his advisers, at the time of the trial. The first line of the new evidence was said to relate to proving that the witness Love had tabled a plea of alibi in a trial in which he was an accused, which, if established, would have placed him at home over the whole of the week-end during which, he had stated in evidence at this trial, he had overheard the appellant, Gray and others discussing in a public house the proposal to set fire to the Fat Boy's house. This, it was said, was crucial to the question of Love's credibility, and Love's evidence was crucial to the Crown's case. No proposed precognitions to support these contentions were produced, the allegations being simply prefaced by the words 'It is understood'. But, perhaps more crucially, the Advocate Depute (who had conducted the prosecution at the trial) pointed out that the witness Love had not been specific, nor could be specific, in his evidence on the actual week-end in March 1984 when the conversation about which he was testifying took place. He started off by saying that it was the 19th or 20th of March or something and then went on to say, when asked, what day of the week it was, that it was towards the end of the week, a Friday or a Saturday (which could have been 23rd or

24th). Moreover, Love's trial had taken place before the present trial, and at the present trial the same solicitor acted for both the appellant and his co-accused Gray. Counsel for Gray had closely cross-examined Love on this point of date but Love remained imprecise. In that situation there was no purpose in the alleged new evidence. It was said that, in any event, the information was clearly available and could have been adduced at the trial. In all the circumstances we are not satisfied that a case had been made out for allowing the new evidence, and we so hold.

Finally the appellant has raised as another ground of 'new evidence' the subject of a statement taken from the witness Granger by Detective Sergeant Patterson. In that connection reference is made by the appellant to a 'discussion' which is so vague and unspecific that it is impossible for us to understand what he is talking about. In any event there is nothing to indicate that this matter could not have been raised at the trial. We also refuse to allow this alleged new evidence to be received. In the result we dismiss the appeal on all points.

Wheatley

There is no way I could provide a precognition of Love from a prison cell while refused Legal Aid. If I had gone within a mile of him I would've been charged with that too. It was for the Crown to disclose the terms of Love's alibi, not me. It was they who continued to refuse to disclose it, not me. For the fact of the matter is that Love was specific and did contradict his alibi. Here the court just accepts the Advocate Depute's word for it that the terms of the alibi were available and that Love was not specific. In fact, the terms of the alibi were a closely guarded secret and Love was specific as the transcripts later showed.

On the Granger point of fresh evidence, the statement was <u>not</u> in fact disclosed to the defence, contrary to the Advocate Depute's argument that it was. This issue and circumstances were clearly printed out in my summary right before them. The Crown had in fact denied the existence of the Granger statement of 23rd April, 1984 even after our trial. Here it is just a case of accepting the excuse not to look deeper and avoiding the controversy by accepting anything the Advocate Depute tells them.

So here was the Crown's Advocate Depute pulling every conceivable stroke in an attempt to sustain conviction, knowing well that access to the transcripts was refused and that without them there was no way anyone could disprove what was said. Reynolds was only one instance where I could do that by using the judge's charge to the jury. That evidence, as submitted against me by the Depute, was dismissed by the court. The case of Mrs Bruce or Degnan's evidence was another instance where the Crown case was founded upon lies other than what the witness' evidence actually was. Mrs Bruce had said that she had finally 'agreed' that the night she'd seen me in Garthamlock was the night Tommy Cooper had died on TV. Had in fact only agreed to that after the police had

pestered her about thirty times to say so. 'Are you sure
that it wasn't the night Tommy Cooper died?' and she
had finally agreed because she wasn't sure which night it
had been and didn't see that it had mattered anyway. Thus
her evidence was discredited and held no significance to
the prosecution case at all. Yet the Advocate Depute, in
absence of transcripts, ignored that significant flaw in
her evidence and used her in the appeal court to say
that she showed me out to be a liar. Nevertheless, the
court deletes her as evidence for the prosecution. Two of
the prosecution points have fallen.

The Advocate Depute had also submitted that I had
been accused of assaulting Andrew Doyle and had as good
as admitted it in my evidence in cross-examination. More
porky pies. This must have been one of the occasions
when I was cross-questioned by the Depute and the judge
simultaneously with conflicting answers,

Advocate Depute:	'Didn't you, Campbell?'
Judge:	'Well, do you deny it?'
Accused:	'Yes.'
Advocate Depute:	'So you admit it then.'
Accused:	'No.'
Judge:	'So you do not deny it then.'

And so on . . .
By the time I had given my evidence I had been acquitted
of all the charges the Depute was listing against me in the
context of having got 'someone else to have done it then'.
He had first tried to refute my alibi and, having failed, had
simply changed tactic and the nature of the charge libelled
by accepting that, 'Well, perhaps you weren't there, then,'
(at the scene of the crime at the time it was committed)
'but you must have got someone else to do it then, didn't
you, Campbell.' Listing those crimes of which I had been
acquitted, no case to answer. Including the assault on

Andrew Doyle and the Marchetti fire. Even although the evidence had shown that the assault was by local boys and the Marchetti fire was an inside insurance job. Now he was, once again, using the indictment itself against me, using the fact that I had been accused of these things as evidence of guilt on the charges which remained. This then became his alleged motive on Charges 9 and 15.

The Advocate Depute also went on about me being an associate of Love who was in the habit of chauffeuring me about. Where did that come from? He denied that Love had given me a lift home and that it had even been put to Love in cross-examination in refutal of my explanation of how the fingerprint may have got into that car. It seems he wanted to keep his cake and eat it too and the court indulged that privilege. In fact, the transcripts now show that it was put to Love. According to their case, then, Love was in the habit of chauffeuring me around but had never given me a lift and both of these points were accepted by the court.

Reynolds' evidence was that his conversation about a car was with Gary Moore and that he had not entered the house of the man they had gone to. It had been obvious to everyone that the man referred to was in relation to the hostage TV incident. The Depute knew that but also knew that without transcripts there was no way I could show that to be the case. Nevertheless, the court dismissed Reynolds' evidence as admissible despite the Depute's argument.

No Reply? (The Presumption of Innocence)

> Black Douglas bled in shackled chains
> In the dungeons of Castle Doon
> As Douglas strained against the chains
> He bled unto his doom.
>
> 'Oh Douglas! Douglas! noble knight,
> What have they done to thee,
> How come that ye no longer fight
> And struggle to be free?'
>
> But no answer came from he . . .

The presumption of innocence goes back a long way in our law, the common law of the people. Jesus Christ made no reply, for example, but they verballed him anyway. 'You said that, Pilate, not I.' The presumptuousness of the innocent then may stem from the fact that the allegation is beneath contempt. That the innocent need not qualify nor credit it with an answer, for they can only be accused by a lie.

High principles indeed but we are not all saints or Messiahs on the path to martyrdom, prepared to be crucified on the cross of injustice for our principles, that others may learn from and be redeemed by the errors of our past case precedents. Yet what have we learned in two thousand years of cruel injustice and mayhem? Nothing! From the warring crusaders and the perverse tortures of the Spanish inquisitions, till today's sectarian wars. In Christ's name! The man was a pacifist, in the presumptuousness of his innocence, died that we might learn from and be redeemed by the understanding of the error in our ways. Yet we still condemn people on the strength of alleged verbals which they deny and wash our hands of the consequences.

The caution before charge reads, 'You have a <u>Right</u> to remain silent but anything you do say may be taken down and used in evidence against you.' Notice that it says 'may be' taken down. For in fact, only incriminating utterances are admissible as evidence. Utterances of innocence are not and therefore are not noted. Nor does it caution you that even that which you don't say will also be taken down and used in evidence against you. Even if, after a dozen hours or so of formal interview under intense interrogation the accused has said nothing incriminating, that is not evidence. But an alleged remark at the point of arrest – precisely when an accused person has no protection or safeguard in law against the vile but standard practice of false verballing will always so happen to be the one point where the accused is alleged to confess. 'Fair cop, Guv' or 'I didn't mean it' provide the essential corroboration which convicts them regardless of however strenuously denied. 'The fire at Fat Boy's was only meant to be a frightener which went too far.' Aye? Well that is probably true but I didn't say it. Coming from a suspect, it can be deemed as a confession. Taken together with Love's alleged overheard conversation in a pub, like Judas and the last supper, Love renders the final kiss-off in condemnation. The two verbals now corroborate each other. There is no real material evidence here. No forensics to tie the accused to the scene of the crime and no eyewitnesses. The court accepts that there was no evidence to say that the accused were near or at the scene of the crime. The prosecution case stands or falls on the evidence the witness Love.

Of course, there was the alleged finding of the map when I was first arrested and shafted. The planting of a map of an area which I can see from my landing window. What would I need a map for? Only a stranger to the area would need or think of using one. The prosecution said that there was a ring around the house and the appeal court accepted that, but it is simply not true. There was a ring on the map in court, but it circled the words 'Bankend Street' allegedly found a month after the fire. Of course it was planted like the shafts by the same police and proven so. But dare you say so in court? The tenant of a household is supposed to sign for items removed from their household as proof of the origin. The only thing signed for was £300 they took from my home. There never was any other such signature on any of the items, including the map, allegedly taken from my home, because I didn't even know about them until we were indicted two months later and they showed up on the productions list.

So much for Charge 15 then, the murder of the Doyle family, but what did the court say? They took the prosecution's word that Love was not specific as to which day or date he overhead this alleged conversation. Well, then we were refused access to the transcripts of the actual evidence to see for sure who was right and who was wrong. So let us just have a quick look at that now. It seems that I was wrong, at least, as to who had gleaned the evidence of specification of time and date. It wasn't Mr Donald Findlay QC, it was . . .

William Love Cross-examined by Mr Stirling QC:

'There couldn't be any mistake about it?'
'No, sir.'
'Surely that particular period of March would be very clear in your mind?'

'Not very clear, sir, no.'

'Was it not?'

'Not date-wise, no.'

'Pardon?'

'The dates are not clear.'

'Are they not?'

'No.'

'That surprises me. Can you tell the ladies and gentlemen of the Jury when you were arrested?'

'25th March.'

'The day after?'

'Two days after, sir.'

'We are talking about the 23rd and 24th March are we not?'

'Yes, sir.'

'And it was a rough idea, you said the 19th or 20th?'

'I didn't pay any particular attention to the date I heard the conversation. I am just trying to give you a rough idea of the date.'

'You were arrested on the 25th March which was the Monday?'

'Yes, sir.'

'Is that right?'

'No, it was a Sunday.'

Obviously then we are talking about Friday 23 March.

With hindsight, it may seem odd that we'd let this evidence of specification of time by Love pass right over our heads. However, it should be recalled that the precise terms of his alibi for that weekend were not known at the time of the trial and not disclosed by the prosecution and were not known for another twelve years. That his alibi for the robbery had covered from the Friday 23rd March to the Sunday 25th March when he was arrested.

'Two days after' he heard the conversation later referred to as 'that night'. Thus, he alleges that the conversation took place on the Friday night of 23rd March, 1984. The prosecutor at our trial was the same prosecutor in his case who had taken his judicial examination and alibi. The prosecution were the only ones aware of the exact terms of his alibi and that he had just provided evidence of his own perjury, even as he uttered it. Hence their case to try to keep the witness as vague and unspecific regarding time as was possible. It is not possible to defend against a witness who is not specific as to date and, in the interests of fairness to an accused person, it is normally the prosecutor's duty to help the witness be as specific as possible. In this case the opposite is true. In their secret knowledge of the terms of his alibi, they went to great lengths to ensure that he was not specific as to the date of the conversation and, when he was specific, they simply covered it up at the appeal court when their deception was revealed. Knowing that the transcripts would not be produced, they could say whatever they liked and get away with it.

According to the law, the Crown prosecution have a duty to investigate all aspects of a case, including that which may tend to exculpate (acquit) an accused. Whilst, on the other hand, it is ruled that, 'There is no obligation in Scots law for the Crown to disclose said (exculpatory) evidence to the accused.' In other words, the Crown retains the privilege and the prerogative to fit-up an accused person by withholding evidence of his innocence.

Those who were involved in the prosecution of Love on the robbery and who judicially examined him were aware of the terms of his alibi and were also those who neglected to have the production labels certified by signature in his case. Thus rendering the material evidence in that case as inadmissible and incompetent in law, leading to Love's acquittal on that charge. Aye right! Auld pals act, Nineteen Canteen.

At least, pages 6 and 7 of the opinion here eliminate Reynolds as evidence and, though it does not mention her, the opinion eliminates Mad Mrs Bruce, Agnes' neighbour, by omitting her from the prosecution's account of the incriminating evidence. All in all, this was not a fair or impartial hearing. It brings evidence against another as evidence against me where I was not present at the time. It says that the excuse of me getting a lift home by Love was not put to the witness in cross-exam whereas the transcripts now show that it was. Though I'd said that I wasn't sure that it was the same car, it is of no real importance. I was not accused of being there at the scene of the crime at the time the crime was committed so a single fingerprint on the car window has no significance at all. It certainly does not, as the prosecution argued, prove beyond doubt that the car belonged to me and that I had loaned it to the perpetrators of the act for the purpose of the act. If it had been my car there would have been evidence of its history traced to me. There would have been evidence from my neighbours that the car was mine. But this was not put to the witnesses on examination because their statements had already said otherwise. I was not aware that the car was supposed to be mine till the Crown prosecution's summation on the close of evidence.

And so it goes on. The Crown case is nothing but a web of illusions created by deceptions, innuendo, inference, and downright lies. My task then became, how do I prove it? And where do I begin from PH S/C buried alive in ice cream war propaganda?

BOOK SIX

Hell Block

Hell Block PH S/C

It was 1985. What did I know what was going on? I couldnae see the world for the prison walls . . .

PH S/C was the official title for Peterhead Prison's Separate Cells. More commonly and aptly known as Peter Hell Solitary Confinement. The digger for short. Dungeons of dire despair for those wretched souls who dwell there.

They are no more than granite vaults with a barred window embedded high in the four-foot thick walls. Steel frames are reinforced by steel bars and stout steel mesh on the inside, four by one inch steel flat bars entwined with razor wire running across on the outside. Every second cell has a brownish black steel plating covering the entire window with air holes drilled therein.

The steel and studded door in the opposite wall is the only other main feature of this tomb. Besides a plastic piss pot and basin on the floor, there is the four inch high granite slab as a bed, one end with a raised stone Jason's Pillow upon which to contemplate one's better days and into which to instil one's hate of a system which keeps men so confined for years without end.

Cut out of the wall above the door is a six-by-six inch square tunnel-like hole with stout Perspex embedded half way to the cellblock gallery beyond. Outside in the gallery is a dim light above each door which casts dull rays through the hole along the arched roof of the dungeon and which remains on twenty-four hours of the day. A one-inch thick rubber mat and two washed out black horsehair army blankets as bedding. A cardboard table and chair are sometimes provided though never used for the purpose intended but as steps to scale the window wall where, clinging to the bars and mesh, a prisoner can whisper in coded language to a neighbouring cell. This place is strict solitary confinement and isolation. Prisoners are not supposed to even see each other far less have a conversation. Yet, what can the screws do? What other punishment can they add other than a bread and water diet and the confiscation of bedding? In which case, it was soon discovered that the alleged indestructible and chemically treated fireproof cardboard table and chairs dissolve and disintegrate under the flow of human urine as dirty protest ensues.

Five times a day the door is opened. Three times for six Darth Vader clad screws in full riot gear, like giant mutant cockroaches in their black gleaming plastic armour, and baseball bat riot sticks to slide a plastic plate of food along the cell floor before slamming it closed again. The effect of these steel doors slamming in the vacuum of the vaulted dungeon can be quite horrendous and devastating on the head, the air pressure often causing the ears to bleed. The then Inspector of Prisons, Buyers, ordered that the practice of slamming doors in these conditions must stop but it was still used as a form of unofficial punishment against any prisoner who raised a whimper of complaint. And as the prisoners there were more inclined to riot rather than whimper the slamming of the doors remained regular and standard despite the squeaks of the toothless inspectorate.

Twice more then the door is opened. Once for slop out and a cup of tepid, dirt-water jail tea. Again for slop out and exercise. Each time when beyond the door you are surrounded by six of Darth Vader's mutant cockroaches to march you to the slop out bin and back. Or to the exercise pen and back. The pens are about twice the size of a cell. Fifteen-foot high walls topped with layer upon layer of coiled razor wire dividing off the screws on the catwalk high above looking down.

Exercise in the open air being a desperately fought for right, entailing many riots and many more martyred casualties, everybody took it regardless of the weather. Hail, sleet or snow it was a welcome change to the four yellow walls and black steel door. The screws hated it, clad in that clumsy awkward riot gear in the hail and sleet blasting in from the North Sea threatening to blow them off the catwalk onto the wire or, worse, into the pen with the prisoner, the equivalent of the lion's den. It was a pure treat to behold.

I was held there for four years. From June 1985 to August 1989. There were some who were there many years before me and who were there for many years beyond, their only break being a temporary transfer to the cages in Inverness for a holiday. Peterhead Prison is the arsehole of the universe. Stuck out on a peninsula in the North Sea, a million miles from anywhere, it may as well be on the dark side of the moon. No telephone. A visit once a month if not snowed in and strict censorship of all outgoing and incoming mail, including legal and European Convention on Human Rights correspondence. Isolation is absolute. For the innocent imprisoned there, and there were many, even Amnesty International could not help. Even if your letter passes the censor, they will tell you that they cannot interfere in cases within the United Kingdom. Something to do with funding no doubt. In the winter, there being no heating, the empty cells are often used as cold storage for the corpses of stab victims until such time as the police and ambulance can get through the snow drifts to examine and investigate that, sure enough, he's dead before hustling back to the warmth of their offices. This then is the modern Scottish prison system.

Don't tell me it has changed because I heard all that before I went there. According to official records, it never existed and doesn't happen. Check then with Buyers' report. Although a whitewash, there still remain traces of the prisoners' original complaints, watered down.

'The whistling must stop,' he says making it sound like prisoners do not enjoy the prison officers' merry dirge. In fact, the 'whistling' was a constant high-pitched, mechanical whine which adjusted in accordance with the time of the day. In the mornings, it would be a high pitched screech, agitating the chamber bound prisoner from sleep, changing tone, winding gradually down in the evening, altering the rhythms of the brain into sleep. So constant, twenty-four hours a day for years that only new prisoners are aware of it, till they too succumb to its constant brainwashing monotony. So much then for the Buyers' report that 'the whistling must stop'. It never even paused for breath. And they wonder why the roof comes off.

On 2nd November, 1985, I had only been there coming on six months when the digger exploded. I was wrapped in a blanket on the mat on the floor, my fingers and face numb with the cold trying to pen a letter to the Scottish Secretary of State regarding my appeal against conviction, struggling in the dull light. It was just after six o'clock of a Saturday night, the main prison being locked down from half four at the weekends. The evening 'supper', that half mug of tepid, dirt-water jail tea, was always early and had just passed me with a full complement of six mutant cockroaches and the so-called nursing officer, a screw with no qualification other than a white coat. Dragging the tea urn along the gallery with a towel on the handle and no wheels, doling out the half mug measures.

Unknown to me then, like the man in the iron mask in my dingy dungeon, there had been a screw do on in their club that night with some stars and cabaret acts up from London to do their turn. The club was almost adjoining the back gate of the prison at the screws' quarters and, this being a show not to be missed, they had an understanding among themselves that they could nip off shift, out the back door to the club after lock up while remaining covered by their comrades on alternating rota. Hence the reason why the tea was early. The digger needing a minimum of six fully clad cockroaches before any one door could be opened was, however, a problem ingeniously overcome by doing the tea run there last. Moving up through the jail from the least to the most potentially volatile halls, gathering the duty screws from each as they went so that they had the mandatory six bodies and the surgery screw by the time they reached the most dangerous men in Scotland, all there together in the Cat-A-List digger of PH S/C. However, that meant there was no one left on wall patrol and no one on guard duty anywhere else in the prison. An ideal time for any enterprising Cat-A-List to make a move on the downfall of the establishment. And he did, with great style. Big Bill Varey captured all the screws and took unchallenged control of Peterhead Prison in attempting to liberate Scotland's toughest from the pits of hell upon the unsuspecting public. May God forever bless and keep him safe for he was the catalyst that closed that door to hell once and for all, where Buyers failed.

Big Bill, an armed robber born in Fife, joined the French Foreign Legion and had settled in Australia for a while. A persistent, ingenious and daring escaper, he started off serving twelve years for armed robbery and ended up serving thirty-one years for his escapes. A Christian and a gentleman, he would never stand idly by and watch a liberty being taken and didn't take kindly to such violations of his own person.

He had been in Sol Con for an escape from the year before I arrived there and was still awaiting sentence on that. Being searched and metal detected every day, he'd managed to hide a pink plastic water pistol, polishing it black and working on it to make it look real. When the cockroaches opened his cell door to tea up, he had stuck it in their faces. I could hear his Australian accent as I shivered there in my cell.

'Get on the fackin floor. I'll blow your fackin head off,' and such choice remarks as the cockroaches clunking and clicking in their armour scurried to hit the floor. Removing their batons, walkie-talkies and keys one at a time, sending them crawling on their bellies into his cell. Last one in slamming the door closed behind him as they all then used their combined body weight to barricade the cell door against him, locking him out before he could order them to strip off their uniforms. Content to leave him with every cell door key in the prison. Every corridor door and double lock security key including the front gate keys and garage key for the prison draft buses.

Every man in the prison could now be opened up with no one to stop them as all the screws in the jail were now locked in Big Bill's cell. The prisoners could then go to the garage and, boarding the busses, drive straight out the front gate unchallenged. The one remaining screw still on duty in the camera room was lying unconscious, drunk at his post. That poor sod who saw nothing was to commit suicide before the trial. Bill was not to know this though. If he had and had released the prisoners there would have been a wave of crime emanating outward from the epicentre of Peterhead Prison throughout the entire country. They would have had to call in the army as Scotland's toughest and most dangerous convicts each headed for their own home turf with whose car? Bus? Lorry? Or tractor? Wearing whose clothes? From whose washing line? Home? Or shop? What would the public have had to say about that? If only they'd ever known or if Bill had taken that option to cover his own tracks. Luckily he didn't and chose a more tight-knit team instead. The Cat-A-List crew of the digger itself. The unrepentant, the undeterred, the irrepressible rebels and the outraged, born to raise hell.

First he opened his good friend, Al Brown, a Londoner born to the chimes of the Bow Bells. An armed robber who shot a have-a-go hero dead in Glasgow during a wages snatch. Originally sentenced to life with a recommended twenty-five years, he ended up with fifty-four years for escape attempts, rioting and, believe it or not, was one of the straightest, most genuine and reliable people you could ever hope to meet. Fearless and intelligent to boot.

Next was Ace Campbell, a west coast loner and armed robber. A handsome Jack-the-lad sometimes known as Jack the Crimper. He started serving ten years, finally escaped while serving twenty-two being sentenced to life for that and a series of armed bank raids whilst on the trot.

Gary McMenamin, the Fifer, a lifer with sentences on top for riot and assault.

Joe McGrath from Glasgow who started serving thirteen years for armed robbery ending up with twenty-five years for riots and escape. Another solid, reliable, intelligent, fearless and resourceful bloke.

Andy McCann, the Paranoid Android. Served three out of three years in solitary and was gate arrested. This guy is the original Rab C. Nesbitt in looks, speech, shape and mentality. Now serving life in the State Mental Hospital, Carstairs.

And me, TC Campbell, Innocent Imprisoned, serving life, twenty years recommended and ten years for mass murder. A motley crew to be set on the loose with control of the entire prison.

My door was open by Bill. 'C'mon, Tom, we're fackin out of here,' said he bouncing on his toes as I dropped my blanket, forgetting the cold and followed. Hell Block seemed strange to see from the outside of the door without six mutant cockroaches around me in the eerie silence. The short back corridor to reception had been accessed and the racks there were dismantled. Long tubular poles were extracted and jammed into doorframes and bent to form hooks long enough to attach to the top of the perimeter wall for easy scaling. Everybody just seemed to know instinctively what needed doing and did it. Working as a unit with very few words spoken, other than, 'Watch what you're doing with that fuckin thing.'

and

'Watch where you're pointing that fuckin thing.'

All directed at Bill who just laughed, twirling his magic gun and pocketing it.

Up onto the wall, straddling it under the starry night sky in the cool fresh November air seemed like the ultimate freedom whilst Bill checked out the route through the fencing. The silent sound alarm had been tripped. The police receiving no call or reply from the prison had telephoned the screws' club asking them to have it turned off. This call was made every half hour for three hours until the compere took the stage asking staff to attend the prison due to the lack of response from there. They did, staggering drunk around the perimeter unable to get in. Finally stumbling upon Bill on his wanders and pleading with him for a key to let them in. Finally, Bill was caught when the Governor arrived with the police and spare key. He was arrested and taken round to the front gate where he once again he drew out his gun, holding dozens of screws, governors and police on the ground till finally tackled and disarmed him while he was trying to make off in a police car. Laughing all the way back to the nick.

Meanwhile, Bill having alerted us by the screws' radio that all had come unstuck, we returned to the cellblock and barricaded the doors. Now the Paranoid Android came into his element smashing anything breakable and generally having a private riot to himself, tormenting the screws who were still barricading themselves in Bill's cell. Lifting the spy-hole:

'Quiet in there. No talking.'

'You'll slop out at the normal times same as every other cunt.'

'Get on your feet when I'm talking to you.'

'Address me as sir or I'll knock your block off, scum.'

'Visit slips on Mondays only.'

'Sore head? See the welfare.'

'One extra sheet per letter only.'

So on and so on.

Someone must have given him some lip back. He became quite upset, grabbing an iron bar and panning in the Perspex window above the door. Snatching a petrol bomb he jumped up on a table trying to light it to throw it in through the gap. 'Right you bastards ye'r kebab,' he screamed trying to light the sodden rag.

Directly above him, I picked up a fire extinguisher, turning it upside down to read the instructions. It was obvious this guy was seriously intent on torching the screws.

'Never mind the instructions,' Joe said beside me. 'If he gets that lit, just drop it on his fuckin' head.' Meanwhile Joe nipped downstairs, jumped up onto the table, planted his forehead on the Android's nose and took the petrol bomb and lighter out of his hands as he staggered back falling off the table. Al Brown looked on, shaking his head, apparently unperturbed. He was already one step

ahead, having poured out the petrol from all of the bottles
(leaving only a spot to retain the smell) and filling them
back up with water, accounting for the Android's difficulty in lighting the bombs. They were non-flammable,
meagre props, but only Al had known that.

There was by now about a hundred screws and police
trying to get in and failing. Negotiations began, just a
load of crap going nowhere and everybody knew it. Still
we had to go through the motions to stall for time to
give Bill a better break, unsure if he'd been captured or
not. That resolved when they displayed him at the hatch
on the cellblock door to prove that he was unharmed.
After that, the game was a bogey. Everyone just armed
themselves with riot batons and shields and waited for
the fight to the death.

The Paranoid Android's demeanour quickly changed.
He went whining to the Governor saying, 'Sir, I've got
nothing to do with any of this, they just opened my door.'
The Governor sympathised, telling him just to go back to
his cell and lock himself in. He did so and was later used as
a witness for the Crown with immunity from prosecution
to testify against the rest of us. However, on the day he
backed out and never did the damage. In the meantime,
that left myself, Joe, Al, Ace and Gary like a handful of
Spartans against the multitudes when they finally came.

Which wasn't until well into the following day. We
were all weary sitting in my cell drinking tea and having
a blether. I had just come back from walking the gallery,
looking in all the cells, all identical. I'd gained the impression of battery hens or pigeon coops and had wondered
how my mind had been tricked into accepting this as a
norm for the fact that it was the usual, day in day out,
routine regime. Leaving Gary on guard I returned to my
cell where everyone had gathered and set about securing
my files from damage.

It started with a bang as one door and barrier was blown with a high-pressure jack. A riot pressure hose through the hatch on the other door sent Gary skiting along the gallery as if on skis. A second hose blasted at the cell door where the screws were holding themselves hostage. The riot troops charged in by the hundreds, slap bang into the first layer of defences. The stone floor had been swamped with gallons of pure liquid soap now added to by water from the cannon. The first wave went skiting and slithering in their armour, whilst the next wave went tumbling over them, creating a heap of upended cockroaches on their back and at the mercy of the prisoners facing them shoulder to shoulder in a row, expecting and prepared for a fight to the death. The Governor ordered a halt to their slow slipping and slithering, comical advance and spoke to us, promising the usual 'no brutality' and ordering his men to form a corridor. They did this, hundreds of them, through the digger, across the corridors through to B Hall.

'One at a time,' I said to Joe. 'Wait and see what happens to me before ye go it alone.' I handed him my riot stick and walked towards the long gauntlet without hesitating, straight into it. A few times, a screw would lift his baton in a jerky movement, expecting me to cringe. I just stopped and stared at them with contempt until they looked away in shame for their cowardice. Straight all the way through without a blow struck. They put me into a cell in B Hall control unit where the rest of the rebels were held. The others followed without further incident. The brutality was yet to come but only while we were alone and in isolation. The Governor had wisely deemed that five determined soldiers were as good as an army and decided to divide us before conquering.

Born Again

It was now Sunday 3rd November, 1985. At least B Hall segregation unit had a bed. I was wakened by a mob of screws in full mufti armour at the door. It appeared that I was being unofficially ID'd for something. They came back later, some of them only semi-clad in armour but all with the three-foot riot sticks. This time they came all the way into the cell, about eight to ten of them moving in single file round the walls. Thus leaving me with my back to the wall under the window. It was quite obvious to me that this was a cosh squad and I was in for the traditional beating usually doled out on such occasions.

'Sorry about this, TC,' said Chief Screw. 'I hope you realise it's nothing personal.'

'I'm due a visit this afternoon, Chief,' I butted in, producing my ace. 'If there's one mark on me they'll go straight to the polis.'

He hesitated. 'Your visit is hereby cancelled, Campbell,' he said, turning away.

'Chief, Chief,' I called, stepping away from the wall, trying to keep him there to reason this out. My visit was important to me. Liz and the weans had travelled a long way through bad roads and treacherous weather for it. 'Ye canny just turn them away,' was about as far as I got. Halfway across the room I felt the first blow as a baton struck me in the back point on in a stabbing thrust, causing my left leg to give way beneath me. I quickly dropped to a squat position to keep my balance, the dead leg kneeling on the floor as I felt the wind of another baton whoosh over my head from behind as they moved in on me. The door was blocked by two screws, shoulder to shoulder holding their riot sticks diagonally across their chests, the Chief, Cormack by name, behind them looking over their shoulders. From an on your mark position I made a mad dash for the door intending to barge my way past the guards out into the main hall with more room to manoeuvre, to shout and bawl to let everyone else know what was happening. A beating in a box has no witness.

My leg didn't work and my attempted barge was a slow feeble effort causing me to half turn as I stumbled forward. The screw at the door simply straightened out his arms, his baton hitting me as a bar and knocking me aside to the left as I fell without balance on one leg. The boots and sticks rained down on me in the corner of the room by the door. They gripped me by each limb, one screw to each foot, one to each leg, one to each shoulder and one to each hand as Chief Cormack gripped my head round the neck in a strangle hold. The others carried on booting as someone squeezed my balls.

Eventually they turned me onto my stomach, twisting my arms up my back and cuffing them there. Back onto my back, never a pause in the beating. The Chief, holding my neck, put his knee under the top of my back holding me in a semi-reclining position while the others held my legs open, standing on my ankles and kneeling on my thighs while Fat Henderson kneeled to squeeze my balls, again and again. Poof! I tried to shout at him, but with the grip on my throat, it came out more like Woof. But he must have got the message. He stood up enraged, placed a hand on each shoulder of the screws at either side of him, heaved his great blubbery bulk up onto his toes, with one foot raised as high as his fat thighs would allow and brought it down, stomping on my stomach and solar plexus. Regardless of how I tensed in expectation, the blow landed expelling air in a hot burning gasp as I felt the tissue of my muscles tear and tasted blood in my mouth. 'Again,' said the Chief, tightening his grip on my throat to prevent the intake of air. Wham! came the next blow. With less resistance from my stomach, I could feel the blow shudder my spine. I could feel it in my teeth. 'Again,' said the Chief next to my ear and the next blow rattled throughout my skeleton. I have a vague memory of a young screw stepping over me and saying something like, 'Yous are killing him,' and a fight breaking out among them before I passed into blissful oblivion.

This had been early afternoon, perhaps one or half one, but I haven't a clue what time I awoke. Still handcuffed up my back and in a pool of water, soaked through. It seemed that someone had been trying to rouse me with a bucketful but there was no one there and the door was firmly closed. I was lying in a foetal position and discovered that to try to straighten out only added agony. It was dark, but that only meant that it was sometime after four in those northern regions. Someone was calling my name, I think it was Ronnie Neeson next door, another innocent imprisoned who'd spent years in Hell Block and these seg units. 'Answer me, for God's sake, big yin . . . Answer me. Tam! Tam! Let us know if you're okay.' He kept repeating, his voice breaking with the emotion of his plea. I finally figured that the sound was coming from the air vent at my head and tried to turn towards it and found that I couldn't move without great pain, the effort causing a groan. I could hear Ron passing on the news that I was alive and that he'd heard me groan, causing him to keep at me with renewed vigour. 'Tam. Tam, they've been in and out trying to rouse you for hours. Are you okay? What happened? Do you need help? Do you need a doctor? Are you doped up or what?'

'Naw! They danced all over me, tried to do me in. I'm still on the floor, still cuffed.' I finished with a growl of pain at the effort. My answer was quickly passed on through the vent systems and it seemed the very fabric of the building buzzed into life as, bit by bit, Ronnie forced me to keep on talking and to stay conscious when all I wanted to do was to slip back into sweet oblivion and escape the pain searing though my entire body. That I was in need of a doctor became obvious and soon the building started to resound with the clatter of banging doors and bars as the prisoners in their cells each had a little riot to themselves.

'One two three four, bang yer pisspots off the door . . . Get a fuckin doctor, ya shower o evil bastards ye's.' The disturbance was spreading from Hall to Hall as the news was passed on from window to window. Soon the entire jail was raising hell fit to be heard in the town many miles away. They would have to do something or there would be no sleep for the bairns tonight. The only time they let up was when the word was passed for quiet for me to speak. As each news was passed on it would break out all over again spontaneously.

I was slipping in and out of consciousness with only the ruckus and Ron's voice reminding me of where I was. Sometimes I was aware that there was pain somewhere in the room but didn't relate it to myself. My dreams were vivid and realistic in contrast from heaven, to hell to return. My body convulsing beyond my control. Rivers of sweat streaming off me, gathering in puddles on the floor.

I became aware of the Chief holding my head again. He was saying something, 'Not make a complaint about assault and we'll not charge you with riot and assault. Deal?' He was making a fuckin deal? About what?

'Anythin you say, mister. Whatever you say, just stop this fuckin pain or kill me.'

'You're a wee bit upset that's all, a wee bit of an upset

tummy. Nothing more, do you hear what I'm saying to you? Nothing more.' He was telling me what to say, going into detail of their version of events which did not include their visit to the cell or the torture session, and if I would agree to that he could get a medic to give me something nice to make me feel fine.

'Whatever you say, Mister,' was all I could muster in reply. He didn't seem to notice that the use of the word Mister in this situation was intended as a mark of disrespect. A Glaswegian would have seen it as intended. He ordered that I be lifted onto the bed but didn't order the removal of the cuffs till his next visit.

The so-called medic arrived. He was one of the screws who'd been there on the beating only now, instead of mufti armour, he wore that magic white coat over his uniform which miraculously transforms a torturer into the doctor who treats the victim he has just tortured. You can imagine how impressed I was at his attempt to test me to see if I would grass them. As If I would? I mean? Hadn't we just struck a fair deal? A wee upset stomach was his diagnosis to Chief Cormack, pleasing him no end to the point where he even ordered the handcuffs removed for good behaviour. 'Something's torn,' I said. 'I felt something tear inside. I need a doctor, it's killing me.'

'Nothing of the kind,' he said as they all left, slamming the door behind them.

The Prison doctor, Mengel Manson arrived after what seemed like an eternity of torture. I told him that something inside was torn but he wasn't having any of it. 'No, you're just a little upset at missing your visit and you have a wee stomach cramp.' He gave me an injection and ordered that I be removed to the prison surgery to quell the rising riot.

I knew and the prisoners knew that he was a waste of time anyway. He had been the prison doctor there for about forty years and was a worse cover-up merchant than the screws. On our last meeting he'd attacked me with a stout walking stick, accusing me of being a 'fucking grass' and had to be restrained by the screws. I had reported sick with the recurrence of an old mastoid infection in my ear. I knew what it was by the smell of the leakage and had explained it to him. I had to stop him from inserting a large steel enema flusher into my ear in an attempt to syringe it. I had then written to the surgeon, explaining my difficulty and asking him if he could instruct this doctor on how to treat this ailment. The surgeon had written back to me, sending a copy to the doctor and the Governor saying, in effect, that any first year medical student would know not to syringe a mastoid infected ear. Such treatment could lead to the death or coma of the patient and under no circumstance was anything to be allowed into that ear, the proper treatment being such and such an antibiotic. The Governor had enquired of me and I had explained what the situation was. He seemed to think the whole thing was so funny, telling me that Doctor Manson wanted to see me but that I should be warned that he was not too stable and I seemed to have upset him by writing to the Medical Council. This is when he'd attacked me with the stick calling me 'a dirty fucking grass' and such like. So we knew there was no point in relying on him.

They dumped me on a table in the surgery wing and left me there with the night shift who didn't bother with the magic white coat any more. The cell door was left open but these cells had an added barred grill gate. The screw could reach through the bars to give you treatment but that's assuming you could walk to the bars. I couldn't move. He would hold his ears for a while against the sounds of pain coming from me then spent an hour throwing paracetemol and aspirin at me through the bars. Going through tubs of them till they were all over the floor. The only time I could reach any was when they landed on my chest. Then

I couldn't swallow them because I was dehydrated with sweating. He wet rags and threw them at me to suck on until they too littered the cell floor. Finally 'he' could stand no more of it and broke rank by phoning a civilian doctor. A godsend to me if ever there was one, but was it too late?

As the prison rioted throughout the night, she appeared to me through the haze of pain and exhaustion as a little angel, examining me for the first time as a doctor would. Getting more and more outraged as first she noted the cuts on my wrists from the cuffs, next the bruising, then the boot prints on my T-shirt and how long I had been left like this. Her dark little elfin eyes flaming, she demanded an emergency ambulance immediately. The screw hesitated – having broken rank to call her, he was already in deep shit. She bustled him aside and did it herself. By that time I was beyond caring.

I remember the ambulance and I remember waking up in the hospital, my body convulsing in a wave of pain, crying out and doctors all rushing around me. The next I knew I was waking up in a private room plugged into all sorts of life support machines and the screws all round me. I had no memory whatsoever. Not even my name or who I was, far less how I'd got there. Apparently I had been there two days when the TV in front of me mentioned my name and that I'd been taken to hospital after suffering an injury when I fell from a wall in an attempt to escape. Suddenly it all started to filter through to me, my brain started to work and I began to remember everything. I straightened my head up realising I'd been drooling like a mindless zombie. Mindless, indeed I had been. On wiping away the spittle from my chin, I noticed I was plugged in and that there were two hospital bracelets on my left arm and one on my right. One had my name and, 'Dead on arrival 4/11/85.' I was thirty-three and had died on my birthday.

I tried to call a nurse only to cry out in pain. The screws

went into high gear bustling about phoning the Governor and the Chief with the news that I was now not only conscious but had spoken. A nurse came running, pressing an emergency button as she did so. Soon I was surrounded by doctors so pleased to be speaking to me. They hadn't thought that they ever would or that I would recover from my stupor. Because my heart and breathing had stopped before I'd convulsed back to life and the blood tests had shown I'd been grossly overdosed with amnesiacs, they hadn't expected me to recover without brain damage. They'd been trying to get a response from me without success.

'Do you know what happened to me!' I started, but they mistook it for a question.

'Apparently you had an accident but we were hoping you could tell us. It's all very odd,' said the doctor.

'Naw,' I croaked, still in terrible pain. ' Him, him, him, and that other one on the phone there danced all over me. Handcuffed me, beat me up and tried to kill me.' The doctor picked up my wrist as if taking my pulse but he was looking at the cuts on my wrists. 'That explains a lot,' he said.

'Tell my family. Let someone know,' I said.

They did and the word got out. The cavalry was coming.

It appears that my charmed life had brought me through again. I had suffered from peritonitis when my gut was ruptured against my spine. There was a maximum of twenty-four hours to live with the pain growing increasingly more intense. They had kept me under wraps for eighteen hours before the hospital had got me 'Dead on arrival'. It also later emerged that my spine had a double fracture to the transverse arch – had broken in two places at the point of impact.

The next official statement from the Scottish Office was that I had suffered from appendicitis. Before long I was kidnapped back to the jail hospital that was condemned as infested. Soon thousands of lice-like creatures were teeming all over me as if it was their first meal in months. Like piranha, they swarmed into my wound and into every orifice of my being, even burrowing into the pores on my arms. I could see them do it but couldn't get up to do anything about it. When the Governor came round, I pulled back the sheets and showed him and he ran from the cell.

The screws came in like space men in germ warfare outfits made in the prison workshop. With big spray guns and canisters, they started at my side of the cell, moving backwards out the door spraying a fine mist of chemicals into the air. Slamming the cell door closed behind them leaving me to choke. I put a sheet over my head and to my mouth and breathed through that. With my broken back, struggling on the bed only to find the window was sealed and didn't open. I then broke the aerial from the radio and used that to smash the window to get some air. I could hear the furnace nearby and could smell dead and decaying flesh like a dead dog. Later the prison said that this could be accounted for by the fact that they had found a dead bird in the air vent. What air vent? There was no air vent in that cell.

The police refused to even hear a complaint against the screws either from me alone or in the presence of my solicitor, John Carroll, when he had arrived at the hospital with a camera. Instead I was charged with riot for the 2nd November incident and assault on Chief Cormack on 3rd November.

So this is what Guilty meant. A small word big on consequence. So, this was the life I'd been sentenced to. Condemned to a wilderness created by people for people. But I wasn't done yet. The beat goes on.

Take Heed

This is the dungeon
in which I reside
these are the bars
which keep me confined.

This is the slab
upon which I sleep
this same cold stone
where the cockroaches feed.

This is the ceiling,
this is the floor,
this is the spy hole
My steel studded door.

These are the walls
all spattered in spite
this is my world
this is my fight.

This is the wind
that roars so loud
these scavenger gulls
that screech all around

This is the salt
I smell from the sea

this is my vault
and yes, this is me.

This is forever
this is for real
the pain of my vision
the anger I feel.

This is my tomb
where the tumbleweed blow
dark side of the moon
where you must not go.

This is my anger
this is my pain
this is my hunger
for freedom again.

These are my bones
my skull, my teeth
this is my heart
I beg you, Take Heed.

(Rip-off from the lost book of passing thoughts by TC.
Peter Hell Sol Con.)

EPILOGUE

Where are They Now?

Chief Cormack, Peterhead Prison – Was convicted of indecent exposure and living off immoral earnings. Was promoted to Governor at Shotts Prison. Retired and died soon thereafter.

Bill Varey – Hit the headlines many more times for his daring escapes. Was finally liberated in the year 2001 and lives a quiet and settled life.

Al Brown – Escaped again but was recaptured accidentally after a couple of years of the quiet life in England. Still serving an eternity of years in Her Majesty's Hells.

Ace Campbell (aka Jack the Crimper) – Escaped but was recaptured and sentenced to life imprisonment for a series of armed bank raids. Still serving an eternity of years in Her Majesty's Hells.

Gary McMenamin – Escaped in a mad car dash and sentenced to a further eight years. Still serving his time in Her Majesty's Hells.

Joe McGrath – Was liberated and settled down. Was working for The Big Issue, the magazine to support the homeless. Last news was he was untried, fitted up for a robbery.

Andy McCann (The Paranoid Android) – Was liberated still fighting with the screws. Was sentenced to four years for tying up and torturing the judge who sentenced him. Later was sentenced to life for murder and is presently a patient at the State Hospital Carstairs.

Liz Campbell – Gave up the ice cream van and went on to raise three wonderful children all on her own.

Stephen Campbell – At nineteen, a six-foot-four honey monster. Working away. Still awaits his Da to fulfil his promise that he will be home soon.

Tamby Gray – Sentenced to fourteen years and liberated in 1993. Caught the Blue Train to Noddyland where this world can't reach him. Still pursues justice against his conviction. There is always tomorrow.

Gardi Loo (Gary Moore) – After liberation from court received a chain of convictions in rapid succession including an eight-year spell for culpable homicide.

Cammy – Completed his three-year sentence. Worked to become a slum landlord. Sold the stock to become a horse farmer. Married and settled somewhere in the wilderness.

The Craw (Thomas McGraw aka the Licensee) – Became infamous as Glasgow's alleged Godfather of crime and head of the Caravel Cartel. Reckoned to be a multi-millionaire. Implicated in many gang war murders but never tried or convicted.

Marchetti family – Went out of the ice cream business and diversified into undertaking.

George Reid – Completed his three-year sentence. Married, built and runs a horse farm in Lanarkshire. Still worships Mammon.

Shadda Lafferty – Completed his three-year sentence and

returned to obscurity. Still contests his conviction and still struggles in battles with demon booze.

Agnes Lafferty (née Campbell) – Abandoned her efforts in the ice cream trade to devote her boundless energies to the struggle for justice and equality for all. Heads the Glasgow Two Campaign.

Thomas Lafferty jnr – Went on to be sentenced to ten years for presenting a firearm at the police. Caught the Blue Train to Noddyland.

Joe Granger – Completed five years for alleged perjury. Fought on for justice and won his case at the European Court of Human Rights. Married Lynne and settled down quietly with their family.

Alex Reynolds – Completed five years for alleged perjury. Caught the Blue Train and contracted full blown AIDS.

Foxy Ferguson (aka the Silver Fox) – Lived an active life for another ten years. Finally died of a real heart attack in 1994.

William Love – Went on to serve a number of prison sentences. Attempted suicide on eleven occasions. Finally admitted perjury to anyone who would listen. Swore confessions to the court, the police, the press and TV. Seems no one wants to believe him now.

Joe Steele – Into his 18th year of imprisonment. Still fighting for justice. Went on to escape three times, gluing himself to the gates of Buckingham Palace and scaling the watchtower at Barlinnie Prison in Glasgow. Ever expects to be home tomorrow.

TC Campbell – Into his 18th year of imprisonment. Still fighting for justice. Ever expects to be home tomorrow.

Epilogue

Riot upon riot ripped the Scottish prison system apart. It was getting heavier and heavier as tactics and counter tactics evolved. As prisoners were being power-hosed off the rooftops, skited slates and hostages would soon put a stop to that malarkey. Peter Hell was erupting into violence on a regular basis finally being burned to a shell and rebuilt. Edinburgh's Saughton went next. Perth Prison went up a few times as did Glenochil and Shotts in Lanarkshire, Barlinnie in the city of Glasgow, Low Moss and Longriggend down Airdrie way and the Young Offenders in Dumfries. A system on its knees and in chaos.

Trial after trial handed out centuries of years in an attempt to keep the lid on but still the revolt raged undeterred. Everywhere the rebel rousers raised the rabble and trouble bubbled. 'Where there was no justice there would be no peace.' They razed the prisons down to rubble on the ground . . .

TC's own other trials would see him acquitted again and again whilst his own counter legal actions against the terror administration were upheld. While amid the chaos, blood, smoke and rubble the other half of The Glasgow Two escaped . . .

In fact, Wee Joe escaped three times. Once to raise a banner on the rooftops of his local housing estate. While TC hungered for justice in a fast for freedom, it was the prison rooftop protests which seized the headlines. Then, once again, in a sensational publicity stunt, wee Joe super-glued himself in a crucifix position to the Palace gates in London – catapulting the justice campaign of the two onto the world stage. Within weeks he was off again. 'Run, Joey. Joey, run run, the cops are on yer trail. Run, Joey, run run, they're gonna take ye back to jail.'

How could it be that an alleged mass murderer on the run was applauded and supported by the public? Could it be that they knew something that the authorities did not? Or did they know it too? The police seemed unconcerned, reassuring the public that he was *not* considered dangerous. So what the hell was going on here? Wee Joe could go, and in fact, did go anywhere he wanted with impunity. As a celebrity people wanted to say they had met him. Palace Gates Joe. He was never taken as any kind of threat to anyone.

Surrendering himself again in another splash of media hype – scaling the vast communications tower at Barlinnie Prison to hold a press conference broadcast live on national television before being dragged back to jail. But Wee Joe isn't done yet. Not while the beat goes on.

Through seventeen years of the Wilderness Years, TC continues his story of apparently endless struggle, terror and heartache, finally gaining freedom only to have it snatched away again by a cruel twist of fate. But it wouldn't end there. Not while there remained a battle to be fought. Not while the beat goes on . . .

Music played in his head as the grating of prison bars ground out his life. Seventeen years divided into months split into weeks cracked into days crushed into hours fractured into minutes but he lived them by the second. Tick . . . tock . . . tick . . . tock . . . tick . . . His innocence sustained him. Raging with injustice he refused to accept others' guilt. They made him pay or thought they could. He would die again and again but revived and lived through his will to spite the bastard system. As long as he lived he kept them worried – the gaolers, the tinsel town prophets and the murders. The Doyles' murders. Easier to die, he lived to serve them justice. And the music played on through The Wilderness Years.